T0324808

Data-Intensive Computing

The world is awash with digital data from social networks, blogs, business, science, and engineering. Data-intensive computing facilitates understanding of complex problems that must process massive amounts of data. Through the development of new classes of software, algorithms, and hardware, data-intensive applications can provide timely and meaningful analytical results in response to exponentially growing data complexity and associated analysis requirements. This emerging area brings many challenges that are different from traditional high-performance computing.

This reference for computing professionals and researchers describes the dimensions of the field, the key challenges, the state of the art, and the characteristics of likely approaches that future data-intensive problems will require. Chapters cover general principles and methods for designing such systems and for managing and analyzing the big data sets of today that live in the cloud, and describe example applications in bioinformatics and cyber-security that illustrate these principles in practice.

IAN GORTON is a Laboratory Fellow in Computational Sciences and Math at Pacific Northwest National Laboratory (PNNL), where he manages the Data Intensive Scientific Computing group and was the Chief Architect for PNNL's Data Intensive Computing Initiative. Gorton is a Senior Member of the IEEE Computer Society and a Fellow of the Australian Computer Society.

DEBORAH K. GRACIO joined Pacific Northwest National Laboratory in 1990 and is currently the Director of the Computational and Statistical Analytics Division and of the Data Intensive Computing Research Initiative. Since joining the laboratory, she has led the research, development, and management of multiple cross-disciplinary, multi-laboratory projects focused in the basic sciences and national security sectors.

Data-Intensive Computing
Architectures, Algorithms, and Applications

Edited by

IAN GORTON
Pacific Northwest National Laboratory

DEBORAH K. GRACIO
Pacific Northwest National Laboratory

CAMBRIDGE
UNIVERSITY PRESS

CAMBRIDGE
UNIVERSITY PRESS

University Printing House, Cambridge CB2 8BS, United Kingdom

One Liberty Plaza, 20th Floor, New York, NY 10006, USA

477 Williamstown Road, Port Melbourne, VIC 3207, Australia

314-321, 3rd Floor, Plot 3, Splendor Forum, Jasola District Centre, New Delhi - 110025, India

79 Anson Road, #06-04/06, Singapore 079906

Cambridge University Press is part of the University of Cambridge.

It furthers the University's mission by disseminating knowledge in the pursuit of
education, learning and research at the highest international levels of excellence.

www.cambridge.org
Information on this title: www.cambridge.org/9780521191951

First published 2013

A catalogue record for this publication is available from the British Library

Library of Congress Cataloging in Publication data
Data-intensive computing : architectures, algorithms, and applications / [edited by]
Ian Gorton, Deborah K. Gracio.
pages   cm
Includes bibliographical references and index.
ISBN 978-0-521-19195-1
1. High performance computing.   2. Database management.   3. Computer storage devices.
4. Software architecture.   5. Data transmission systems.   I. Gorton, Ian.
II. Gracio, Deborah K., 1965–
QA76.88.D38   2012
004.5–dc23   2012015720

ISBN 978-0-521-19195-1 Hardback

Contents

List of Contributors

ʹGhaleb Abdulla Lawrence Livermore National Laboratory

Justin Almquist Pacific Northwest National Laboratory

Magdalena Balazinska University of Washington

Jacek Becla Stanford University

Daniel M. Best Pacific Northwest National Laboratory

Shawn J. Bohn Pacific Northwest National Laboratory

Daniel Chavarría-Miranda Pacific Northwest National Laboratory

Terence Critchlow Pacific Northwest National Laboratory

Scott Dowson Pacific Northwest National Laboratory

Ian Gorton Pacific Northwest National Laboratory

Deborah K. Gracio Pacific Northwest National Laboratory

Wes Hatley Future Point Systems

Bill Howe University of Washington

Chandrika Kamath Lawrence Livermore National Laboratory

Sam Lang Pacific Northwest National Laboratory

Anna Liu National ICT Australia (NICTA), University of New South Wales

Kerstin Kleese-Van Dam Pacific Northwest National Laboratory

Douglas V. Love Pacific Northwest National Laboratory

Lee Ann McCue Pacific Northwest National Laboratory

Jason McDermott Pacific Northwest National Laboratory

Deborah L. McGuinness Rensselaer Polytechnic Institute

Patrick Nichols Pacific Northwest National Laboratory

Christopher Oehmen Pacific Northwest National Laboratory

William A. Pike Pacific Northwest National Laboratory

Sherif Sakr National ICT Australia (NICTA), University of New South Wales

Antonino Tumeo Pacific Northwest National Laboratory

Oreste Villa Pacific Northwest National Laboratory

Bobbie-Jo Webb-Robertson Pacific Northwest National Laboratory

1

Data-Intensive Computing: A Challenge for the 21st Century

Ian Gorton and Deborah K. Gracio

1.1 Introduction

In our world of rapid technological change, occasionally it is instructive to contemplate how much has altered in the last few years. Remembering life without the ability to view the World Wide Web (WWW) through browser windows will be difficult, if not impossible, for less "mature" readers. Is it only seven years since YouTube first appeared, a Web site that is now ingrained in many facets of modern life? How did we survive without Facebook all those (actually, about five) years ago?

In 2010, various estimates put the amount of data stored by consumers and businesses around the world in the vicinity of 13 exabytes, with a growth rate of 20 to 25 percent per annum. That is a lot of data. No wonder IBM is pursuing building a 120-petabyte storage array.[1] Obviously there is going to be a market for such devices in the future. As data volumes of all types – from video and photos to text documents and binary files for science – continue to grow in number and resolution, it is clear that we have genuinely entered the realm of data-intensive computing, or as it is often now referred to, big data.[2]

Interestingly, the term "data-intensive computing" was actually coined by the scientific community. Traditionally, scientific codes have been starved of sufficient compute cycles, a paucity that has driven the creation of ever larger and faster high-performance computing machines, typically known as super-computers. The Top 500 Web site[3] shows the latest benchmark results that characterize the fastest supercomputers on the planet. While this fascination with compute performance continues, scientific computing has been gradually coming to terms with the challenges brought by ever-increasing data size and

---

[1] http://www.technologyreview.com/computing/38440/page1/.
[2] http://en.wikipedia.org/wiki/Big_data.
[3] http://www.top500.org/.

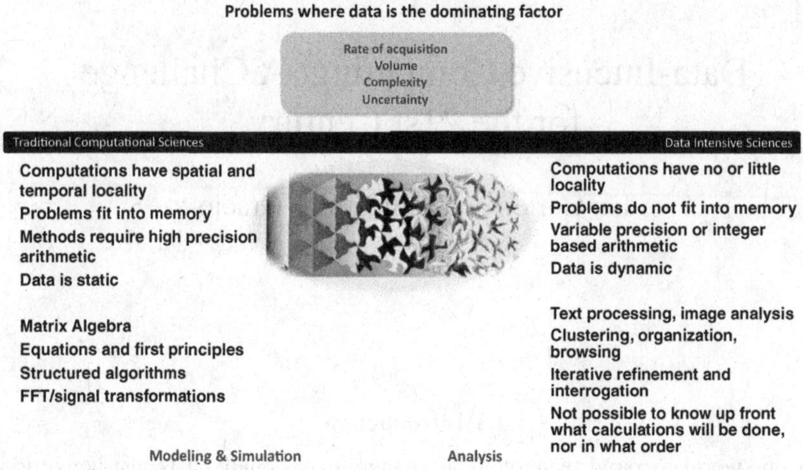

Problems where data is the dominating factor

Rate of acquisition
Volume
Complexity
Uncertainty

Traditional Computational Sciences	Data Intensive Sciences
Computations have spatial and temporal locality	Computations have no or little locality
Problems fit into memory	Problems do not fit into memory
Methods require high precision arithmetic	Variable precision or integer based arithmetic
Data is static	Data is dynamic
Matrix Algebra	Text processing, image analysis
Equations and first principles	Clustering, organization, browsing
Structured algorithms	Iterative refinement and interrogation
FFT/signal transformations	Not possible to know up front what calculations will be done, nor in what order

Modeling & Simulation   Analysis

Figure 1.1. The major concerns of computational and data-intensive applications.

complexity. In 1998, William Johnston's paper at the Seventh IEEE Symposium on High Performance Distributed Computing [1] described the evolution of data-intensive computing over the previous decade. The achievements described in that paper, while state of the art at the time, now seem modest in comparison to the scale of the problems that are routinely tackled in present-day data-intensive computing applications.

More recently, others including Hey and Trefethen [2], Bell et al. [3], and Newman et al. [4] have described the magnitude of the data-intensive problems faced by the e-science community. Their descriptions of the *data deluge* that future applications must process, in domains ranging from science to business informatics, create a compelling argument for research and development (R&D) to be targeted at discovering scalable hardware and software solutions for data-intensive problems. While multi-petabyte data sets and gigabit data streams are today's frontier of data-intensive applications, no doubt ten years from now we will fondly reminisce about these problems, and will be concerned about the looming exascale applications we need to address.

Figure 1.1 lists the general features of traditional computational science applications and their data-intensive counterparts. The former focuses more on solving mathematical equations for static data sets, whereas the latter is concerned with more exploratory search and processing of large, dynamic, and complex data collections.

1.2 Some Examples

The challenge of managing massive and complex data sets is one faced by many enterprises already. The following are some examples of the current state of the art that illustrate the magnitude of what is currently possible.

1.2.1 Internet Search

Internet search is the current poster child for data-intensive computing. While the precise amounts of data held by Google, Yahoo!, Microsoft, and other search providers is a closely guarded commercial secret, it is pretty obvious that "building a copy of the Internet" to answer Internet searches is going to result in a daunting data archive. In 2008, it was reported that Google processed about 24 petabytes of data per day [5], but other hard facts from the search engine providers are difficult to come by. As of November 2011, an estimate of the number of Web pages indexed by Google is in the vicinity of 50 billion.[4] We'll leave it to the reader to extrapolate an actual data size from this value, but discussions at a recent workshop (overheard by one of the authors) strayed into descriptions of 70 petabytes (PBs) of data in a single Google BigTable.[5]

In order to manage and rapidly search these multi-petabyte repositories to answer searches, Google has custom built a specialized file system and indexing scheme that allows queries to execute in parallel across clusters of thousands of commodity machines. As a contrast, and slightly tangential to Internet search, the Internet Archive (http://www.archive.org/) contained about 5.8 petabytes of data as of December 2010 and was growing at the rate of about 100 terabytes per month in March 2009.

1.2.2 Internet Applications

Of course, the Internet is much more than search. Many Web sites manage and deliver data to millions of users around the world, and each faces its own data challenges. In May 2010, YouTube, for example, had more than 14 billion views of videos and more than 48 hours of new videos are uploaded to the site every minute. Given the size of video files, this inevitably leads to a repository of many, many petabytes. In 2009, YouTube was serving 1 billion page views

---

[4] http://www.worldwidewebsize.com/.
[5] http://en.wikipedia.org/wiki/BigTable.

per day.[6] In a similar vein, Netflix has more than 1 petabyte of data stored on Amazon's EC2 cloud.

Not all large data repositories on the Internet store video. eBay, for example, holds its data in multi-petabyte databases, using technology from Teradata. In 2010, these databases were of the order of 15 petabytes, spanning user data and Web and network event logs.[7] Facebook relies heavily on MySQL databases and the distributed object cache, Memcached (http://memcached.org/). While no data sizes are known, the Facebook infrastructure is reported to divide its MySQL database into 4,000 shards in order to handle the site's massive data volume, and runs 9,000 instances of Memcached to process the number of transactions the database must serve.[8]

1.2.3 Business Applications

Large businesses such as financial institutions, telecommunications operators, and retail outlets all must deal with daunting complex data collections. In 2010, AT&T carried 19 petabytes of data each day on its network[9] and was one of the first organizations to report having a petabyte data warehouse. Others include Walmart, Dell, and Bank of America, and there are no doubt many more. Traditionally, large business data collections execute on data warehouse technology from organizations such as Teradata, Oracle, and IBM. These data warehouses integrate key business data (such as call records or sales records across regions) from multiple operational systems in each business and make the data available for querying and reporting through specialized business intelligence tools.[10] More recently, Hadoop-based data warehouses are making an impact; the most prominent example is Facebook's 21-PB warehouse.[11]

1.2.4 Science

Modern science is becoming increasingly data intensive, driven by modern instrumentation and high-fidelity simulations running on ever-growing supercomputers. In terms of data generation, CERN's Large Hadron Collider (LHC)[12] particle accelerator is currently the most challenging experiment in

---

[6] http://www.datacenterknowledge.com/archives/2009/10/09/1-billion-page-views-a-day-for-youtube/.

[7] http://www.dbms2.com/2010/10/06/ebay-followup-greenplum-out-teradata-10-petabytes-hadoop-has-some-value-and-more/.

[8] http://gigaom.com/cloud/facebook-trapped-in-mysql-fate-worse-than-death/.

[9] http://www.att.com/gen/press-room?pid=4800&cdvn=news&newsarticleid=30623.

[10] http://en.wikipedia.org/wiki/Business_intelligence_tools.

[11] http://hadoopblog.blogspot.com/2010/05/facebook-has-worlds-largest-hadoop.html.

[12] http://lhc.web.cern.ch/lhc/.

terms of data size, producing around 13 PBs of data per year. Detectors in the LHC generate approximately 300 gigabytes (GBs) per second of data. This data is processed to search for events of interest, which reduces the data that is stored for further processing to about 300 megabytes per second (MB/s). Processed data from experiments is distributed from CERN to several other institutions around the world, which act as backups for CERN data and serve as regional data centers to support a whole range of science with universities in their region. Within a decade, astronomy may take over as the largest generator of scientific data when the Square Kilometer Array radio telescope is built.[13] This massive project will create a telescope fifty times more sensitive than exists today. The anticipated 1-TB/s data stream (or an exabyte of data every thirteen days when in full operation) will need to be processed in real time to reduce it to a size that can be meaningfully stored and processed. Even then, estimates are that a 100-petaflop supercomputer, an order of magnitude more powerful than exists today, will be needed for scientific analysis.

Simulations are also generators of complex and massive data sets. For example, climate simulations executing on petaflop supercomputers produce thousands of data sets that contain the predicted values of various climate variables (temperature, wind speed, and so on) for the duration of the simulation, often for hundreds of years. These data sets fuel scientific investigations around the world on the effects of climate change. To address the challenge of managing the results from multiple simulations with different characteristics (scale, time, or initial conditions), the climate community has invested in the Earth System Grid (ESG).[14] ESG provides a gateway to a data collection of hundreds of terabytes of results from climate simulations that are physically hosted at data centers across the United States and supports 2,500 users.

Systems biology is another scientific discipline that is heavily data dependent. The discipline is characterized by numerous GB-TB data collections, typically accessed through applications made available to users for downloading and processing specified data sets. Examples of such sites are GenBank[15] and KEGG.[16] Currently, these applications are hosted at institutional sites and accessed through Web-based interfaces or custom-built software applications. The range of features supported by each application for interactive users varies in range and quality, as does the extent of programmatic facilities for building access to the data collections into complex and multistage analyses. As the size and complexity of biological data sets continue to grow, this approach to

[13] http://www.skatelescope.org/.
[14] www.earthsystemgrid.org.
[15] http://www.ncbi.nlm.nih.gov/genbank/.
[16] http://www.genome.jp/kegg/.

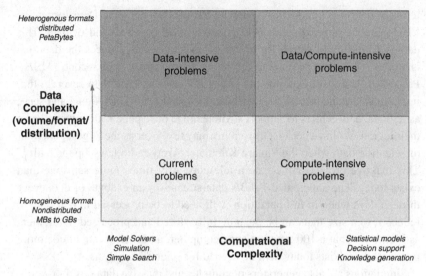

Figure 1.2. Data-intensive computing dimensions.

data analysis is becoming increasingly demanding, and new architectures for serving data and providing analytics are required. An early example of this is the iPlant Collaborative [6] at the University of Texas.

1.3 Characterizing Data-Intensive Applications

As the previous section illustrates, data-intensive computing challenges can be found in many different application domains. Across these domains, the specific challenges vary in their characteristics, scale, and complexity. Fundamentally, however, data-intensive applications have two major challenges:

1. Manage and process exponentially growing data volumes, often arriving in streams from sensors, networks, or outputs from simulations.
2. Significantly reduce data analysis cycles so that timely analyses and decisions can be made.

Undoubtedly, there is an overlap between data- and compute-intensive problems. Figure 1.2 shows a simple diagram that can be used to classify the application space between data and compute intensiveness.

Existing and purely data-intensive applications process multi-terabyte to petabyte size data sets. This data is routinely distributed and in heterogeneous formats, requiring multistep processing by analytical pipelines that incorporate various transformations and fusion of data. Processing typically scales near-linearly with data size, and is often amenable to straightforward parallelization. Key research issues involve data management, filtering and fusion techniques, and efficient querying and distribution.

In addition, combined data/compute-intensive problems exhibit an increase in computational complexity. Processing typically scales super-linearly with data size and requires complex searches, analyses, and fusion in order to produce key insights from the data. Application requirements may also place time limits on producing useful results. Key research issues include new algorithms, signature generation, and specialized processing platforms for algorithm acceleration (such as reduced memory latency and hardware accelerators like GPGPUs).

To offer another perspective on data-intensive application characteristics, we've defined a number of key criteria that enable the quantitative and qualitative assessment of different applications. These criteria are as follows:

Data Size: The absolute size of the data that must be processed for an application is a key characteristic. As data sizes grow, issues that are straightforward for small data sets become problematic. As a simple example, it takes a minute or so to upload a low-quality video of thirty seconds from your phone to YouTube. But try uploading a 5-GB high-definition video and you'll find that at the very least it takes a few hours and greatly increases the chance of encountering a network error (or loss of battery power). Massive data sets take longer to write, search, and transmit over a network, and any bottlenecks in your software or hardware are cruelly exposed, which limits overall system performance.

Complexity of analysis: Single pass algorithms through a data collection – for example, a search through a text file for keywords – scale linearly with size. Building indexes over data sets in a single pass can speed up subsequent access if the index can be used. Using the text search example again, Lucene[17] is an open-source technology for full text indexing and searching and is widely used behind many Web sites to power fast text searches. Indexes in databases serve a similar purpose. However, many applications require complex analysis where algorithms do not scale linearly with data size. For example, sorting large data sets is expensive, with a Bubble sort having a time complexity of $O(n^2)$ for n items being sorted. Breadth-first graph searches have a worst-case time complexity of O(number of edges + number of nodes). Of course, parallel implementations of algorithms and specialized hardware architectures can be

[17] http://lucene.apache.org.

used to reduce execution times, but data set sizes are still a significant factor in the speedups that can be achieved.

Space complexity also plays a part in analysis complexity. Attractive algorithms minimize the amount of memory and disk space that an algorithm needs. However, there is often a trade-off between time and space complexity for an algorithm. Classic examples of such trade-offs are:

- the space taken by an index in order to speed up search time;
- storing data in compressed formats at the expense of the time taken to uncompress the data when processing is needed; and,
- storing images of commonly accessed charts and analyses, for example historical rainfall amounts, instead of calculating the images from raw data each time a request is made.

Number of data sources: An additional complexity factor in data-intensive applications is the number of data sources that must be accessed. For example, processing network packets to determine connections between machines is nontrivial on a high-speed network, but life gets much more complex when a recognized IP address must be correlated with data from other sources to try to determine the identity of a user. Multiple data sources also exacerbate the complexity of application reliability, as a required data source may fail independently and, therefore, be unavailable when needed.

Heterogeneity of the data: Another key challenge is the heterogeneity of the data required by an application. For example, many bioinformatics applications must query several external databases and relate the returned data to experimental data from sequencing machines. Also, the proliferation of formats, both proprietary and standardized, greatly complicates this task. Even data in the same format, for example NetCDF, may have data items that represent different concepts that need correlating in an application. Appropriate metadata, controlled vocabularies, and ontologies are all key components of making handling data heterogeneity both tractable and scalable.

Distribution of data: Distributed data sources bring both reliability and latency challenges. Applications that access external distributed data must deal with possible failures, and access to data over wide area networks incurs latency costs that can become prohibitive as data sets grow in size, even when compression is used.

Timeliness of processing: Most data-intensive applications, such as searching for new stars from telescope data, just need to execute as fast as possible in producing a result. Others have time constraints within which analyses must complete in order to produce useful results. Video processing is a good example. Loading a video onto YouTube is an example of the former, whereas

Table 1.1. *Using the assessment framework for two different data-intensive applications*

Application Characteristic	Cyber-Security	Bioinformatics
Data size	10s of TBs per day from network sensors, in the form of processed raw network data	TBs of data in experimental databases
Complexity of analysis	Multistage, comprising signature generation, clustering, anomaly detection, and visualization	Multistage, comprising input data transformations, HPC analysis code, and interactive visualization
Heterogeneity of data	Correlation of Web-mined text information with structured network data	Need to process both proteomic and genomic data
Number of data sources	For core processing pipeline, there is one major source that receives reduced data from many network sensors that perform preliminary processing.	Databases for relevant gene and protein data sets
Distribution of data	Core processing pipeline handles one incoming data stream from network sensors and stores results in a single database.	Processing pipeline needs to retrieve data sets from geographically distributed databases. This can be costly if transfers occur over the Internet.
Timeliness of processing	Results of analysis required in seconds to a minute	"As fast as possible" processing requirements, but ideally a few 10s of seconds or less for interactive exploration of data

automated recognition and tracking of vehicles by citywide surveillance systems obviously has time constraints for processing. For low-latency real-time constraints, specialized hardware is often the only solution for a given application. When constraints are of the order of seconds to minutes, parallel processing and high-speed networks can often meet the necessary deadlines.

As an example of how this framework can be used, we classify the major characteristics of two applications that are described in later chapters in Table 1.1. As can be seen, this framework gives a concise representation that can be used to compare applications across the broad spectrum of data-intensive and big data computing.

1.4 Summary

This chapter lays out the broad landscape of data-intensive computing, describing example application domains where such problems are prevalent and presenting a framework for characterizing data-intensive software systems. Given the exponentially increasing data volumes being generated, and the new and innovative ways being discovered for analyzing and exploiting that data, we are now only at the beginning of the data-intensive, or the big data computing era.

The future will require the creation of breakthrough technologies to address many key data-intensive computing problems, bringing together results from various disciplines in computer science, engineering, and mathematics. For example, the following are all pieces of the puzzle required by data-intensive computing solutions:

- New algorithms that can scale to search and process massive data sets.
- New metadata management technologies that can scale to handle complex, heterogeneous, and distributed data sources.
- Advances in high-performance computing platforms to provide uniform high-speed memory access to multi-terabyte data structures.
- High-performance, high-reliability, and petascale distributed file systems.
- Flexible and high-performance software integration technologies that facilitate "plug and play" integration of software components running on diverse computing platforms to quickly form analytical pipelines.
- Data signature generation techniques for data reduction and rapid processing.
- Mobile code-based analytics, where processing is moved to the data.

The remainder of this book describes the current state of the art and potential futures in many of these areas. The next chapter dissects the anatomy of data-intensive applications, describing the various computational methods, software components, and technologies that are relevant. The following collection of chapters delves into detail on hardware architectures, data management approaches, and cloud-based technologies that are all fundamental application building blocks. Next, the book contains chapters on fundamental algorithms for data classification, clustering, and dimensionality reduction. Finally, data-intensive applications in biology and cyber-security are described, giving insights into how the various building blocks covered in earlier chapters can be brought together to create innovative solutions to challenging big data problems.

References

1. Johnston, W. "High-Speed, Wide Area, Data Intensive Computing: A Ten Year Retrospective." Presented at 7th IEEE Symposium on High Performance Distributed Computing, Chicago, July 1998.
2. Hey, A. J. G. and Trefethen, A. E. "The Data Deluge: An e-Science Perspective." In Berman, F., Fox, G. C. and Hey, A. J. G. (eds.), *Grid Computing – Making the Global Infrastructure a Reality.* 809–24. Wiley and Sons, 2003. From http://eprints.soton.ac.uk/257648/.
3. Bell, G., Gray, J., and Szalay, A. "Petascale Computational Systems." *Computer* 39, no. 1 (2006): 110–12.
4. Newman, H. B., Ellisman, M. H., and Orcutt, J. A. 2003. "Data-Intensive e-Science Frontier Research." *Commun. ACM* 46, no. 11 (Nov. 2003): 68–77.
5. Dean, J., and Ghemawat, S. "MapReduce: Simplified Data Processing on Large Clusters." *Commun. ACM* 51, no. 1 (Jan. 2008): 107–13.
6. Stanzione, Dan. "The iPlant Collaborative: Cyberinfrastructure to Feed the World," *IEEE Computer* (Nov. 2011), 44–52.

2

Anatomy of Data-Intensive Computing Applications

Ian Gorton and Deborah K. Gracio

2.1 An Architecture Blueprint

As the previous chapter describes, data-intensive applications arise from the interplay of ever-increasing data volumes, complexity, and distribution. Add the needs of applications to process this complex data mélange in ever more interesting and faster ways, and you have an expansive landscape of specific application requirements to address.

Not surprisingly, this breadth of specific requirements leads to many alternative approaches to developing solutions. Different application domains also leverage different technologies, adding further variety to the landscape of data-intensive computing. Despite this inherent diversity, several model solutions for contemporary data-intensive problems have emerged in the last few years. The following briefly describes each one:

Data processing pipelines: Emerging from scientific domains, many large data problems are addressed using processing pipelines. Raw data that originates from a scientific instrument or a simulation is captured and stored. The first stage of processing typically applies techniques to reduce the data in size by removing noise and then processes the data (such as index, summarize, or markup) so that it can be more efficiently manipulated by downstream analytics. Once the capture and initial processing takes place, complex algorithms search and process the data. These algorithms create information and/or knowledge that can be digested by humans or further computational processes. Often, these analytics require large-scale distribution or specialized high-performance computing platforms to execute, making the execution environment of most pipelines both distributed and heterogeneous. Finally, the analysis results are presented to users so that they can be digested and acted upon. This stage can utilize advanced visualization tools, and ideally enables the user to step back through the processing steps that have been executed in order to

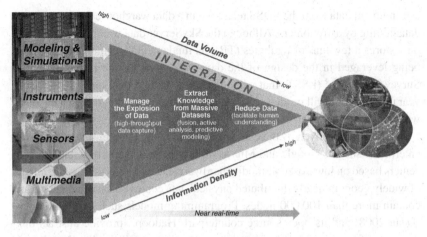

Figure 2.1. Blueprint for a data-intensive processing pipeline.

perform forensic investigations to validate the outcome. Also, users typically need functionality to modify parameters on some of the analytics that have been performed and reexecute various steps in the processing pipeline.

As Figure 2.1 depicts, processing pipelines start with large data volumes with low information content. This data is reduced by the subsequent processing steps in the pipeline to create relatively small data sets that are rich in information and are suitable for visualization or human understanding. In many applications, for example the Atlas[1] high-energy physics experiment, large data sets are moved between sites over high-speed, wide-area networks for downstream pipeline processing.

Data warehouses: Commercial enterprises are voracious users of data warehousing technologies. These are supplied by mainstream database technology vendors to provide archival storage of business transactions for business analysis purposes. As enterprises capture and store more data, data warehouses have grown into the petabyte (PB) range. Best known is Walmart's, which in more than a decade has grown to store more than a petabyte in 2007, and is fueled by daily data from more than 800 million transactions generated by its 30 million customers.[2]

The data warehousing approach is now finding traction in science. The Sloan Digital Sky Survey[3] (SDSS) SkyServer stores the results of processing raw

---

[1] http://atlas.web.cern.ch/Atlas/index.html.
[2] Information Week, August 6, 2007 issue.
[3] http://cas.sdss.org/dr6/en/.

astronomical data from the SDSS telescope in a data warehouse for subsequent data mining by astronomers. Although the SkyServer data warehouse currently only stores a few tens of terabytes (TB), its fundamental design principles are being leveraged in the design of the data warehouse for the Large Synoptic Survey Telescope[4] (LSST) that will commence data production in 2019. Each year the telescope will produce 6.8 PBs of raw data, requiring the resulting data warehouse to grow at an expected rate of 300 TBs per year.

Data centers: Driven by the explosive growth of the Internet, Internet search enterprises such as Google and Microsoft have developed multi-petabyte data centers based on low-cost commodity hardware. Data is stored across a number of widely geographically distributed physical data centers, each of which might contain more than 100,000 nodes. Programming models such as MapReduce (Dean 2008) and its open source counterpart, Hadoop,[5] provide abstractions that simplify writing applications that access this massively distributed data collection.

Essentially, MapReduce distributes data and processing across clusters of commodity computers, and processes the data in parallel and locally at each node. In this way, massively parallel processing can be simply achieved using clusters that comprise thousands of nodes. In addition, the supporting run-time environment provides transparent fault tolerance by automatically duplicating data across nodes and detecting and restarting computations that fail on a particular node.

This approach is also attracting interest from the scientific community. The National Science Foundation is partnering with Google and IBM to provide a 1,600 node cluster for academic research.[6] Supported by Hadoop's open source software, this provides an experimental platform for scientists and researchers to investigate new data-intensive computing applications.

Regardless of the style of data-intensive solutions, there are a number of stages that are common to most, if not all, data-intensive applications. These include data acquisition, reduction, analysis, and visualization. In addition, applications leverage scalable software infrastructures for data management and workflow orchestration that enable the various components of a solution to communicate and share both intermediate and final results.

The following sections delve into each of these areas and present overviews of the general approaches that are widely utilized. They also describe some of the state-of-the-art technologies that are prominent in today's data-intensive applications.

---

[4] www.lsst.org.
[5] http://hadoop.apache.org/.
[6] http://www.nsf.gov/news/news_summ.jsp?cntn_id=111186.

2.2 Data Acquisition

Data acquisition is concerned with making the required input data available for a data-intensive application and is typically the first step in a processing pipeline. In large experimental facilities such as the Large Hadron Collider, highly specialized hardware and software systems are used to deal with streams of data coming from instruments at a rate of several gigabytes per second (GB/s) [1]. Data from these experiments are stored in large archives and subsequently become the input to further downstream data analyses.

In many applications, data acquisition consists of gathering together data sets from multiple sources to perform an analysis. Bioinformatics is an example where multiple distributed data bases are often accessed by biologists to download data sets to local servers where they can be easily processed. For example, MG-RAST[7] is a system for annotation and comparative analysis of metagenomes (genetic material recovered directly from environmental samples that contain multiple genes). MG-RAST users upload raw sequence data, which is normalized and processed, and subsequently made available to users through several tools, for example to compare the metabolism and annotations of one or more metagenomes and genomes. Users can also download all the data generated by the MG-RAST pipeline in a variety of common formats using protocols such as FTP and HTTP. Many other bioinformatics databases operate in an analogous fashion, providing biologists with a rich, albeit fragmented, collection of public data sets for their work.

Downloads of large data sets over the Internet can be an extremely time-consuming exercise. In fact, much data is still shipped around on disk (see http://aws.amazon.com/importexport/ for how one cloud provider handles this). Ensuring that all the data sets are ready and available for processing is an important element in data-intensive applications. This is especially true when computations have to be scheduled, for example on a supercomputer, or you are paying for cycles from a cloud provider. Waiting for a few TBs of data to download while you hold compute resources idle is never a desirable situation.

2.3 Data Reduction

Simply put, data reduction is the transformation of data into a simplified form, which is more amenable to downstream processing. An extreme example of this is found again in the realm of high-energy physics, in which the Belle II

---

[7] http://metagenomics.anl.gov/.

accelerator[8] is projected to produce approximately 250 PB of raw data for processing. It is estimated that only 1 percent of this data will contain events that are interesting for various analyses, representing a large-scale data reduction challenge.

In fact, data-intensive applications demand that data-reduction techniques are one pass in order to be scalable. It is simply not computationally efficient to process massive data sets many times in their entirety in order to produce a reduced form. In network packet processing applications, simple reduction techniques such as throwing away acknowledgement packets can be used. In many experimental domains, data is often reduced during acquisition from an instrument, and further techniques are used to cluster, collate, or index the remaining data for efficient processing. Indexing is particularly efficient in applications where the raw data cannot be thrown away. Indexing using a database or some file-system based approach provides an efficient way for applications to search over very large data collections.

Google's search engine works using a combination of data reduction and indexing. Crawled Web pages are passed to an indexer function that indexes each word in a document, storing a list of documents in which the term appears and the precise location of the word in the text. Stop words such as *the* and *it* are not indexed, reducing data volumes. This design supports rapid access to the documents that contain user query terms in response to Google searches.

Another common data reduction technique is the generation of mathematical signatures. A signature is a unique or distinguishing measurement, pattern, or collection of data that identifies a phenomenon (object, action, or behavior) of interest. Signatures are analogous to people's fingerprints – providing compact and computationally efficient representations of complex data sets.

Across multiple domains, signatures are used in a variety of ways:

- biomarkers can be used to indicate the presence of disease or identify a drug resistance;
- acoustic signals distinguish one maritime vessel from another; and
- anomalous network traffic is often an indicator of a computer virus or malware.

Useful signatures often exist at the boundary of knowledge domains. For example, signatures created from text, multimedia, and sensor data can be used to produce new ways of summarizing key features in large, heterogeneous data sets. Signature attributes may be generated from underlying data through

[8] http://belle2.kek.jp/.

very complex and nonlinear relationships, and typically require expert domain knowledge to help identify the characteristics of useful signatures.[9]

Data reduction is an integral part of any data-intensive application. Chapter 6 presents an in-depth description of data reduction techniques for streaming that illustrates many of the fundamental principles required for effective data reduction.

2.4 Data Analysis and Visualization

Once data has been reduced to a manageable size, applications perform various analyses to recognize patterns in the data and often find obscure relationships between data items. Even with reduced data sizes, efficient processing can typically only be achieved by using data parallel algorithms that exploit underlying computational clusters. Data parallel applications partition the data into multiple segments, which can be processed independently and concurrently across multiple compute nodes, and then reassemble the partial results to produce the outputs.

A wide range of algorithms are commonly used for data-intensive applications, and precise needs are obviously application-specific. The following are some examples we often use:

- **Classifiers:** The ability to classify data using some application-defined classification scheme is widely used across domains, from Internet search to biology. Many classification algorithms exist, based on statistical (such as regression or Bayesian Networks) or structural (such as rule-based or neural networks) techniques. Classifiers require a training phase based on reference structures that divide the space of all possible data points into a set of non-overlapping classes. An example of a classifier in action is in Chapter 7, which describes using a highly efficient implementation of Support Vector Machines for data-intensive biological applications.
- **Clustering:** Clustering assigns sets of data items into groups (called clusters), such that the data items in the same cluster are more similar (in some application-defined sense) to each other than to those in other clusters. Many clustering algorithms exist, each with their own strengths and weaknesses in terms of efficiency and exactly what characteristics of data constitute a cluster. Examples are centroid- (such as k-means), distribution- (such as multivariate normal distributions) and connectivity-based (such as hierarchical) methods.

---

[9] Signature discovery, generation, and validation are active research areas. See http://signatures.pnnl.gov/ for more details.

- **Search:** Searching large and complex data sets efficiently is necessary in many data-intensive applications in order to find a data object with specified properties among a collection of objects. Search approaches abound, but the most effective is dictated by the organization of the data being searched. For simple structures, brute-force searches can be made to scale on massively parallel platforms. Heuristic searches, where knowledge about structure of the data is exploited to increase search efficiency, are also widely used. Numerous algorithms exist for searching graph-based data. However, traversing large graphs is not computationally efficient on commodity clusters, and specialized hardware can be exploited gainfully to increase graph algorithm performance. Chapter 3 includes a description of the Cray XMT, a thread-based hardware architecture for processing graph-based data.

Providing meaningful visual representations of the results of data-intensive applications helps users understand and explore the results, distilling complex relationships into graphs, images, and charts that communicate information clearly and effectively through graphical means. As an everyday example, Figure 2.2 shows a visual representation of Facebook relationships. The tight clusters of nodes represent groups of people who are more closely related in Facebook; sparsely connected nodes are visualized on the edge of the graph, indicating they are less connected to others in this group. This is a common data visualization technique. Tools such as InSpire[10] enable users to visually explore such representations through panning and zooming, and then by selecting nodes to view the data associated with a specific node in the graph.

Visualization is a reasonably mature area of investigation in computer science and mathematics. This means that a data-intensive application developer can draw upon a rich collection of open source and commercial tools for their specific visualization needs. Scientific visualization technologies such as VisiT[11] and ParaView[12] provide many capabilities for advanced data visualization and can run in *client-server* mode, whereby the server processes the data on the compute node it resides and transmits only the generated visualization to the user. This provides a highly attractive and efficient approach for visualizing massive data sets without incurring the costs of moving the data to a site for visualization. Other powerful visualization tools and libraries, which

---

[10] http://in-spire.pnnl.gov/.
[11] https://wci.llnl.gov/codes/visit/.
[12] http://www.paraview.org/.

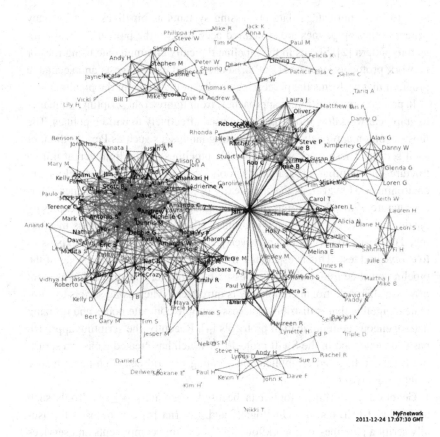

Figure 2.2. Visualization of Facebook relationships.

are routinely used in all data-intensive domains, include gnuplot,[13] Java 3D,[14] MATLAB,[15] and OpenGL.[16]

2.5 Data Processing Pipeline Infrastructure

Data-intensive applications inevitably comprise a number of processing steps to transform massive and complex data sets into information that is usable by humans and other computational systems. Scientists and engineers commonly

[13] http://www.gnuplot.info/.
[14] http://java3d.java.net/.
[15] http://www.mathworks.com/index.html.
[16] http://www.opengl.org/.

refer to these multistage data-processing systems as pipelines, and in many instances these pipelines are structured according to the pipe and filter architecture pattern [2]. Stages in the pipeline typically communicate using files or network protocols such as HTTP or sockets, and each stage is an executable program that performs the processing needed at that stage in the pipeline.

In practice, many different approaches, from lightweight scripting languages to graphical workflow tools, have been used effectively to build pipelines. The most common approach is to use scripting languages such as Perl, Python, or shell scripts. These work well for simple pipelines, as the lightweight infrastructure and familiar programming tools provide an effective development environment. However, as the complexity of pipelines grows, the general purpose nature of the abstractions in these languages make it difficult to explicitly handle concurrency, distributed communications, and asynchronous messaging. This leads to scripts that are overly complex and increasingly expensive to evolve and test. This is especially true when the outputs of one stage of the pipeline must be routed to and processed by multiple, concurrent downstream processes [3]. Additional complexity is introduced when using scripts to automate a pipeline that is distributed across multiple compute nodes and utilizing heterogeneous communication protocols [4]. Recently, the scripting approach has been extended in the Swift project [5], which has created a custom scripting language targeted at applications running on grid and high-performance computing platforms.

Generalized workflow tools can be used to create pipelines. Tools such as Kepler, BPEL-based technologies, and Taverna [6] can be used to visually script a pipeline-style workflow, link in existing components and services through a variety of protocols, including Web services, and then deploy and orchestrate the pipeline. These tools and approaches can be used to describe pipelines, but similar to scripting languages, they must explicitly describe concurrency and buffering requirements. This can add considerable complexity to pipeline descriptions. In addition, they are heavyweight in terms of development infrastructure (that is, they require visual programming with custom languages) and run-time overheads. The run-time overheads make them particularily inappropriate for building pipelines that need to process high-volume data streams, where fast context switching, lightweight concurrency, and buffering are paramount.

Custom approaches also exist for building pipelines. Prominent in this category are Pipeline Pilot [7] and the MeDICi Integration Framework (MIF) [8]. Pipeline Pilot provides a client-server architecture similar to that of BPEL-based tools. The client tools are used to visually create pipelines in a custom graphical language, based upon underlying service-oriented components. The server executes pipelines defined by the client, orchestrating externally defined components through SOAP-based communications. The client also provides a proprietary scripting language to enable custom manipulation of data as it flows between the main steps of the pipeline. In contrast, MIF is built upon a commercial-grade enterprise service bus, Mule,[17] and represents pipeline stages as components that are connected into pipelines using connectors that can utilize any protocols through simple configuration. Concurrent processing and buffering between stages are implicit in a MIF application and are tuned through configuration parameters. Explicit abstractions for handling large data sets and moving them between distributed compute nodes in the pipeline greatly ease the difficulty of creating high-performance and data-intensive applications for pipeline designers.

As data-intensive applications continue to grow in both scale and fidelity, the demands placed on the computational pipeline infrastructures proportionally increase. In the last five years, we have frequently seen the following application drivers for change in deployed pipeline-based systems:

- **Scalability:** Pipeline-based applications need to scale to handle larger and more complex data sets without significant increases in processing times.
- **Modifiability:** Scientists and engineers wish to experiment with different algorithms at various stages in the pipeline, and hence need to easily change the algorithms for a given pipeline stage.
- **Complexity:** New codes need to be incorporated into the pipeline, resulting in a more complex pipeline topology based on processing path forks and joins.

2.6 Data Management

Architectures and technologies for data management play essential roles in data- intensive applications. Chapter 1 describes how petascale repositories exist already and are built upon technologies ranging from relational data ware-houses to column-oriented data stores such as HBase, parallel file systems such as Lustre, and specialized hardware storage appliances such as Netezza. Many factors dictate the most appropriate solution for given application requirements. Chapters 4 and 5 explore such factors in depth.

Often, different data persistence mechanisms are used at different stages of the data processing pipeline. During data acquisition, it may be necessary to

---

[17] http://www.mulesoft.com/.

write data using simple structures to a high-performance file system so that data capture can keep up with data production from an instrument, simulation, or sensor. The data reduction phase, perhaps in parallel with data capture, will operate on these structures, and write its outputs to a structured data store such as a column-oriented database, upon which downstream analytics can more efficiently operate. The results from the analytics stage may subsequently be loaded into a relational data warehouse so users can explore the data using the interactive query tools that are packaged with the data warehousing technology.

2.7 Summary

This chapter breaks down data-intensive applications into their constituent stages and describes various approaches, techniques, and technologies that are appropriate at each stage. Although not every stage in this abstract data-intensive processing pipeline will be equally applicable in every application, the underlying pipeline-based architecture can be viewed as a blueprint, or pattern [9], for designing such applications.

Exactly how specific data-intensive applications are conceived and implemented depends very much on the application characteristics, deployment environment, and the skills of system architecture and development team. The range of alternative concrete software architectures (such as MapReduce or MPI), deployment infrastructures (such as public cloud or private HPC cluster), and data management platforms (such as column-oriented data stores or parallel file systems) is daunting, requiring the design team to take a broad view of the application requirements, and crucially explore how it is expected to evolve in terms of data sizes and analytical needs. Big data problems have a habit of quickly teasing out any inherent bottlenecks and performance weaknesses in an application design and implementation. This calls for careful design, prototyping, and stress testing of potential solutions so that unpleasant surprises are minimized in sometimes merciless production environments.

References

1. Roukoutakis, F., S., Chapeland, and Cobanoglu, O. "The ALICE-LHC Online Data Quality Monitoring Framework: Present and Future." *Real-Time Conference, 2007 15th IEEE-NPSS*, (April 29 2007–May 4 2007): 1–6. http://ieeexplore.ieee.org/xpl/articleDetails.jsp?reload=true&arnumber=4382730&contentType=Conference+Publications.
2. Shaw, M., and Garlan, D. *Software Architecture: Perspectives on an Emerging Discipline.* Upper Saddle River, New Jersey: Prentice-Hall, Inc., 1996.

3. McPhillips, T., Bowers, S., Zinn, D., and Ludascher, B. "Scientific Workflow Design for Mere Mortals." *Future Generation Computer Systems 25*, no. 5, (May 2009): 541–51.
4. Ludscher, Bertram, Mathias Weske, Timothy Mcphillips, and Shawn Bowers. "Scientific Workflows: Business as Usual?" In *Proceedings of the 7th International Conference on Business Process Management* (BPM '09), edited by Umeshwar Dayal, Johann Eder, Jana Koehler, and Hajo A. Reijers. 31–47. Berlin, Heidelberg: Springer-Verlag, 2009.
5. Wilde, I. F., Iskra, K., Beckman, P., Zhang, Z., Espinosa, A., Hategan, M., Clifford, B., and Raicu, I. "Parallel Scripting for Applications at the Petascale and Beyond." *Computer 42*, no. 11, (2009): 50–60.
6. Barker, A., and van Hemert, J. "Scientific Workflow: A Survey and Research Directions." In *Lecture Notes in Computer Science*, Volume 4967/2008. 746–53. Berlin, Heidelberg: Springer-Verlag, 2008.
7. Yang, Xiaoyu, Richard P. Bruin, and Martin T. Dove. "Developing an End-to-End Scientific Workflow," *Computing in Science and Engineering*, (May/June 2010), 52–61.
8. Gorton, I., Wynne, A., Liu, Y., and Yin, J. "Components in the Pipeline." Software, *IEEE 28*, no. 3 (May-June 2011): 34–40.
9. Gorton, I. *Essential Software Architecture (2nd ed.).* Berlin, Heidelberg: Springer-Verlag, 2011.

3

Hardware Architectures for Data-Intensive Computing Problems: A Case Study for String Matching

Antonino Tumeo, Oreste Villa, and Daniel Chavarría-Miranda

3.1 Introduction

Data-intensive applications have special characteristics that in many cases prevent them from executing well on traditional cache-based processors. They can have highly irregular access patterns with very little locality that do not match the expectations of automatically controlled caches. In other cases, such as when they process data in streaming, they do not have temporal locality at all and only limited spatial locality, therefore reducing the effectiveness of caches.

We present an application-driven study of several architectures that are suitable for data-intensive algorithms. Our chosen application is high-speed string matching, which exhibits two key properties of data-intensive codes: highly irregular access patterns and high-speed streaming data. Irregular access patterns appear in string matching when traversing graph-based representations of the pattern dictionaries being used. String matching is typically used in cybersecurity applications to scan incoming network traffic or files for the presence of signatures (such as specific sequences of symbols), which may relate to attack patterns, viruses, or other malware.

3.1.1 String Matching

String matching algorithms check and detect the presence of one or more known symbol sequences inside the analyzed data sets. Besides their well-known application to databases and text processing, they are the basis of several other critical, real-world applications. String matching algorithms are key components of DNA and protein sequencing, data mining, security systems, such as Intrusion Detection Systems (IDS) for Networks (NIDS), Applications (APIDS), Protocols (PIDS), or Systems (Host based IDS [HIDS]), anti-virus software, and machine learning problems. All of these applications process large quantities of textual data and require extremely high performance to produce meaningful results in an acceptable time: for NIDS, modern Ethernet connections can provide more than 10 GB of data per second. In addition, the number of patterns of malicious threats to search nowadays is well over 1 million, and is exponentially increasing [16]. Furthermore, in cases like NIDS, string matching should also allow for real-time behavior, guaranteeing predictable performance independently of the size of the input streams and the number of symbols to search, without hindering the overall performance of the system by reducing the available bandwidth or raising the latency.

Performing string matching with real-time or predictable performance has always been a problem for software-based solutions, because of their tendency to exhibit large performance variabilities when dealing with different sizes of inputs and matching patterns. This behavior is exacerbated by modern Central Processing Units (CPUs), which integrate advanced and complex cache architectures. Intuitively, if a pattern resides in the cache, the matching is fast. If it does not, it has to be retrieved from memory and the algorithm performs poorly. With small dictionaries, or when the same few patterns are matched, the processor accesses only the cache with very high performance. With large dictionaries, when many patterns are matched, they cannot fit all in the cache. If the patterns matched progressively change (for example, there is not locality), this may generate many cache misses and many cache replacement operations. Consequently, the data in the cache are constantly thrashed and the cache becomes ineffective. In many applications, when the input is not known and the data cannot be adequately preprocessed to guarantee some locality, such as network traffic, the matching algorithm accesses pattern data in unpredictable locations of the main memory, leading to highly variable performance.

For these reasons, a large amount of research has been done to design efficient implementations of string matching algorithms using Field Programmable Gate Arrays (FPGAs) [3, 4, 8, 15], highly multithreaded architectures like the Cray XMT [19], multicore processors [11], or heterogeneous processors like the CELL Broadband Engine [14, 20]. Recently, Graphic Processing Units (GPUs) have been demonstrated as a suitable platform for some classes of string matching algorithms for NIDS such as SNORT [6, 12, 18]. Designers of string matching solutions are challenged at the same time along a multi-dimensional space: performance (throughput), performance variability, dictionary size, and flexibility (system customization). FPGA solutions are limited because of their lack of flexibility and difficulty of customization; in addition, they typically cannot support large dictionaries in result of their limited memory sizes. CELL-based implementations require a significant programming effort to extract the performance, therefore making them difficult to integrate and modify for different application areas.

With the emergence of multicore and multithreaded architectures, full software-based approaches have become feasible for high-throughput string matching applications. Architectures such as the multithreaded Sun Niagara 2 and Cray XMT hide memory latencies, common applications with irregular access patterns, by scheduling multiple thread contexts on a cycle-by-cycle basis. Multicore architectures such as the Nehalem-based Intel Xeon and the AMD Opteron processors today contain up to six cores in the same die and twelve on the same socket. Nehalem processors can even use multithreading to maximize the utilization of each core. In the last few years, GPUs have become more flexible and more easily programmable for nongraphic-related computing through interfaces such as CUDA or OpenCL. Because of their large amount of functional units and the high memory bandwidth, GPUs have become an appealing platform for the acceleration of some massively parallel, throughput-oriented applications, and have been appearing more frequently in high performance system configurations. String matching is usually a good candidate for execution on all these parallel architectures. Depending on the specific algorithm, the matching process can be parallelized by dividing the input data set in smaller subsets, each one processed by a single thread. However, maximizing its performance on different architectures requires different optimization techniques that accurately exploit the features of each platform. Even doing so, it may not be sufficient to reach the desired trade-off among throughput, performance variability, dictionary size, and flexibility.

3.1.2 Application Study

In the remainder of this chapter, we present and compare several software-based implementations of the Aho-Corasick string searching algorithm for high-performance systems. We look at how each solution achieves the objectives of supporting large dictionaries, obtaining high performance, enabling flexibility and customization, and limiting performance variability. We discuss the implementation of the algorithm on a range of high-performance architectures, with shared or distributed memory, and with homogeneous or heterogeneous processing elements. For the shared memory solutions, we consider: a Cray XMT with up to 128 processors (128 threads per core), a dual-socket Niagara 2 (8 cores per processor, 8 threads per core), and a dual-socket Intel Xeon 5560 (Nehalem architecture, 4 cores per processor, 2 threads per core). For the distributed memory systems, we evaluate a homogeneous cluster of Xeon 5560 processors (10 nodes, 2 processors per node) interconnected through Infiniband QDR and a heterogeneous cluster where the Xeon 5560 processors are accelerated with Tesla C1060 GPUs (10 nodes, 2 GPUs per node).

3.2 Background

We analyze the problem of string matching using the Aho-Corasick algorithm on high-performance systems. We consider a typical situation where the input is coming from a single source. For example, this is the case of NIDS, where the data is streamed from the network connection. In this scenario, the input set must initially be buffered in memory, and then sent to the processing elements. There is no possibility to prepartition the data, so that in distributed memory architectures they cannot be preallocated to the different nodes. These applications need to reach very high performance to match the bandwidth of today's internet connections (over 10 Gbps). In particular, with NIDS the string matcher should perform well in order to guarantee real-time behavior, without slowing down the network to perform the analysis or letting packets pass uninspected to maintain the connection rate. An aspect that is often not thoroughly considered with NIDS is that for these reasons the performance should not only be high, but also predictable and stable, independent of variations in the dictionaries or the input streams. In fact, as previously introduced, in many implementations the throughput of the matching algorithm depends on the number and the distribution of matching strings in the input, and may significantly change during the matching process itself. An attacker may exploit this weakness by overloading a NIDS with packets that contains specific packets, forcing it to leave subsequent packets unchecked or completely blocking the whole network it is monitoring.

Another crucial element is the size of the dictionaries. Modern high-performance pattern matching applications use dictionaries that contain well over hundreds of thousands, if not millions, of patterns, so approaches that provide a limited amount of memory are not suitable for them or require a significant effort to make the dictionaries fit in the tight constraints. High-performance machines are appealing for pattern matching because they have large memory pools, compared to custom architectures, which can be effectively utilized for software implementations without giving up on the performance or increasing the complexity of the software implementation.

The focus of our evaluation has been the Aho-Corasick string matching algorithm [1]. The algorithm scans an input text T of length m and detects any exact occurrence of each of the patterns of a given dictionary, including partially and completely overlapping occurrences. A detailed presentation of the algorithm can be found in [1] and descriptions of its high-performance implementations can be found in [14 ,19, 20].

The following sections describe the architectures that we used for our evaluation of the Aho-Corasick string matching algorithm.

3.2.1 Cray XMT

The Cray XMT is the commercial name for a shared-memory multithreaded machine developed by Cray under the code name "Eldorado" [2, 5]. The system is composed of dual-socket Opteron AMD service nodes and custom-designed multithreaded compute nodes with *Threadstorm* processors. The entire system is connected using the Cray Seastar-2.2 high-speed interconnect. The XMT system can scale up to 8,192 *Threadstorm* processors and 128 TB of shared memory.

Each Threadstorm processor is able to schedule 128 fine-grained hardware threads to avoid memory-access generated pipeline stalls on a cycle-by-cycle basis. At runtime, a software thread is mapped to a hardware stream comprised of a program counter, a status word, a target register, and thirty-two general purpose registers. Each Threadstorm processor has a Very Long Instruction Word (VLIW) pipeline containing operations for the Memory functional unit, the Arithmetic unit and the Control unit. The Arithmetic unit is capable of performing a floating-point multiply-add per cycle. In conjunction with the control unit doubling as arithmetic unit, a Threadstorm is capable of achieving 1.5 GFlops at a clock rate of 500 MHz. A 64 KB, 4-way associative instruction cache helps in exploiting code locality.

Each Threadstorm is associated with a memory system that can accommodate up to 8 GB of 128-bit wide DDR memory. Each memory controller is complemented with a 128 KB, 4-way associative data cache to reduce access latencies (this is the only data cache present in the entire memory hierarchy). Memory is structured with full-empty-, pointer forwarding-, and trap-bits to support fine grained thread synchronization with little overhead. The memory is hashed at a granularity of 64 bytes (see Figure 3.1) and fully accessible through load/store operations to any Threadstorm processor connected to the Seastar-2.2 network, which is configured in a 3-D toroidal topology. Although memory is completely shared among Threadstorm processors, it is decoupled from the main memory in the AMD Opteron service nodes. Communication between Threadstorm nodes and Opteron nodes is performed through a Lightweight Communication Library (LCM). Continuous random accesses to memory by the Threadstorm processor will top memory bandwidth at around 100 M requests per second.

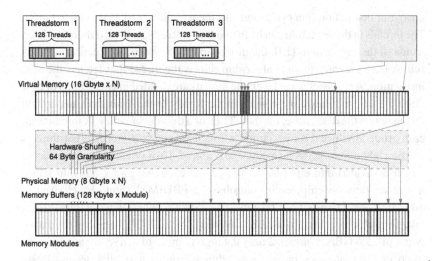

Figure 3.1. Cray XMT Threadstorm memory subsystem.

The software environment on the Cray XMT includes a custom, multi-threaded operating system for the Threadstorm compute nodes (MTX), a paral-lelizing C/C++ cross-compiler targeting Threadstorm, a standard Linux 64-bit environment executing on the service and I/O nodes, as well as the necessary libraries to provide communication and interaction between the two parts of the XMT system.

The XMT machine used in our analysis is composed of 128 nodes, with ThreadStorm processors at 500 MHz, and has 1 TB of memory.

3.2.2 Niagara2

The Niagara 2 processor (also known as the UltraSPARC T2) is the follow on to the Niagara 1 (UltraSPARC T1), a power-efficient chip processor based on the Chip MultiThreading architecture (CMT) optimized for Space, Watts (Power) and Performance (SWaP) [9]. The Niagara 2 has 8 SPARC cores, and each core supports the concurrent execution of 8 threads, for a total of 64 threads per chip. The cores implement the 64-bit SPARC V9 instruction set and have one Load/Store Unit, two execution units, one FPU and a Cryptographic/Stream Processing Unit. The cores have an 8-way 16 KB instruction cache, a 4-way 8 KB data cache, and fully associative 64-entry instruction-TLB, and 128-entry data-TLB. The integer pipeline is eight stages long whereas the floating point pipeline has twelve stages for most operations. The eight threads share the instruction cache, but have their own instruction buffers. The Fetch unit loads up to four instructions per cycle, and puts them in the thread's instruction buffer. The threads in the fetch unit can be in two states: Ready, or Wait if there has been a miss in the instruction-TLB, the instruction cache, or the instruction buffer is full. A least-recently-fetched algorithm selects the thread that fetches the next instruction. At the execution level, the threads are divided in two groups of four threads each, and they can be again in the Ready or the Wait state, depending on misses on the data cache, the data-TLB, or a data dependency. A thread from each group is selected for execution with a least-recently-picked algorithm.

The eight cores access a shared 4 MB level 2 16-way set associative cache, which is divided into eight banks of 512 KB each. Niagara 2 has four memory controllers on chip, each controlling 2 FBDIMM channels, clocked at 400 MHz. Read transactions take two clock cycles, whereas write transactions take four clock cycles, for a read bandwidth of 51.2 GB/s and a write bandwidth of 25.6 GB/s. Niagara 2 uses the high number of active threads per core to cover miss latencies in the cache, thus tolerating a smaller second Level cache compared to other processors.

Our Niagara 2 system is an UltraSparc T5240, which is composed of 2 processors at 1165 MHz (for a total of 128 threads) and 32 GB of memory, and runs SunOS 5.10. In the following, we refer to the whole system as the *Niagara 2*.

3.2.3 Nehalem

Nehalem is the codename for the latest Intel microarchitecture for x86 processors. Nehalem-based processors have currently two, four, six and eight cores, depending on their target market. The processors used in our machines are all four-core implementations, manufactured at 45 nm. Nehalem has a powerful out-of-order core, able to decode up to four x86 istructions per clock cycle through its four decoders (three simple and one complex), and to issue up to 7 μops per cycle. The processor has a 128-entry reservation station and a 128-entry reorder buffer, dispatching up to 6 μops to the execution units through its six ports. Three of these ports access three 128-bit SSE (Streaming SIMD Extension) units, two 128-bit floating point units, and three 64-bit integer units, the other three access the memory units, respectively the store data unit, the store address unit, and the load address unit. Each core has a 32 KB level 1 instruction cache, a 32 KB level 1 data cache, and a 256 KB level 2 cache. All the cores share, in the 4-core implementations, an 8 MB level 3 cache. The caches are inclusive, meaning that the data from a lower level is contained in the higher level. Nehalem has a two-level data TLB hierarchy, where the first level has 64 entries and the second level 512 entries, both 4-way associative.

The cores support Simultaneous Multithreading (commercially named HyperThreading), which allows executing multiple threads per core. In these complex cores, multithreading is used to maximize the utilization of the execution units of the processor by choosing the instructions to execute from multiple threads. Nehalem integrates a memory controller, supporting up to three channels of DDR3 SDRAM and four FB-DIMM channels. Multiple processors and Intel's Northbridge are interconnected through the integrated QuickPath Interconnect (QPI).

For the performance analysis presented in this chapter, we used a system composed of 2 Nehalem-based Xeon 5560 processors, with 24 GB of DDR3 memory at 667 MHz (1333 mega-transfers per second). In the following, we refer to this machine as the *x86 SMP*.

3.2.4 CUDA-Based GPUs

The Compute Unified Device Architecture (CUDA) [10] is defined by NVIDIA both as an architectural paradigm and a programming model for developing General Purpose applications on Graphic Processing Units (GPGPU). NVIDIA provides a toolkit with a C compiler (C for CUDA) that supports some custom extensions for mapping the program onto the architecture. The GPU is considered as a coprocessor to which parallel parts of the application are offloaded. The portion of the program offloaded to the GPU, known as kernel, is divided in a *grid* of up to 65,356 *thread blocks*. Each thread block is composed of up to 512 threads.

We consider the Tesla T10 GPU architecture, which supports compute capability 1.3 and is used in the Tesla C1060 solution. The basic blocks in the architecture are the Streaming Multiprocessors (SM), which are composed of 8 Streaming Processors (SPs), 2 Super Function Units (SFUs), a Dual Precision Streaming Processor (DP), a shared memory of 16 KB, the instruction unit (I-Unit), the instruction cache (I-Cache), and a constant cache (C-Cache). The SPs are the basic single precision Arithmetic Logic Units (ALUs) that perform the basic integer and floating point computations, the SFUs instead are used for the computation of special functions such as transcendental and trigonometric operations. The I-Unit fetches a single operation for a group of thirty-two threads (or, a *warp*) at a time, which are executed by a single SM in a Single Instruction Multiple Data (SIMD) fashion. This means that in a branch, if threads of the same warp takes different directions (*divergence*), the I-Unit must fetch the instructions for all the sides of the branch and the threads must wait for each other, making the execution time equal to the sum of the execution times for all the directions taken. A thread block contains up to sixteen warps, and does not migrate from the SM where it started. Multiple SMs are combined in a Texture Processor Cluster (TPC), which provides a Texture Unit and a Texture Cache. In the T10, three SMs form a single TPC.

All SMs in the GPU access a unified, globally shared memory space known as *global memory*, which is typically on the order of several GB in current implementations. This memory is built out of GDDR RAM, specialized for the bandwidth and access pattern requirements of GPUs. The SMs communicates with the global memory through a crossbar connected to several 64-bit memory controllers. The global memory is accessed also by the host CPU through the PCI Express bus, whereas the shared memory can be read and wrote exclusively by the GPU threads running on the specific SM. The global memory contains kernels and data shared among all SMs. Shared memories, instead, work like scrathpads (for example, they are managed by the programmer) and can contain data shared only among the threads of the same thread block. The memory operations to the shared and the global memory are issued for a half-warp (sixteen threads). The latency of the global memory is in the range of 400-600 cycles, whereas the shared memory, when accessed without bank conflicts, is as fast as the registers (single clock cycle). It is very important to correctly align the accesses of a half-warp to the global memory to coalesce them in a single memory transaction, whereas for the shared memory it is useful to minimize bank conflicts.

Each SM of a device with compute capability 1.3 has 16,384 registers and can keep simultaneously active up to 1,024 threads from different thread blocks. The registers are statically partitioned among all the active threads, whereas the shared memory is allocated per thread block. A low register utilization and a correct sizing of the shared memory are crucial for maximizing the number of active threads. Keeping more threads active means having more warps available to switch in and out of the execution units for covering the latency of the memory operations.

3.2.5 Clustered Machines

Clusters are by far the most common approach for implementing high performance systems today. A compute cluster is composed of individual nodes interconnected together through a dedicated network. The *de facto* standard for programming these machines is the Message Passing Interface (MPI). For our Aho-corasick distributed memory implementations, we used a high-performance cluster with a homogeneous and a heterogeneous configuration of the nodes. The homogeneous configuration uses nodes composed of two Nehalem-based Intel Xeon 5560 at 2.8 GHz on SuperMicro motherboards.

Each processor has 4 cores with 2 threads per cores and 8 MB of second level cache. Our homogeneous cluster has 10 nodes, with 24 GB of DDR 3 memory each (triple channel) at 667 MHz, interconnected through Mellanox Connect X QDR Infiniband.

Our cluster uses 4 Infiniband links (2.5 Gbps each) with quad data signalling rates, reaching a peak rate of 40 Gbps (32 Gbps worth of data) in each direction. For the heterogeneous configurations, we use 5 Tesla S1070 boxes. A Tesla S1070 presents 4 Tesla C1060 GPUs with 4 GB of GDDR3 memory each. The Tesla C1060 is composed of 30 Streaming Multiprocessors (240 Streaming Processors), working at 1.3 GHz. In our 20-GPU cluster, 2 Tesla GPUs are connected to a single node through a switch with a PCI Express 2.0 x16 connection, so they both share a peak bandwidth of 8 GB/s.

3.3 Aho-Corasick Algorithmic Design and Optimization

The basic implementation of the Aho-Corasick Algorithm starts from similar principles for all the architectures analyzed in this work. However, there are aspects in the implementations and the optimizations that are obviously different. In this section, we present the overall basic algorithmic design and then focus on the specific modifications and optimizations for the various platforms.

Starting from the same basis, we designed shared memory implementations using `pthreads` for the Niagara 2, x86 SMP, and the proprietary programming model of the Cray XMT. For the GPU kernel, we used NVIDIA CUDA. For the heterogeneous and homogeneous cluster, instead we designed a MPI load balancer, which can be used alone, or integrated with `pthreads` or CUDA.

3.3.1 Basic Design

Our algorithm design is based on the following cornerstones:

- minimize the number of memory references
- reduce memory contention

This is true for all the implementations. The searched patterns are represented as a Deterministic Finite Automaton (DFA). As the input symbols are scanned, the search algorithm traverses the different nodes of the DFA. For each possible input symbol, there is **always** a valid transition to another node in the graph. This key feature guarantees that for each input symbol there is always the same amount of work to perform. In detail, the Aho-Corasick string matching algorithm works as shown in Algorithm 3.1.

Algorithm 3.1 Basic steps of the DFA-based Aho-Corasick string matching algorithm.

1. **Load** node "0" (or root) from main memory (DFA) in *current_node*.
2. **Load** one input symbol from main memory in *symbol*.
3. **Load** the *next_node* from main memory (DFA) (following the link from the *current_node*, labeled by *symbol*).
4. **Check if** the transition to *next_node* is final (if it is, the last symbols are a matching pattern).
5. **Assign** *next_node* to *current_node*.
6. **Repeat** starting from step 2 **until** there are no more input symbols.

For a given dictionary the data structures in main memory (DFA and input symbols) are readonly. For all the implementations, the common parallelization stategy is to use multiple threads or processes that concurrently execute the algorithm. Each thread or process has a *current_node* and operates on a distinct section of the input.

For each input symbol, there are conceptually two loads to perform, one for the *symbol* itself (Step 2 in Algorithm 3.1) and one for the *next_node* in the DFA (Step 3 in Algorithm 3.1). Step 4 could also involve an extra load for checking if the transition is final or not, but in our implementation it does not, as we explain later.

Step 2 loads contiguous symbols of 8-bits each (ASCII alphabet in our experiments) from main memory. In 32- or 64-bit architectures, the frequency of this load can be reduced respectivively to only one load for every four or eight symbols, shifting and masking to extract the right symbol. Furthermore, accessing the scanned symbols has very high spatial locality.

The load in Step 3 (for *next_node*) is quite different. It is not predictable because it depends on the *symbol* just loaded and on the *current_node*. This load is the main cause of performance degradation on conventional cache-based architectures for this class of algorithms. If the input text contains a large number of patterns that are present in the dictionary, then the entire graph will likely be accessed during the matching process ("heavy" matching). On the other hand, if there is "light" or no matching (such as a dictionary against a random pattern) most of the time the search algorithm will stay on the DFA's node 0 (root) because the failure transitions jump again on node 0 itself.

As already presented in [19], our first algorithmic decision was to implement a scanning engine that performs Step 3 with only one load per symbol. To achieve this goal, we represent the DFA graph as a sparse State Transition Table (STT). The STT is large table composed of as many rows as there are nodes in the DFA and as many columns as there are symbols of the alphabet. Each STT line represents a *node* in the original DFA. Each entry of a STT line (cell) (indexed by a *current_node* and a *symbol*) stores the address of the *beginning* of the STT line that represents the *next_node* for that transition in the DFA. This sparse STT representation is somewhat expensive in terms of the amount of memory required, but it guarantees that Step 3 will only require one load operation. The boolean information indicates if a transition is For the Cray XMT and `pthreads` pattern matchers, the STT lines are 256-byte aligned such that the least significant byte of the address is equal to zero. This property allows us to store in the least significant bit of each STT cell the boolean information indicating if that transition is final or not, removing the need for the extra load in Step 4.

As discussed previously, the load in Step 3 is crucial because this operation could have the highest performance variability. In fact, Step 1 is executed only once, Step 2 loads contiguous symbols that most likely are in the cache, Steps 4, 5, and 6 are arithmetic/logic operations on registers. This basic design is at the core of the `pthreads` implementation for the x86 SMP and the Niagara 2 platforms. Because one of the objectives of our work is to verify if content-independent performance can be provided, we need to obtain a relatively uniform latency for this load.

3.3.2 Cray XMT Implementation

In comparison to other solutions where absolute latency matters, the approach for exploiting the highly multithreaded architecture of the Cray XMT focuses mostly on reducing latency variability. If the latency is constant or low variable, the system is able to schedule a sufficient number of threads to hide it.

On the Cray XMT, the main cause of variability in the memory access time is the presence of hotspots. Hotspots are memory regions frequently accessed by multiple threads simultaneously. Nevertheless, the Cray XMT employs a hardware-hashing mechanism which spreads data in all the system's memory banks with a granularity of 64 bytes (block) [5]. However, if different blocks corresponding to different memory banks have different access ratios, the "pressure" on the memory banks is not equally balanced, producing variability in the access time. In our implementation, there are two reasons why this can happen:

- Each 64-byte block in the XMT's memory can contain multiple STT cells. Thus, it is possible that for, say English text, there might contention and hotspotting on the same memory block for contiguous ASCII symbols.

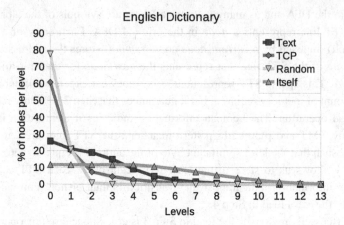

Figure 3.2. Access distribution for an English dictionary with different inputs.

- The first few states of the top levels of a Breadth-First Search (BFS) of the DFA graph are responsible for most of the accesses. Thus, there can be hot-spotting if too many threads are reading those entries simultaneously. Figure 3.2 shows, for an English dictionary with 20,000 patterns, the distribution of the accessed nodes in the DFA as function of the levels when scanned against English Text, a TCP traffic dump, random input, and the dictionary itself.

In order to alleviate the preceding problems, we propose two solutions as shown in [19]:

- **Alphabet shuffling:** The alphabet symbols in a STT line can be shuffled using a relatively simple linear transformation, to ensure that symbols that are contiguous in the alphabet (such as standard English characters in ASCII) are spread out over multiple memory blocks.
- **State replication:** We replicate the STT states corresponding to the first two levels of the BFS exploration of the DFA.

The details of how these mechanisms are implemented on the XMT are discussed in [19]. On cache-based architectures (x86 and Niagara 2), these optimizations would not bring significant benefits, but rather reduce the spatial locality of the cache.

3.3.3 GPU Implementation

The GPU implementation starts from the same principles of the basic design, but requires some specific adaptations. Each CUDA thread independently performs the matching on a chunk of the input text. This allows reasonably sized chunks, while maintaining a high utilization of each thread. The main differences reside in the STT: the rows still represent the states, columns, and symbols, but states are addressed by indices, not by pointers. Each cell of the table, which in our GPU code has a size of 32-bits, contains the index of the next state in the first 31-bits and the flag that tags final states in the last bit. Therefore, we thus reduce memory usage, which is critical for GPUs that can address only up to 4 GB of memory. However, the organization of memory controllers on CUDA-based GPUs requires to further optimize the STT layout. In fact, similar to the basic Cray XMT implementation, it is possible to generate memory hotspots. The reasons are that each memory controller manages a 256-byte wide memory partition, and depending on the number of memory controllers and partitions, the input set and the pattern dictionary, the accesses may concentrate only on a single partition (single memory controller). This problem is known in the GPGPU community as partition camping [13]. To solve this problem, we added padding to each line of the STT corresponding to the size of a partition, allowing a more even access pattern.

The unpredictable nature of the loads on the STT makes it impossible to coalesce the accesses of half-warps in a single memory transaction: with high probability, they are not sequential and not aligned. Thus, we decided to bind the STT to the texture memory. Binding data to texture memory allows fetching the data through the texture units, which do not require coalescence (but still suffer from partition camping), and using the texture caches, which are optimized for 2-D locality. Depending on the particular input set, we underline that the benefits in using the texture cache derive mainly from the hits on the first levels, as shown in Figure 3.2. Textures have a limit on their size (2^{27} elements) in CUDA, so we only bind the first few levels of the STT to textures, which gives the most performance benefits.

In applications with a single point of input, where the data is streamed from the input connection, the symbols are saved in memory sequentially. This means that if they are moved in the same layout to the global memory of the GPU, and each thread starts processing its own chunk, the accesses by a half-warp of threads will be uncoalesced. In fact, each thread will start reading input symbols with the stride of a chunk. Figure 3.3a shows the situation. To offset this problem, we transpose the input in groups of four characters. With this transformation, blocks of four symbols each from each chunk are interleaved so that threads from the same half-warp can read from sequential memory locations four characters at a time with a single 32-bit load. The transformation on the input is shown in Figure 3.3b.

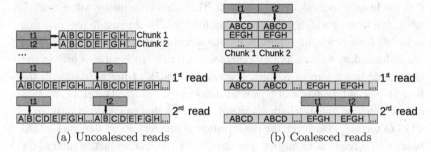

(a) Uncoalesced reads   (b) Coalesced reads

Figure 3.3. Uncoalesced versus coalesced reads on a GPU.

The matching results are collected per chunk. A reduction is applied to gather all the results and send them back to the host through a single memory copy operation. The complete details on the GPU implementation are described in [17].

3.3.4 Distributed Memory Implementation

For distributed memory architectures, we wrapped our string matching engine in an MPI load balancer. MPI is the *de facto* message passing application programming interface for distributed memory machines and it is the dominant model used in high-performance computing today [7]. We developed a master/slave scheduler, where the master MPI process distributes the work, and the slaves perform the effective computation. From the same scheduler, we developed three slightly different implementations for the various configurations of the clustered architectures:

- A **MPI-only** solution for the homogeneous x86 cluster, where each slave process is mapped to a core and wraps a single-threaded version of our string matching engine.
- A **MPI with** `pthreads` solution, where each slave process is mapped to an entire node of the cluster and wraps a multithreaded version of our string matching engine.
- A **MPI with CUDA** solution, where each slave process is mapped to a GPU and wraps a CUDA kernel.

In the basic master/slave implementation, the master divides the input in several chunks and sends data to the slaves as they progressively finish previous chunks. As previously explained in cache-based architectures, the performance of pattern matching strictly depends on the number of matches in the (unknown) input stream. This is also true for our GPU implementation, which uses the

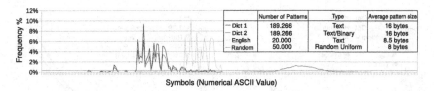

Figure 3.4. Distributions of the symbols in the dictionaries.

cached texture memory to store the STT. The MPI load balancer uses dynamic assignment of fixed chunks of input to each MPI slave to avoid load imbalance between them.

Generally, communication bandwidth among the nodes of a cluster is limited with respect to the computing resources available on each node. If the computational kernels are well optimized for the target computing resources and can reach high throughputs, communication bandwidth may become a significant bottleneck for an application. To overcome this problem, in our distributed string-matching implementations we use multibuffering coupled together with non-blocking MPI communication, allowing overlapping of communication with computation.

3.4 Experimental Results

We have implemented various versions of the Aho-Corasick parallel algorithm as previously described for the Cray XMT multithreaded system, the x86 SMP architecture, the Niagara 2, the GPU cluster, and the x86 cluster. Our implementations are composed of two phases: building the State Transition Table (STT) and executing string matches against the built STT. The STT building phase is performed offline and stored in a file representation. Therefore, we focus our experiments on the string matching phase, because this is the critical portion in the realistic use of this algorithm for network content analysis.

Our experiments utilize four different dictionaries: **Dict 1:** an ≈ 190, 000-pattern data set with mostly text entries with an average length of 16 bytes; **Dict 2:** an ≈ 190,000-pattern data set with mixed text and binary entries with an average length of 16 bytes; **English:** a 20,000-pattern data set with the most common words from the English language, with an average length of 8.5 bytes; and, **Random:** a 50,000-pattern data set with entries generated at random from the ASCII alphabet with an uniform distribution and an average length of 8 bytes. Figure 3.4 presents the distribution of ASCII symbols present in each of the experimental dictionaries. Dictionaries with more text-like entries have higher frequencies of alphabetical ASCII symbols. We also use four different

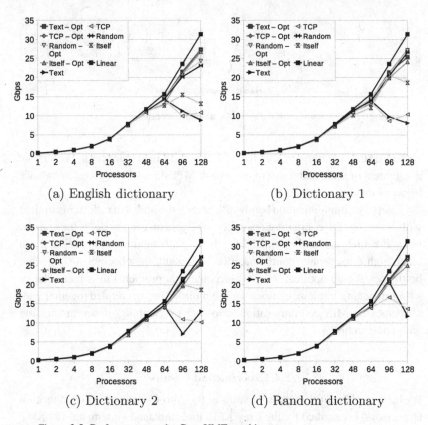

(a) English dictionary

(b) Dictionary 1

(c) Dictionary 2

(d) Random dictionary

Figure 3.5. Performance on the Cray XMT machine.

input streams for each dictionary: **Text**, which corresponds to the English text of the King James Bible; **TCP**, which corresponds to captured TCP/IP traffic; **Random**, which corresponds to a random sample of characters from the ASCII alphabet; and **Itself**, which corresponds to feeding the dictionary itself as an input stream for string matching. As previously discussed, using the dictionary itself as an input will exhibit the "heaviest" matching behavior, thus significantly influencing the performance of the algorithm.

Figure 3.5 shows the performance obtained by the XMT implementations, and compares the basic design to the optimized version which exploits both alphabet shuffling and state replication. With the basic implementation, when using more than 48 processors, the performance remains far from the linear scaling curve, and often the tests with 64 and 128 processors results in slow downs, in particular with the *text* and *TCP* input sets, because of the memory hotspots present in accessing the STT representation by a large number of threads.

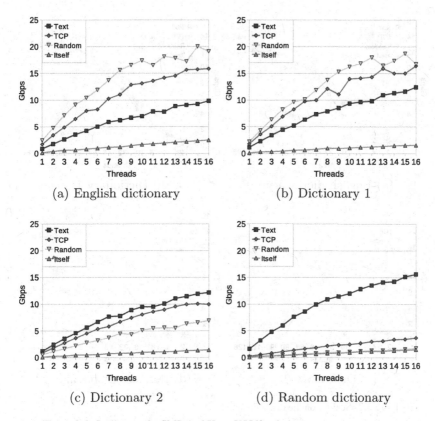

Figure 3.6. Scaling on the SMP dual Xeon X5560 solution.

We can see how, when the optimizations are used, the performance instead is very close to linear scaling, with little differences among the different input sets for all the dictionaries.

The results on the XMT should be compared with the performance of the algorithm on the x86 SMP and the Niagara 2, both with shared memory. We implemented a pthreads-based version of the basic algorithm, which has been compiled with the Intel C Compiler (icc) 11.1 for the x86 SMP and with the Sun C compiler 5.9 for the Niagara 2. Figure 3.6 shows the performance of the x86 SMP. On this system, we executed the benchmarks with HyperThreading enabled, raising the number of threads from 1 to 16 (8 per processor). Figure 3.6 shows that the scaling is not linear and that, in a few low matching cases, raising the number of threads, can slightly reduce the performance. The main reason for this behavior is the complex hierarchy of caches of the Nehalem solution, in particular the shared L3, which may get different access patterns

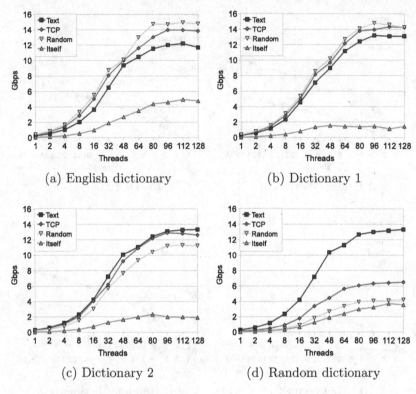

(a) English dictionary

(b) Dictionary 1

(c) Dictionary 2

(d) Random dictionary

Figure 3.7. Scaling on the dual Niagara 2.

when changing the number of threads and the chunks processed by each thread. Figure 3.7 presents the performance of the Niagara 2. On this system, we executed the algorithm raising the number of threads one by one from 1 to 128, but in the figure we report only the most relevant runs. Niagara 2 obtains significant speedups, albeit not linear, with up to 80 threads. At 80 threads, we start getting reduced speedups and over 96 threads the speedups are marginal as the system gets clearly saturated. The Niagara 2 architecture does not seem to be able to cope with heavy matching conditions (dictionaries matched with themselves, and STTs thorougly accessed), because of thrashing of the small second level cache and memory hotspots. For the x86 platform, instead, the performance is more evenly distributed, depending on the type of input streams matched against the dictionary.

It is also worth comparing the best results on the these three shared memory machines with the throughputs obtained by our optimized GPU implementation on a single Tesla C1060 GPU, which may be considered a shared memory

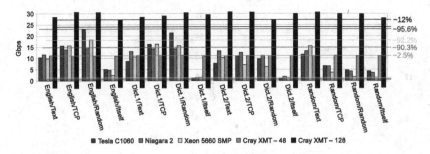

Figure 3.8. Comparison among all the shared memory solutions.

platform, because the STT data structure is shared among the various processing elements. We compiled the kernel with CUDA 3.0. Figure 3.8 presents
this comparison and also shows the performance variability on the various
architectures with our data sets.[1] All the implementations that exploit caching
for the STTs show high variability. The GPU implementation's worst performance is 95 percent slower than the best, the x86 SMP implementation 92.2
percent slower than its best and the Niagara 90.3 percent slower than its best.
Thus, even if GPUs and Niagara exploit multithreading to cover the memory
latencies, they remain still limited by their memory subsystem. The Cray XMT
solution with 48 processors, instead, shows a performance variability of only
2.5 percent with the different combinations of dictionaries and input stream,
and on average is faster than the GPU, the x86, and the Niagara systems.
On the Cray XMT solution with 128 processors, the performance rises up to
28 Gbps, the highest reported in the literature for a software solution with very
large dictionaries, with a variability of only ≈ 12 percent.

For the scaling tests with the full, 10-node x86 cluster, we only show the
pthreads implementation with the MPI load balancer. Instead, the GPU cluster
implementation, uses an MPI process for each CUDA device, thus each node
runs two MPI processes. Figure 3.9 shows the performance obtained while
raising the number of nodes on the x86 cluster from one to ten (thus, from
two to twenty CPUs), while Figure 3.10 shows the performance of the GPU
cluster, again moving from one to ten nodes, corresponding to two to twenty
Tesla C1060 GPUs. In the clustered implementations, the master MPI process
streams the input text to the other nodes in blocks of 3 MB each.

The plots show some interesting behavior. First of all, we notice that the
GPU-accelerated cluster reaches a saturation point with all the datasets. With

---

[1] Note that without the optimizations presented earlier the GPU would hardly obtain speed ups
with respect to a sequential x86 implementation, in particular for the noncoalescent accesses.

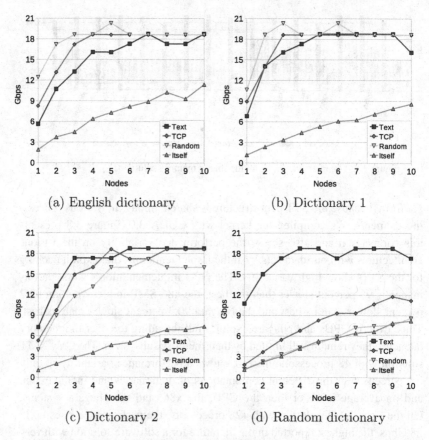

Figure 3.9. Scaling on multiple nodes of the x86 cluster.

an adequate number of nodes, also the heavy-matching benchmarks reach the performance of the light matching benchmarks. This does not happen for the x86 tests, where the heavy-matching benchmarks (the dictionary matched with itself) continue to scale but never reach the performance of the light matching tests. The main bottleneck here appears to be the Infiniband bandwidth.

More detailed analysis of these experimental results appears in [17].

3.5 Conclusion

We have presented several software implementations of the Aho-Corasick pattern matching algorithm for high-performance systems, and carefully analyzed their performance. We have considered the various tradeoffs in terms of peak performance, performance variability, and dataset size. We presented optimized

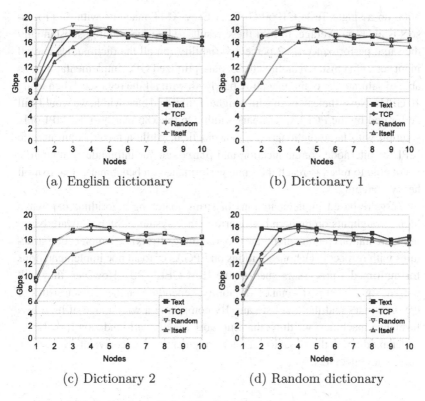

Figure 3.10. Scaling on multiple nodes of the GPU cluster.

designs for the various architectures, discussing several algorithmic strategies for shared memory solutions, GPU accelerated systems, and distributed memory systems.

We found that the absolute performance obtained on the Cray XMT system is one of the highest reported in literature, at ≈ 28 Gbps (using 128 processors) for a software solution with very large dictionaries, and because of its multithreading and memory hashing features the machine is able to maintain stable performance across very different sets of dictionaries and input streams. The Niagara 2 multithreaded solution obtains stable performance only in low and medium matching conditions, whereas a dual Xeon X5660 machine has more varied results, obtaining high peak rates for low-matching conditions, but progressively reducing its performance as the number of matches increases. Our optimized GPU implementation, which exploits the texture cache, obtains varied results depending on the dictionaries and the input streams, but is able to reach on average the same performance as a dual Niagara 2 and a dual Xeon

5660 on a single Tesla C1060 GPU. A Cray XMT machine with 48 processors is able, on average, to beat these results, while maintaining substantially the same performance ($\approx$ 2 percent variability) on all the dictionaries and all input sets. On clustered architectures, our optimized GPU implementation was able to saturate the communication bandwith with all the data sets when using 10 GPUs. Nevertheless, even with a higher Infiniband bandwidth, we would still be limited by the PCI-Express bandwidth. On the x86 platform, an MPI-only solution with large dictionaries is not practical, while a mixed solution with MPI for internode communication and `pthreads` for intranode computation is not able to reach to reach the same performance on benchmarks that exhibit heavy matching.

Software-based implementations of string matching algorithms can reach high throughputs on modern high-performance systems. Such software-based implementations require moderate programming efforts and simpler code structures with respect to custom solutions on FPGAs or to ad hoc implementations for multimedia processors such as the IBM CELL/B.E. However, they still present significant performance variability, depending on the characteristics of the dictionary and the input stream. By comparing a wide range of high performance machines, we think that our work may lay a foundation for a better understanding of the behavior of such irregular, data-intensive algorithms on current architectures.

References

1. Aho, A. V., and Corasick, M. J. "Efficient String Matching: An Aid to Bibliographic Search." *Communications of the ACM* 18, 6(1975): 333–40.
2. Chavarría-Miranda, D., Marquez, A., Nieplocha, J., Maschhoff, K., and Scherrer, C. Early Experience with Out-of-Core Applications on the Cray XMT. In *IPDPS '08: 22nd IEEE International Parallel and Distributed Processing Symposium* (April 2008), pp. 1–8.
3. Cho, Y. H., and Mangione-Smith, W. H. "Deep Packet Filter with Dedicated Logic and Read Only Memories." In *FCCM '04: 12th Annual IEEE Symposium on Field-Programmable Custom Computing Machines* (April 2004), pp. 125–34.
4. Clark, C. R., and Schimmel, D. E. "Scalable Pattern Matching for High Speed Networks." In *FCCM '04: 12th Annual IEEE Symposium on Field-Programmable Custom Computing Machines* (Apr. 2004), pp. 249–57.
5. Feo, J., Harper, D., Kahan, S., and Konecny, P. Eldorado. In *CF '05: Proceedings of the 2nd conference on Computing frontiers* (New York, NY, USA, 2005), ACM, pp. 28–34.
6. Jacob, N., and Brodley, C. "Offloading IDS Computation to the GPU." In *ACSAC '06: 22nd Annual Computer Security Applications Conference* (Dec. 2006), pp. 371–80.

7. Message Passing Interface Forum. MPI: A Message-Passing Interface Standard. Version 2.2, September 2009.

8. Mitra, A., Najjar, W., and Bhuyan, L. "Compiling PCRE to FPGA for accelerating SNORT IDS." In *ANCS '07: The 3rd ACM/IEEE Symposium on Architecture for Networking and Communications Systems* (2007), pp. 127–36.

9. Nawathe, U., Hassan, M., Yen, K., Kumar, A., Ramachandran, A., and Greenhill, D. "Implementation of an 8-Core, 64-Thread, Power-Efficient SPARC Server on a Chip." *Solid-State Circuits, IEEE Journal of* 43, 1 (Jan. 2008): 6–20.

10. Nvidia *Nvidia Cuda: Compute Unified Device Architecture*. Programming guide. Version 2.0, July 2008.

11. Pasetto, D., Petrini, F., and Agarwal, V. Tools for Very Fast Regular Expression Matching. *Computer* 43 (2010): 50–58.

12. Roesch, M. Snort: Lightweight Intrusion Detection for Networks. In *LISA* (1999), pp. 229–38.

13. Ruetsch, G., and Micikevicius, P. "NVIDIA Whitepaper: Optimizing Matrix Transpose in CUDA."

14. Scarpazza, D. P., Villa, O., and Petrini, F. "Exact Multi-Pattern String Matching on the Cell/B.E. Processor." In *CF '08: Proceedings of the 2008 conference on Computing frontiers* (New York, NY, USA, 2008), ACM, pp. 33–42.

15. Sourdis, I., and Pnevmatikatos, D. Fast, Large-Scale String Match for a 10Gbps FPGA-Based Network Intrusion. In *FPL '03: 13th Conference on Field Programmable Logic and Applications* (September 2003), pp. 880–89.

16. Symantec Global Internet Security Threat Report. *White Paper* (April 2008).

17. Tumeo, A., Villa, O., Chavarria-Miranda, D. "Aho-Corasick String Matching on Shared and Distributed-Memory Parallel Architectures," IEEE Transactions on Parallel and Distributed Systems, pp. 436–43, March, 2012.

18. Vasiliadis, G., Antonatos, S., Polychronakis, M., Markatos, E. P., and Ioannidis, S. "Gnort: High Performance Network Intrusion Detection Using Graphics Processors." In *RAID '08: 11th international symposium on Recent Advances in Intrusion Detection* (2008), pp. 116–34.

19. Villa, O., Chavarria-Miranda, D., and Maschhoff, K. "Input-Independent, Scalable and Fast String Matching on the Cray XMT." In *IPDPS '09: The 2009 IEEE International Symposium on Parallel & Distributed Processing* (2009), pp. 1–12.

20. Villa, O., Scarpazza, D. P., and Petrini, F. "Accelerating Real-Time String Searching with Multicore Processors." *Computer* 41, 4 (2008): 42–50.

4

Data Management Architectures

Terence Critchlow, Ghaleb Abdulla, Jacek Becla,
Kerstin Kleese-Van Dam, Sam Lang, and
Deborah L. McGuinness

Data management is the organization of information to support efficient access and analysis. For data-intensive computing applications, the speed at which relevant data can be accessed is a limiting factor in terms of the size and complexity of computation that can be performed. Data access speed is impacted by the size of the relevant subset of the data, the complexity of the query used to define it, and the layout of the data relative to the query. As the underlying data sets become increasingly complex, the questions asked of it become more involved as well. For example, geospatial data associated with a city is no longer limited to the map data representing its streets, but now also includes layers identifying utility lines, key points, locations, and types of businesses within the city limits, tax information for each land parcel, satellite imagery, and possibly even street-level views. As a result, queries have gone from simple questions, such as, "How long is Main Street?," to much more complex questions such as, "Taking all other factors into consideration, are the property values of houses near parks higher than those under power lines, and if so, by what percentage?" Answering these questions requires a coherent infrastructure, integrating the relevant data into a format optimized for the questions being asked.

Data management is critical to supporting analysis because, for large data sets, reading the entire collection is simply not feasible. Instead, the relevant subset of the data must be efficiently described, identified, and retrieved. As a result, the data management approach taken effectively defines the analysis that can be efficiently performed over the data. To support the variety of complex query specifications required by different types of analysis, specialized data management architectures have evolved over time. These predominantly software-centric architectures enable efficient searching across large data sets for well-defined subsets of the data. This chapter gives an overview of the approaches to large-scale data management currently in popular use.

48

The first section presents an overview of large-scale file systems, including the standard interfaces and libraries that have been designed to support large-scale experimental and simulation data sets as well as the challenges these systems face. This is the most general data management architecture, but also the hardest to use effectively. It is particularly suitable for problems where either raw throughput is critical, or where data can be easily organized into files that will be read in their entirety. For many applications, significant increases in efficiency can be found by optimizing the layout of data on disk through a preprocessing step. Geospatial information is not only large, but often requires complex analytics such as computing distance and overlap between regions. To address these needs, geospatial database systems have been developed and deployed. Typically these systems use specialized data structures hidden from the user to efficiently support the complex queries they perform. No discussion of large-scale data management technology would be complete without an overview of relational and next-generation database management systems. Relational systems form the basis for most business data management infrastructures as well as for many scientific environments. These systems use a layer of abstraction, called relational tables, to hide the complexity of storing and accessing categorical data. The third section discusses why this basic abstraction is being extended to manage multi-modal data as well as queries beyond the traditional standard SQL select-project-join specifications. Finally, this chapter concludes with a discussion of the role of metadata in supporting data access. The fourth section demonstrates how the effective use of metadata can determine whether or not a problem is tractable.

4.1 Data Storage and Architectures

A major part of the data management picture includes storing data persistently and reliably on behalf of the application. Large computing systems include a storage area known as *the storage system* for placing data sets. In data-intensive computing, the storage system plays a vital role of not only providing a location for persistent and reliable storage of data, but also the means to organize information that enables efficient access and analysis. The hardware devices and network connections that make up the storage system consist of many storage components, provide the capacity necessary to store massive data sets, and enable parallel access to data.

Data-intensive computing applications often distribute one large coordinated computation across many compute elements and periodically dispatch I/O accesses from these compute elements in parallel. The underlying data-intensive computing architectures vary widely, from high-performance

computing systems used for computational science and advanced computation to massive enterprise data centers that run complex data mining codes on
petabyte data sets. These architectures differ in their capacity, performance, and
workload requirements, but they all share basic design principles fundamental
to supporting and managing massive data sets common to the various types
of data-intensive applications. To frame our discussion of the storage system,
we focus on storage architectures typically deployed within high-performance
computing. Many of the design principles we describe in the HPC storage
system carry over into large enterprise data centers and other systems as well.

Computational science focuses on solving problems in science and technology that are too large or too complex to be addressed through laboratory
experiments. These applications generate massive quantities of data and have
a wide variety of data models and access patterns. A typical I/O workload in
HPC might consist of mining a large data set for desired information, with
many queries on the same data set executing concurrently. Data sets could be
anywhere from terabytes (TB) to a few petabytes (PB) in size and so are too
large to fit entirely in memory. The storage system that supports this workload
must not only provide enough capacity to store terabytes of data, it must provide enough parallel bandwidth to allow access to these large data sets quickly.
It must also provide a degree of reliability, ensuring that data will not be lost
or corrupted should failures of various storage system components occur. The
challenges of capacity, performance, and reliability are seen across all areas of
data-intensive computing and as a result, the various storage architectures built
to meet these challenges have similar design criteria.

Storage systems in HPC are built from many individual hardware components, enabling parallel access and preventing single points of failure. The
storage hardware is often physically partitioned from the compute system, with
separate machines dedicated to managing secondary storage for the cluster.
These machines, shown as the *storage nodes* in Figure 4.1, are connected to the
compute cluster or front-end nodes through a high-speed I/O network. Each
storage node manages a subset of the storage devices, which may consist of
directly attached RAID controllers and a few disk drives, or network attached
enterprise storage controllers with hundreds of disks. The I/O network, storage
nodes, and collection of storage devices make up the storage system of large
data centers and HPC clusters, providing persistent data storage for applications. This design enables high performance from all the compute elements in
the cluster, and allows the I/O system to scale as needed. Current installations at
some of the largest supercomputing centers in the world consist of hundreds of
storage nodes and thousands of disk drives [31, 63], whereas some of the largest
enterprise data centers manage petabytes of data across thousands of storage
nodes [8].

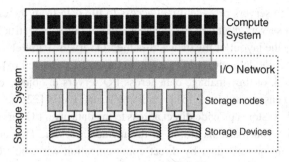

Figure 4.1. Typical I/O system in high-performance computing.

Computational science applications typically store their data sets in files. As an unstructured stream of bytes, a file can be easily split up by the storage system to optimize performance and provide versatility for a wide variety of I/O workloads. Some applications lay out data so that each compute element stores parts of a data set in a separate file, or they may store all the application data sets in only a few files.

A parallel or distributed file system brings together the various components of the I/O hardware to provide applications with a single file interface to secondary storage. It is designed to provide parallel and high-performance access to data and ensure a consistent view of the data across all the compute elements in the cluster. Figure 4.2 illustrates the parts of the parallel file system (PFS) software running on the hardware components of the I/O system. The PFS client software executes on the compute elements, and communicates over the I/O network to the PFS I/O and metadata servers running on the storage

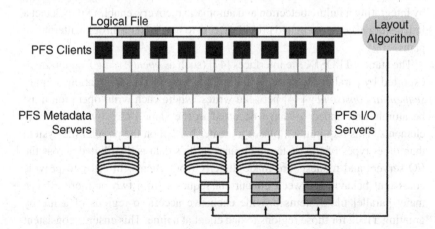

Figure 4.2. Components of the parallel file system.

nodes. The I/O servers provide direct access to file data from the clients, and the metadata servers maintain file metadata and the directory structure. They also organize the layout of file data across the I/O servers. Parallel file systems either manage file data across I/O servers in units of fixed sized bytes (known as blocks) [57], or they manage data across I/O servers in objects of variable size, as is the case with Lustre [51], PanFS [67], and PVFS [32].

Parallel file systems provide direct access to the data at an I/O server through well-defined layout patterns stored at the metadata server. This allows PFS clients to write or read data by direct communication with the I/O servers, avoiding the metadata server as a potential bottleneck. In most cases, the parallel file system uses a simple round-robin layout scheme, so that a file becomes uniformly distributed across I/O servers as the file grows. This allows an application to access different regions of the file from different I/O servers, ensuring that no single I/O server becomes bottlenecked by a multitude of I/O requests from many compute elements. This performance optimization is so ubiquitous in parallel file systems that it has been adopted by the NFS specification [56], a standard file system networking protocol. The specification includes standardized layout schemes (collectively called parallel NFS or pNFS) allowing direct access to I/O servers from file system clients.

Parallel file systems must be resilient to failures. Storage node or storage device failures should not cause data loss or prevent applications from accessing their data. To provide this degree of resilience, parallel file systems rely partly on the storage devices to be fault-tolerant. Large supercomputing centers invest in expensive storage devices with built-in redundancy mechanisms to ensure that a failed disk drive does not cause a loss of data. Multiple paths to the data guard against failures of controllers and specialized hardware performs rebuilds of failed disk drives. The parallel file system provides high-availability by integrating a failure detection and automatic recovery, enabling it to detect a failed storage component and provide access to needed data through alternative paths.

The standard POSIX file interfaces [47] (such as *open()*, *read()*, and *write()*) exported by parallel file systems and used by many HPC applications require *sequential consistency* [14] between writes, where each write operation must be atomic and appear to have occurred in the same order by all compute elements. This requirement places a greater burden on the parallel file system than other types of file systems, because a file's data is distributed across the I/O servers and requests are made directly from clients. In order to provide consistent behavior between concurrent requests from two or more clients, many parallel file systems provide exclusive access to regions of a file by granting a lock for those regions to one client at a time. This ensures consistent

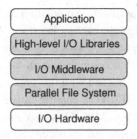

Figure 4.3. The I/O software stack in HPC.

behavior, but can limit performance as clients must first acquire a lock from a lock manager running on a separate server before performing requests to the I/O servers. Although locking regions of the file can hinder performance for some I/O workloads, it does allow the PFS client to cache the locked file regions, which has shown to improve performance for applications that perform many small I/O requests. With a lock acquired, small requests to a file can be aggregated together so that a single large request can be sent to the I/O servers. Still, file systems that implicitly lock file accesses to provide sequential consistency not only require extra communication to grant lock requests, but must also coordinate between competing compute elements, adding significant complexity to the file system. Sequential consistency is necessary in some distributed applications, but for computational science it most often provides stronger guarantees than are usually required. Extensions to the POSIX I/O standard have been proposed to address this issue, known as *Lazy I/O*. Lazy I/O relaxes POSIX sequential consistency for certain I/O accesses, allowing applications to choose the degree of consistency required.

Because the I/O workloads of computational science have such intensive and unique data requirements, a simple POSIX interface on top of the parallel file system is usually not enough to provide high-performance I/O to the application. Instead, a suite of I/O libraries and software are utilized to improve performance and convenience for applications as they perform I/O to storage. Figure 4.3 shows the HPC I/O software stack. As discussed, the parallel file system manages the I/O hardware components. Above the parallel file system, I/O middleware aggregates and optimizes I/O accesses from the application to the file system. MPI-IO [62] and ADIOS [35] are examples of I/O middleware used in HPC. Lastly, the high-level I/O library provides I/O interfaces that fit with the application's data models, allowing it to access data based on multi-dimensional variables instead of as a flat stream of bytes. The following describes each of these software interfaces in more detail.

HPC applications often coordinate computation and share state between compute elements using the message-passing interface (MPI) [20]. This provides an opportunity for coordinating accesses to files directly instead of requiring the file system to perform that coordination on the application's behalf. The MPI-IO interface [62] was designed with this goal in mind. By leveraging the existing MPI framework, MPI-IO is able to ensure consistent access across process in the MPI application. MPI-IO is also able to optimize I/O through message passing. Multi-dimensional arrays can be distributed across compute elements with individual processes getting many small regions of the data set. This leads to many small I/O accesses, which are not optimal for parallel file systems. MPI-IO optimizes these small I/O accesses by designating a few compute elements as buffering nodes so that many small requests can be aggregated into a single large I/O request before sending the request to the file system [61]. In MPI-IO, this is known as *collective buffering* because the compute elements act collectively to perform I/O through the buffering nodes.

High-level libraries (HLLs) allow computational science applications to store their data sets in a much more natural way than writing bytes to a file. Instead, applications using HLLs can generate and store data directly into *variables*, and the library takes care of converting the structured data of a variable into a flat stream of bytes to be stored in a file. This not only simplifies the task of storing large data sets, it also allows the HLL to optimize the layout of the structured data sets in the file for performance. Two common HLLs used in computational science are pNetCDF [33] and HDF5 [24]. Both libraries support parallel I/O access to structure data sets using MPI-IO to aggregate and optimize I/O accesses to the parallel file system.

Computational science applications tend to generate data sets that match the scale at which they run. Larger scales allow applications to examine problems at finer granularities, or solve larger, more complex systems. This means that applications will generate larger and larger data sets as supercomputing systems increase in capability and performance. Data sets generated on the largest systems today are terabytes in size and are often stored in millions of files. If trends continue, by 2020 the largest supercomputing systems will consist of 100 million application tasks and have somewhere between 20 to 50 petabytes of memory [28]. This presents a challenge to the storage system to provide not only the bandwidth required to generate and store these large data sets, but also to place the data within the storage system efficiently so that it can be easily accessed during analysis. Storage systems will need to organize and manage data that improves locality of access as well as continue to provide reliability and performance.

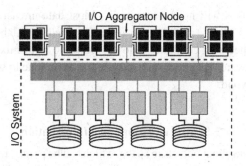

Figure 4.4. I/O Aggregator nodes.

Many of the challenges arising in HPC storage systems today are performance related. Parallel file systems often struggle with applications that choose to share a data set in a single file across thousands of compute elements in the system. This type of workload can cause contention for locks to shared data regions and reduce system throughput to a fraction of peak bandwidth. Storage systems also struggle to support simultaneous parallel access to millions of files, because of the heavy load on the metadata server this workload creates [12]. As the number of individual compute elements increases exponentially over the next decade, these problems will only get worse. To address the increase in core counts, storage systems researchers have added a buffering layer for the file system. Similar to collective buffering in MPI-IO, *I/O aggregation* provides dedicated nodes within the compute system to perform I/O on behalf of a portion of the compute elements. Instead of the parallel file system receiving I/O requests from each of the compute elements, it receives fewer and larger requests from the I/O aggregator nodes. Figure 4.4 shows the architecture of an HPC system with I/O aggregator nodes. Along with separate hardware components, I/O aggregation requires special I/O forwarding software to efficiently aggregate and buffer the I/O requests from compute elements. The *I/O forwarding scalability layer* (IOFSL) [4] is a joint project to provide portable and highly efficient I/O forwarding software.

The I/O demands of data-intensive computing create other challenges as well. To support capacity and performance requirements, systems are being deployed with tens of thousands of disk drives and thousands of storage nodes. Storage systems will only be able to scale with compute performance by continuing to increase this count of individual components, in turn increasing the likelihood of failure of any single component. Storage systems face a daunting challenge to provide storage that is resilient to failures yet still maintaining the highest possible degree of performance.

These challenges will not be met easily. Most data-intensive applications quickly consume all I/O and storage resources made available and experts anticipate that they will continue to do so. Only the right mixture of system designs and software will allow storage systems to continue to scale to exabyte data sets and beyond.

4.2 Spatial and Temporal Information

Spatial data is data about objects in space, which can be points, lines, regions, or volumes. A feature set defines attributes that are associated with spatial objects; for example, date, temperature, humidity, altitude, longitude, and latitude are features that could be associated with a city. The object's feature values and spatial location can be updated over time, adding a temporal dimension. An instance in the time dimension captures the state of the object at that time and the feature values for an object over multiple time instances represent the history of that object as it evolved over time. The time dimension can quickly cause a data explosion. For example, high-resolution environmental sensing and high-resolution satellite or telescope imaging can produce terabytes to petabytes of data each day (the LSST is expected to collect 20 TB/night [37]); the amount of data stored increases linearly with the number of days recorded. This in turn introduces several challenges: reliable spatio-temporal data storage, efficient and scalable retrieval algorithms, efficient data analysis algorithms, and data provenance management (including defining, querying, and controlling access to provenance data) [26].

If a spatial object has fixed location overtime then it is referred to as a *static* object; otherwise, it is a *moving* object. We will motivate the spatio-temporal data management challenges using tracking of moving objects as an example. Data sets for moving objects and trajectories for moving objects (such as GPS-tracks or celestial objects' tracks) are either collected from devices such as cell phones or GPS's or extracted from spatial images. In the case of GPS or cell phones, the data can be used to create hour-by-hour census for cities to facilitate understanding human behavior in urban areas. In the case of Astrophysics or medical images, behavior modeling is not as important, however, keeping track of objects, their location, and how the attributes' values change is still important. Tracking of moving objects and predicting future locations for these objects can introduce several challenges, especially because the behavior of the moving object depends on the application domain. For example, movement of astronomical objects is predictable in most cases (a planet or a comet will follow a certain trajectory). Theoretically, three spatial data points can be used to predict the next location of the spatial object; however, several real-world complexities could make the prediction erroneous. First, simply identifying which objects are the moving objects is challenging [30] and requires matching objects with high certainty using non-spatial features. Then, if the object passes behind or in front off another spatial object non spatial features need to be used to help resolve the objects identity. For objects such as cars or trucks, predicting the next location is even harder because the object can make sudden turns or stops. Fusing data with other information sources such as road maps or traffic information could help in tracking a moving object and predict its next location.

Spatio-temporal data poses several interesting research challenges and it is useful to classify the research challenges into categories:

1. Data management algorithms, which include algorithms for efficient data storage and retrieval.
2. Spatio-temporal data mining.
3. Query processing and optimization for spatio-temporal data.
4. Hardware and software architectures for spatio-temporal data.
5. Algorithms for real-time sensor spatio-temporal data.
6. Ontology and structure of spatial data.
7. Data provenance.
8. Uncertainty quantification, representation, and propagation in spatio-temporal databases.
9. Formal models and languages for representing spatio-temporal data.

Although there is a lot of work that spans these nine areas, there is little work that has been done with respect to large data sets, with scalable data mining algorithms as one exception. For space considerations, we consolidate these nine research areas into the following three general challenges and present the current state of the art in these areas in relation to anticipated exascale data sets.

1. Performance related challenges, which include categories 1, 3, and 4.
2. Spatio-temporal data analytics and real-time analysis, which includes categories 2 and 5.
3. Uncertainty quantification representation and propagation in spatio-temporal databases.

After discussing the ongoing research in these areas, this section concludes with an example of spatio-temporal analysis based on work done for the Large Synoptic Survey Telescope project (LSST). This example illustrates how these approaches may be applied in a real-world setting.

4.2.1 Performance-Related Research and Challenges

This area of research includes, but is not limited to, benchmarking of spatio-temporal databases, query processing and optimization, and efficient data storage and indexing. After observing that existing spatio-temporal benchmarks lack the ability to thoroughly evaluate the temporal capabilities and assume that temporal events are evenly spaced in time, [48] proposes a new set of spatio-temporal queries that require significant temporal processing and evaluate the ability of a database to handle three-dimensional data. In addition to evaluating the database performance, the proposed thirty-six queries can evaluate the impact of the operating system enhancements including file systems, virtual memory management, and process scheduling enhancements on the query performance. It has been shown that success in designing efficient database-indexes relies on empirical studies and proposes a benchmark for evaluating the indexing of current and near-future positions of moving objects. Although benchmarking measures the performance of the data management systems, the underlying spatio-temporal access methods implemented in these systems are a major factor in affecting the performance.

Mokbel et al. [41] is a short, yet excellent, survey of spatio-temporal access methods and it provides a classification of these methods that distinguishes between access methods that index the past (static data) and ones that indexes current and future predictions (streaming data). Static access methods deal with time in three different ways. First, as another dimension where the focus is on handling spatial queries efficiently whereas temporal queries are considered less important. The RT-tree, which is based on the R-tree for spatial indexing and the TSB-tree for temporal indexing, are examples of this class of access methods [68].

Second, the temporal dimension is dealt with as a separate dimension and each time instance has its own spatial tree. The MR-tree, which is an optimized implementation using overlapping B-trees of a series of R-trees over time, implements this data structure.

Third, access methods are focused on objects that move over time and the data structure is optimized for trajectory queries. For indexing current position, several access methods have been proposed, however, the differences between these methods are primarily because of scalability of these algorithms. Most of these methods, however, try to separate the historical data from the current data. An example of such access methods is the LUR-tree. For indexing current and predicting future positions, extra information, such as velocity and destination, needs to be stored. In some cases, the object's movement can be modeled by a linear equation, whereas in other cases it could have multiple future locations (such as a car coming to an intersection) that needs to be updated in real time once more information is available. The PMR-quadtree is an example of an access method that can be used to index future trajectories. The survey concludes that more work should be done to support operators that are important to the spatio-temporal domain such as nearest-neighbor queries and spatio-temporal joins.

Most of the work in industry focuses on building specialized distributed systems that will scale traditional DBMS's. For example, Oracle TimesTen [OT] is an in-memory database that uses a traditional database architecture, and its main advantage is that it relies on large memory to cache the data that will be processed. Netezza [44], on the other hand, took a different direction by using "active disks" to speed up database operations. Netezza is distinguished by employing FPGAs and PowerPC processors rather than standard disk controller chips and Intel CPUs to build their own customized hardware. A Netezza system distributes data across the disks and queries it in parallel, at the disk level, using the FPGAs.

In summary, to meet the exascale data analysis challenge, more spatio-temporal benchmarks and use case studies are needed to explore and uncover the weaknesses in the current database architectures. Specifically, proposed benchmarks should be able to uncover weaknesses of a data management system with respect to the specific data-intensive application requirements. For example, if the application will need to answer a set of different spatio temporal queries with both space and time constraints, the time to rebuild the index or redistribute the data must be considered in the benchmark. More use cases are clearly needed in the distributed data processing area; for example, there is a need for efficient and dynamic declustering algorithms to improve parallel data analysis performance. Similarly, data preparation (loading or redistributing), which can be time consuming and expensive, has a significant impact on query performance. Finally, R-tree indexing is implemented in most of the modern database systems; more complex indexing schemes may be implemented as customized stored procedures within the database system, but at the cost of performance. The trade-off between making these algorithms (such as the zones algorithm [22]) native to the database versus building customized solutions must be thoroughly evaluated.

4.2.2 Spatio-Temporal Data Analytics Research and Challenges

Spatial data mining is the application of data-mining techniques to spatial data with the objective of finding patterns in spatial data. Spatio-temporal data mining is similar, but with the goal of finding patterns across both spatial and temporal domains. The work in this area is motivated by the need to identify complex and time-sensitive patterns hidden in large data sets in domains as varied as sensor streams, climate data, astrophysics, and traffic monitoring. Currently, the work in this area handles spatio-temporal data the same as any other type of data without special consideration for the semantics of the spatial and temporal dimensions. This approach is attractive because the clustering and other data analytic algorithms can be used to immediately explore the data. However, the semantics of the spatio-temporal relationships are lost. Ideally, a theoretical framework can be developed to capture the relationships of the spatio-temporal components to the other data, providing a powerful analysis capability.

Spatio-temporal data mining is a very active field and there are an increasing number of publications in the popular data-mining conferences such as SIGKDD. Roddick et al. [49] developed a bibliography of the publications in the spatio-temporal data-mining field divided into nine categories that reflects the wealth of research in this area. Among the identified categories are time series mining, association rule mining in spatio-temporal data, and discovery of temporal patterns.

There are several new domains of science to benefit from spatial-temporal data mining in particular. For example, Twa et al. [64] discusses an interesting, but small-scale clinical application of spatial data mining: a classification tree is used to classify a sample of normal patients versus patients with corneal distortion caused by keratoconus. Spatial features that can help classify normal patients versus patients with corneal distortion are extracted from images of patients' eyes. The shape of the cornea is modeled using Zernike polynomials and the coefficients of the polynomial are used as features for a decision tree classifier.

Nanni et al. [45] provides an overview of spatio-temporal data mining research. It uses highway traffic to introduce spatio-temporal queries and concepts that need to be supported by a spatio-temporal database. The authors distinguish between local pattern mining, where the objective is to search and find interesting spatio-temporal patterns (for example, a periodic pattern for a group of people travelling together from one city to another), and global pattern mining where the objective is to mine the full data for all patterns or to create predictive models. The first task is similar to information retrieval where the objective is to match a specific pattern within a specific context, whereas the latter task uses clustering and classification techniques to extract global patterns across the data (exploratory activity).

To move beyond the current state of the art and enable complex spatio-temporal analysis, a systematic approach that integrates spatio-temporal semantics (for example, the notions of proximity and temporal order define when an event comes before or after another event) into data management frameworks is needed. Formally defining these relationships and operation (such as intersects, overlaps, and contains), allows data-mining algorithms to reason over the relationships between spatial objects and to identify interesting and emerging spatio-temporal patterns.

4.2.3 Uncertainty Quantification, Representation, Visualization, and Propagation in Spatio-Temporal Databases

The literature includes several approaches to support uncertainty in spatial data, including visualizing uncertainty [43], models and data types for uncertainty in spatial databases [52], and spatial data mining with uncertainty. What uncertainty means for spatio-temporal data is still unclear, with at least two common definitions being used. In the first, uncertainty is defined in terms of fuzzy spatial objects, or objects that do not have well-defined boundaries such as polluted areas. The location, center, and boundaries of these objects can be represented with range of values or with error bars. In [52], an abstract data model to handle fuzzy objects introduces fuzzy operations that can be used to manipulate these objects. As a first step, spatial objects can be defined with an uncertainty measure as one of the attributes. For example, a fuzzy *point* that belongs to an air-polluted cloud can have a numeric attribute that measures the degree of pollution of that point. In turn, this decides the strength of membership of the point to the cloud and helps define the cloud's (or region's) boundaries. Spatial operations, such as intersects or contains, can also be implemented while considering the uncertainty. A fuzzy spatial *algebra* is proposed that can be used to address the uncertainty in the spatial operations.

Realizing the challenges of visualizing uncertainty in spatial data, [43] reviews and assesses progress toward visual tools and methods to help analysts manage and understand information uncertainty. The paper discusses the value of visualizing uncertainty and raises two related questions: "Is it helpful to include uncertainty in the visualization?" and "Do users with different knowledge level use uncertainty differently?" For example, do domain experts understand a particular visualization of uncertainty better than a novice user?

Similar to other research areas in the spatio-temporal domain, the area of spatio-temporal data mining with uncertainty is an open research area. More work on the semantics of uncertainty with respect to the spatial objects is needed to fully develop the field. For example, formal models, such as the one suggested in [52], need to be extended, generally accepted, and ultimately standardized. Before gaining acceptance, these models need to be evaluated against new use cases to test their completeness. In the context of database design, more work is needed on data structures that can support fuzzy manipulation of spatial objects and indexing techniques.

4.2.4 Crossmatching of Astronomical Objects

This section describes our experience evaluating different database architectures to implement the crossmatch algorithm (such as identification of the same moving object across different images taken at different times) for a large data set. The LSST is an example of a data-intensive application that drives towards examining new hardware/software data-intensive architectures because it combines two important challenges: large data volumes and real-time or near-real-time data querying and analysis. Moreover, when fully operational, the multi-petabyte data set captured by the LSST is expected to be used by many research studies from the astronomy community. As a result, efficient solutions to the LSST data capture, processing, cataloging, and analysis pipelines are likely to have broad scientific impact.

Our task is to identify the same object in different images of the sky. In addition to the object moving relative to other objects within the image, these images are taken at different times, possibly days or weeks apart, and under different conditions (such as cloud cover or angles). To do this, we start by comparing objects based on their distances from each other. This requires fast retrieval of candidate objects from a large historical catalog. Once the candidate objects have been retrieved, the crossmatch operation tries to match the new object to this historical data. The focus of our evaluation is to determine the best architecture to identify the candidate historical objects.

We examine different database system configurations and indexing strategies to speedup the data access and processing operations. First, we investigate techniques for constructing spatial indices on large streaming data. We look at the performance of a spatial index library (SaIL [25]) for creating spatial indices on large data volumes as they are ingested, and for efficiently searching and retrieving objects using these indices. We then develop parallel versions of the index creation and querying steps provided with the library distribution. The spatial indexing is customized – by selecting an appropriate value for the fan-out factor of the tree-based index – for optimal performance based on the analysis steps that follow it. Although this is a promising direction, we conclude that the performance of the spatial index is limited by the query selectivity. In our case, we have to rebuild the distributed index to get the targeted performance. Unfortunately, this is a very expensive operation and cannot be avoided.

Second, we evaluate a set of database systems with different architectural configurations and identify performance differences and bottlenecks in these

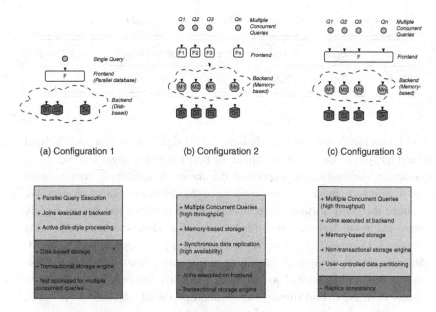

Figure 4.5. Alternative database architecture configurations, their pros and cons.

systems for spatial crossmatch operations. We investigate the execution of two database-oriented crossmatch algorithms, the zones algorithm [22] and the optimized zones algorithm [6], on three different architectures (see Figure 4.5).

- Netezza Performance Server R, a parallel database management system with active disk architecture support for certain types of database operations;
- MySQL Cluster, a database system designed for high-availability and high-throughput; and,
- A distributed collection of independent database system instances with support for data replication. In this configuration, we combine the best features from the two previous configurations to achieve the best performance for this use case. The achieved performance is not specifically unique to the MySql server and it can be obtained using other database engines if used in the same way.

The tested algorithms are very well known to the astronomy community and were developed by a team from the computer science and the astronomy fields. For test data, we use the USNO-B catalog (a public astronomy catalog generated by U.S. Naval Observatory at Flagstaff containing more than a billion objects) because it closely emulates the LSST data when it becomes operational [30]. Our experimental evaluations are based on real queries put forth by the

Table 4.1. *Crossmatch time using 16 × 1 strategy and OptZone*

	Prepare	Transfer Time	Query Time	Total Time
High	1.9 s	5.6 s	1.3 s	7 s

LSST astrophysicists and provide important insights about how architectural characteristics of these systems affect the performance of these techniques. In particular, our evaluation shows that the choice of a database configuration can significantly impact the performance of the object association process. We evaluate the queries using different FOV region densities, but we are mostly interested in the high-density fields because of its closeness in density to the average LSST case. This case involves searching for approximately 30,000 detections in approximately 30 million objects using spatial attributes. These objects need to be matched within 5 to 10 seconds. For brevity, we show the results from the hybrid (third) configuration previously described. However, the reader is advised to go to [30] for greater details of the work.

In our evaluation, the algorithms behave differently on different database system configuration. On the Netezza system, one of our benchmarks performed poorly because of the overhead of creating disk-based tables on-demand for each of the spatial regions and the lack of support for stored procedures in the system, which results in overheads because of external scripts being treated as independent queries. On the MySQL system, however, neither algorithm performs as well as it does on the first configuration because it does not execute a query in parallel and executes JOINs on the frontend. This drawback is remedied to an extent by partitioning a query into a set of smaller queries and executing these subqueries as a batch query. This takes advantage of the high-throughput-oriented design of the second configuration. The third configuration enables different partitioning and replication of the catalog tables across a collection of the independent database system instances. Although query performance is enhanced for this configuration, the data preparation phase and distribution remains a challenge and adds to the time of the query.

Table 4.1 shows the results from running the query on a 16-node cluster with data replicated on all nodes. The table also lists the three different important phases that data has to go through before getting the results. We measure the time for data movement and preparation because in some cases it could delay the query results and we believe this should not be ignored. These results show that we can satisfy the high-speed matching requirements for the application.

Realistic evaluations are key to understanding the performance of complex and data-intensive applications. To that end, there is a need to develop benchmarks and realistic use cases in order to help evaluate data-intensive algorithms and architectures. These benchmarks should include a detailed description of how the data is queried and used, and should cover all nine of the research challenges previously mentioned.

4.3 Relational Databases, On-Line Analytical Processing, and Nontraditional Database Environments

Relational database management systems (RDBMS) are the standard, nearly ubiquitous, technology used to store and search categorical data. The relational model was first outlined by Cobb [13] and is based on relational algebra. Many books have been written on the design and use of relational databases and the interested reader is directed to [58] for a more detailed overview. For our purposes, it is sufficient to know that in the relational model all concepts are mapped to a set of two-dimensional tables, where the columns represent attributes of concept and the rows represent a specific instance of that concept, and queried through a standard language called SQL. Relational database implementations support definition of keys and indices to enforce integrity constraints and enable efficient querying of the data.

Beyond the ease with which these complex tasks can be performed, the popularity of databases in commercial environments can be traced to three guarantees they provide. The first is ensuring atomicity: a set of commands can be grouped into a single transaction that will either be completed in its entirety or not at all, but under no circumstances will only part of the transaction be performed (specifically, the collection is treated as an atomic instruction). Second, multiple transactions are serializable: the result of executing a set of transactions must correspond to a sequential execution of the transactions, even if the individual commands are performed concurrently. Finally, databases are highly fault tolerant, with checkpoints supporting long-running series of transactions by enabling rollbacks and restarts if the database is interrupted. These benefits of relational databases come at a cost; throughput on these systems is typically far from the raw disk bandwidth because of locking and synchronous disk writes.

Traditional relational databases are extremely useful for applications that take advantage of their guarantees. However, they do have significant limitations as well. A database is typically designed to serve a specific function (such as tracking sales) and is isolated from other databases. As a result, it is not uncommon for an organization's data to be distributed across multiple databases; for example, for each store to keep its own sales data. Furthermore, the resulting record-centric view is often optimized for data ingest, making it less useful for higher-level data analysis and reporting. To enable multi-terabyte or petabyte database analysis alternative data management approaches, specifically data warehouses and data cubes, have been developed.

Data warehouses [5, 15] may still be stored within an RDBMS, but have several important differences from traditional transaction-oriented databases.

- They are updated on a regular schedule, not as transactions occur, and thus may not have the most current information. Whether they are updated hourly, daily, weekly, or monthly depends both on the number of transactions being processed and the reporting requirements.
- They are focused on summary information. Aggregations, for example sales by item by store by day, are often created to reduce the size of the database and enable faster query responses. Although this removes access to the detailed records, these aggregations are usually all that is needed for reports and analysis.
- A star or snowflake schema [21] is used to organized data around facts and specified dimensions (columns in the original database). By reducing the number of dimensions and organizing the data around them, it is easier to generate the summarizations and views of the data required to perform analysis or generate reports.
- Data warehouses often integrate information from multiple transactional databases to provide a more comprehensive view; for example, from each store within a chain.

Data warehouses have been popular in business for more than a decade, and have resulted in some of the first multi-terabyte data sets. Although integration of the underlying data should be a simple process, in practice a significant data cleaning step is required to resolve semantic inconsistencies between the databases (such as converting data when an update has not been consistently applied). Despite this additional cost, analysis over data warehouses has allowed businesses to better understand their data and become significantly more efficient.

Unfortunately, even with a star schema, it can be challenging to interact with data warehouses because of the volume and relational organization of the data. Online Analytical Processing (OLAP) [9], otherwise known as data cubes, are a non-relational data structure in which the N-dimensional cube, derived from the dimensions of the associated star schema, is stored in a format that supports fast projections of data summaries onto a small number of dimensions. Conceptually, the cube stores metrics, such as counts, totals, or averages in an efficient, but sparse N-dimensional matrix, a representation that is often several orders of magnitude smaller than the original database. Queries then project this data onto a view comprised of a relatively small number of dimensions (typically two to four), further aggregating the information. Identifying informative views is typically performed by an expert. However, some research in user guided view discovery has been performed [27]. Because the projection can be efficiently computed, data cubes, through the associated interfaces, provide an interactive way to explore large data sets. Several vendors provide excellent graphical interfaces to data cubes, enabling drag-and-drop data selection tied to charts and maps of the data.

Although relational databases are extremely important for managing data that requires atomicity and serializability, as much business information does, these benefits apply primarily to categorical data. The associated overhead and table-oriented structure makes RBDMS less than ideal for other types of information:

- **Temporal data:** Time is represented as a singular value (in particular a timestamp), and as a result relativistic queries (such as age or three days ago) can be asked, but are not directly supported by SQL. More complex temporal queries (such as identifying overlapping periods or sequences of events) can be challenging to perform in a relational environment.
- **Semi-structured data (XML):** Semi-structured data does not map well to a traditional relational format, although it can be represented using *Name-Value* pairs to map attributes to the associated entities. Unfortunately, this type of structure makes it harder to do complex searches across objects and usually requires a significant number of (costly) joins. If the information being represented is primarily structured, adding semi-structured tables to a standard relational format may be acceptable. Because of the popularity and importance of this type of data, many RDBMS vendors are providing the ability to read, store, and write semi-structured data in an optimized data structure.
- **Image or video data:** Images do not map well to the table structure of relational environments, and thus are usually treated as single and binary large objects (BLOBs). This type of information can be read, but not searched, compared, or otherwise analyzed within the database.
- **Text:** Unstructured data such as text data can be stored within a relational database, in a form similar to a BLOB. Simple keyword searching is typically supported and many vendors provide additional search capabilities. However, more complex analysis (such as entity extraction, version control, or clustering) are not generally supported. Document management systems

are evolving to address this need and will likely become integral components of future database systems.

Scientific data has also remained a significant challenge for relational database technology. In part, this is because the associated applications typically require extremely fast I/O and are not concerned about serializability or atomicity [39]. Additionally, a simulation typically maps its data to a small number of extremely large tables. Analysis would require these tables to be repeatedly searched, joined, and sorted, which are expensive operations even with indices. Nonetheless, there have been some clear examples where relational technology has been extremely beneficial to scientific domains. One of the best known examples, is Jim Gray's release of the Sloan Digital Sky Survey (SDSS) server using a relational database backend [59]. The SDSS is a digital map of the northern sky that has enabled detection of hundreds of millions of new objects. Concluded in 2005, the initial SDSS project generated several terabytes of data, which was freely accessible to both astronomers and the public through a web-based query interface. Follow-on projects have brought the total data set size up to 49.5 TB, with approximately half of that representing the raw data. The key to the success of this project was to define the specific queries that need to be enabled and to develop an appropriate set of metadata. The queries focused the database design leading to a more efficient implementation than would be possible if the database was required to fully support *ad hoc* queries. The metadata provided additional semantic information (such as from post-processing the data, tracking provenance, and soliciting user annotations) about the data, which were then stored and used to efficiently answer these queries.

Despite these limited successes, there remains a disconnect between what the relational data model offers and what scientific data analysis needs that hampers widespread adoption. Most modern experimental science makes extensive use of *sensor arrays* to measure whatever physical phenomenon is the subject of study, be it an astronomical star, a wild fire, or diseased tissue.[1] Each of these observable features are typically represented as co-located pixels or *objects* derived from pixel data. Multiple observations of the same phenomenon are often recorded, yielding *time series* – in some cases with frequency exceeding hundreds of observations per second. In other words, data tends to have well-defined neighborhoods, and is inherently *ordered* in both space and time. For these reasons, an *array data model*, with implicit ordering and notions of

---

[1] Similar challenges can be observed in certain types of commercial applications such as risk management systems in financial applications, analysis of web log data, deep sequencing analytics for drug discovery or digital medical imaging analysis.

"adjacency" or "neighborhood," is far more desirable than tabular tables offered by relational technology.

Moreover, because of many factors, including imperfect observing conditions, detector misalignments, and hardware limitations and failures, data is typically sparse and imperfect ("noisy" and uncertain). To process such data, specialized, mathematically, and algorithmically sophisticated processing methods are required. Expressing these sophisticated algorithms through rich-but-constraining SQL is often next to impossible – allowing scientists to "package" their algorithms into reusable *user defined functions* (UDFs), and executing these functions where the data resides is far more desirable.

To illustrate the reasoning behind the preceding claims, consider a few typical scientific analyses: pairwise comparisons of observation or entity records, such as searching for near-neighbor entities; computing regional densities; or, finding spatial patterns. A naïve implementation for these analysis requires $O(N^2)$ comparisons, and with N measured in billions or trillions this becomes too expensive and slow to be practical. A common solution to dealing with a large data set is to partition it and analyze each partition in parallel. This approach is particularly popular for noncorrelated data sets, as evidenced by the popularity of the map/reduce paradigm. Scientific observational data, however, is *highly* correlated and thus a naïve partitioning into chunks, and processing these chunks in parallel is not a viable option. For example, pairwise analyses near partition edges requires "adjacent" partitions, leading to unbearably large internode data transfers needed to compute results across the edges. An effective data "de-correlation" can be done at the expense of small data duplication, commonly called overlapping partitioning. Unfortunately, overlapping partitioning is not implemented in any existing off-the-shelf data management system.

To illustrate need for new data abstractions and associated interfaces, consider analyses that involve finding pairs of objects within "similar" time series: because measurements of different objects are typically taken at different times, some measurements are missing, and those not missing are uncertain. Expressing an algorithm that compares these imperfect time series through SQL is a daunting task. Consequently, scientists tend to run data analyses using an extract-transform-load (ETL) approach: data is extracted from database, processed using a procedural language in custom application software, and results are pushed back to the database. This means data is *moved* to the computation – something that was works well on megabytes or gigabytes of data, but fails miserably when terabytes or petabytes of data are required. For large data sets, moving computation to data is highly preferred, and this is typically achieved through UDFs. Although UDFs have been implemented in DBMSs for many years, they were never extensively used for scientific analyses.

As a result data-intensive applications typically perform extreme-scale data analytics by building systems from the "bare metal" up. In some cases, work-flow management tools [2, 31, 34] have been used to simplify the process of organizing large-scale analytical systems. These tools work best when data collections involve large numbers of moderately-sized files and are not optimized for observational data sets that contain immense number of relatively small records. Analyses involving processing entire data sets are typically planned and scheduled as production jobs, prohibiting curiosity-driven, what-if, and ad-hoc analysis further delaying scientific discoveries. For this reason, many data-intensive industrial users, in particular Internet companies, have turned to the map/reduce (MR) model. The MR approach works particularly well on uncorrelated and unstructured data sets: segments of data are randomly distributed (hashed) across the available nodes and processed in parallel. This approach is less well-suited for the type of spatial or temporal correlations previously described. Additionally, the MR model leaves the record structure for the user to define in code.[2]

This recent trend, observed in industry and underlined by MR, departs from traditional, highly-centralized database architectures. Instead, a system is deployed over a network of computers, each with its own locally attached storage. Each compute/storage node runs a semiautonomous instance of a database engine, providing communications, query processing, and a local storage manager. All instances share access to a centralized system catalog database (which could be logical) that stores information about the nodes, data distribution, user-defined extensions, and so on. This architecture allows for incremental (horizontal) upgrades of the system and provides dramatically better resilience against failures as well as simplifying recovery.

SciDB [11, 55], is one example of a new breed of database management systems designed to overcome these shortcomings and extend the benefits of database management systems to a broader community.[3] SciDB is an open source system currently under construction focused on addressing the challenges present in scientific analytics on highly dimensional, correlated, large-scale data sets. SciDB is not a traditional database: it is not optimized for online transaction processing (OLTP) and only minimally supports transactions at all; it does not have a rigidly-defined and difficult-to-modify schema. Instead, everything is designed to support analytics. Storage is write-once, read-many with bulk loading, rather than single-row inserts as the primary input method.

---

[2] This has been addressed to some extent by implementing limited RDBMS functionality on top of MR, including Hive and HadoopDB.
[3] See [3] for additional references on column-oriented databases.

Functions and procedures can execute in parallel as close to the data being operated on as possible. SciDB natively supports an array data model and query language with facilities that allow users to extend the system through new scalar data types and array operators.

4.4 Metadata and Provenance Management

Metadata captures and provides information about other objects, often digital ones. This information can include details such as the following:

- **Topic:** Keywords describing the domain the object belongs to.
- **Description:** natural language comment about the object.
- **Access conditions:** information concerning who and how the object can be accessed.
- **Structure:** Description of the organization (physical or virtual) of the object.
- **Content:** Key parameters distinguishing and characterizing the content of the object.
- **Location:** Navigational information to where the object can be found (often geospatial in nature).
- **Related material:** References to other objects into the literature and community providing context about the object.

In data-intensive computing, metadata is of particular importance because it can be used to help organize and characterize the data and to enable effective discovery, access, and analysis of relevant data. In addition, it can be used to help to document important links between different data sets, scholarly publication, or other sources of complimentary information, providing vital background and guidance for the exploration of a particular data-intensive environment.

Repeatability, reproducibility, and transparency are qualities that are at the heart of good research practices. In data-intensive environments with high levels of distribution of data and/or compute resources, complex computational analysis, and evaluation pipelines and processes, these qualities become even more important. In order to support repeatability, reproducibility, and transparency in such complex settings, it is important to provide for the automated capture of information about the data creation process as well as information concerning potential later additional analysis and manipulations. Provenance metadata provides the history of ownership and creation of an object, and thus is a well-suited means to capture, manage, and make accessible this kind of information to enable future use and reuse with confidence. The analysis of the provenance metadata can help to ascertain data quality and the rigor of the research process, establishing the data's "pedigree," in both human and machine-readable form. Moreover, an increasing number of data generators are interested in having their authorship and affiliation associated with their data. Provenance metadata can help to provide attribution information along with data thus helping data generators begin to gain and maintain credit for their contributions.

Metadata provenance information is best captured in a structured and well understood format so that programs and humans accessing the information can understand what it means. It is also important for the metadata to be accessible. Thus, a preferred solution is often to store it in what appears to be a centralized repository that is web accessible. Such a repository may truly be centralized or it may just have interface options that support centralized search and access over what may be a distributed backend.

Although metadata and provenance are critical across a broad range of settings, this section focuses on how effective metadata and provenance management plays an essential role in data-intensive simulations and analysis. Given this discussion, the relevance and applicability to other areas should become apparent.

4.4.1 Support for Data-Intensive Application Execution

Researchers today rarely engage any longer directly with their research object, but do so via digitally captured, reduced, calibrated, analyzed, synthesized, and visualized data. Often at least some of the data is generated by other researchers and then reused. Advances in experimental and computational technologies have led to an exponential growth in the volumes, variety, and complexity of this data, resulting in a growing number of petabyte and soon exabyte scale collections, predicted to outstrip the volumes of data available on the Internet [16]. Leading examples of data-intensive simulations are:

- Climate models, expected to reach exascale by 2020.[4]
- Computational astrophysics – including predictions for the gravitational lensing signal – could reach 20 petabytes per simulation in 2012 (today 0.03 petabytes).
- New experimental facilities, for example the LSST will produce a multi-petabyte data set to include 10 billion galaxies and a similar number of stars. Therefore, energy research such as the European XFEL will require near

---

[4] *Challenges in Climate Change Science and the Role of Computing at the Extreme Scale*, http://extremecomputing.labworks.org/climate/report.stm.

real-time analysis of experimental results produced at multi-petabytes per day from 2014 (today 3 petabytes per year at comparable facilities).

- The U.S. Department of Defense is expecting yottabytes (10^{24}) of sensor data by 2015.
- Internet services such as Google, Yahoo, and Microsoft have already reached data volumes of hundreds of petabytes.

A wide range of supporting technologies is required to allow applications to effectively utilize these large data sets. Metadata plays an essential role in most of these enabling technologies, making them effective in reducing the data space and volume as well as enabling them to exploit relevant relationships between different, often heterogeneous, and potentially distributed data objects. Challenging areas of data-intensive computing support, where metadata and provenance have a crucial impact include: data identification and assessment, data subsetting, monitoring and control of the simulation, provenance for simulation, data management for distributed applications, and the annotation of the results for future analysis, reuse, and attribution. The following explore each of these areas.

Data identification and assessment: With exponentially growing data diversity and volumes, the selection of the most suitable data for any task at hand can be time consuming. Appropriate metadata and metadata systems can cut efforts dramatically, providing easily searchable summary information on provenance, content, quality, and access conditions. Depending on the extent of the metadata, it can be possible to make very detailed assessments and comparisons between data sets, without the need to download and access the data directly. This is because provenance and key parameters from the data have been captured in the metadata systems and can themselves be analyzed. An example of the type of question that can be asked about provenance is:

> give me only data sets where value Z is in the range of F-G produced by radar A, with positions a Lat c – long D, at altitude X, which worked 100% during the selected period, and shows high quality verified data . . .

In data-rich environments, metadata is fundamental to this kind of automated processing, because it identifies relevant data effectively and efficiently. One emerging trend in virtual observatories is to use exactly this strategy to support two levels of queries – one identifying sources that contain data of interest and another query to actually obtain (and often plot) data (such as VSTO [40]). In contrast, however, to the World Wide Web, only selected scientific communities offer this type of identification and assessment support across organizational boundaries [36, 42, 53].

Data subsetting: It is very common that only a subset of a particular data file is required to initialize a simulation, and the simulation might need similar subsets from a collection of files or databases. In less data-rich environments, with smaller data volumes, it is still possible at times to download the complete data object and filter out the required data during preprocessing. However, in data-intensive applications the volumes become prohibitive. For these applications, remote preselection and filtering is required to reduce the data to only the necessary subset, thus reducing the volume that needs to be transferred. Metadata guided identification, assessment, and selection reduces the volume of data to be accessed. Further metadata describing the structure, specific content, and coverage of each data file allows algorithms to identify and extract the specific subset of the file(s) or databases that the user requires. Some communities have taken the concept further and provide the capabilities to:

- Capture specific data requirements of an applications through metadata;
- drive repackaging of the data by matching data file and application metadata information (including execution environment); and,
- deliver the right data to the right place for the simulation run such as in the cloud, on a campus grid computing environment, or on a leadership class computing facility requiring parallel I/O.

Metadata makes it possible here to create and guide automated processes that can respond flexibly to changing user requirements.

Monitoring and control of the simulation: Complex simulations require coupling simulation models that span different domains and different levels of theory, time, and scale to provide increased simulation fidelity. Computing environments themselves are also increasing in complexity with distributed data sources, leadership class computer systems, and grid and cloud computing. The factors combined make it increasingly difficult to manage, monitor, and control the execution of a particular simulation run – or even more so a combinatorial or ensemble run with tens to hundreds of runs. Computational workflows and accompanying dashboard applications [1] can support the automation and monitoring of single applications, and do so usually based on the simulation output. However, for data-intensive applications the volume of the output makes it very difficult to quickly identify the relevant information directly from the outputs. The incorporation of metadata can make it more efficient to capture and track the progress of applications. Metadata can be used to capture key derived values from simulation runs, enabling a quick assessment of application progress and correctness without the need to analyze voluminous simulation output files. By collecting and analyzing this metadata not only for single runs, but also across a larger number of simulations, metadata can help identify both important trends in the scientific results and areas of operational concern. If key parameters of the simulation run have been collected, simple analysis or visualization programs can be used to give an overview of the result spread or trends across potentially thousands of runs, allowing the user to hone in on the important executions, without the need to analyze all resulting data sets in full [65]. Similarly potential problem areas and trends in the code can be easily identified and tracked, some of which would otherwise be impossible to pin down. Scientists who have extensively collected this type of metadata have reported that they have been able to improve the quality and accuracy of their code significantly [29] because of the ability to track both intermittent errors and to spot trends in their calculations. Scientists found that with the support of provenance metadata they were able to carry out and analyze many more simulations in a shorter time, leading to greater accuracy of their results because of more complete information. Again, metadata is used to identify relevant information more quickly, aiding the monitoring, analysis, and improvement of applications and simulation processes. If stored, this information also forms a critical part of the provenance of a simulation run, allowing users to assess a workflow execution after its execution.

Provenance for applications: With the increase in data and complexity of compute environments, there has been a corresponding increase in the number of applications carried out (such as for scenario analysis, parameter sweeps, ensemble runs, distributed applications, or large scale collaborative projects). In each of these scenarios, it is of fundamental importance for the assessment of the results to have information available on how the results are obtained:

- Which code and code versions were used?
- What was the input set and code configuration?
- Where and how was it compiled and executed?
- Were there any special occurrences such as restarts, warnings, or errors?

Provenance metadata is designed to capture and make this type of information available; ideally any such provenance information should be captured automatically as it becomes available to ensure ease of use for the scientists and reliable quality and accuracy of the data. This metadata enables scientists to retrace an execution, and for example verify if some unexpected findings are potentially caused by a problem in the code or input values. Further, at the time of execution additional information such as key parameters in the output could be captured.

Data management for distributed applications: A particular class of data-intensive applications run in highly distributed environments, where data and/or computing are found in many different locations. Examples are climate simulations driven by a variety of observational data reaching from NASA satellite data to sensor network measurements, or meta genomics analysis in biology, which results from many different experimental results. Given the volumes of data involved in data-intensive applications, it is not feasible to move all data into a single location, either before analysis or afterward. Therefore, it is paramount to support applications in locating and managing their data, in particular for highly distributed applications. Metadata available for input data locations and captured during the application run can help to track the location of input and output data for particular simulations or related to particular simulation components. It can provide an easy-to-use logical link to each data object, independent of its physical location to enable access to the data at any stage. In addition, the metadata can capture detailed information about the actual physical location of each data object and the organization of any compound data set. It can be used to support services to resolve the logical link to the data used by applications into the data's actual physical location and accompanying access mechanism at any given point in time. This information can be used both during and after the simulation run to coordinate access to the data and support scheduling of computational tasks close to the data, whether for further analysis, data exchange, or final data collection for archival if required. This type of metadata can also be used to add an additional layer of monitoring, control, and audit for complex data movement processes.

Annotation of results for analysis and future reuse: Closing the circle with the large volumes of data produced by data-intensive application codes, it is paramount to annotate the results appropriately to allow for further analysis and potential future reuse of the data by students, collaborators, and the wider scientific community. In this step, a range of different metadata components are combined, including those described in the previous sections as well as topic, access conditions, and content and related materials, all of which form a full descriptive record.

To make the capture of the metadata and provenance information practical and reliable, it is essential to automate most of the processes involved in its capture, management, and analysis. Furthermore, these metadata-related processes are best tightly integrated into computing environments, as studies have shown that the usage of metadata is most beneficial and transformational when seamlessly integrated into the research process. An excellent example is the U.S. Earth Systems Grid (ESG) [53].

U.S. Earth Systems Grid: This project provides scientists with access to essential climate data from worldwide distributed resources as well as analysis capabilities. It uses community agreed data and metadata formats and standards to describe data content and structure. International resources are linked through mappings between their own data formats and the ESG formats, giving scientists seamless access to all resources. To allow users to explore the large number and size of the different data holding the project has developed a multi-tier metadata-based approach for data discovery and assessment. Further, standardized services allow the user to select particular subsets of the data to minimize the size of data that needs to be transported; these subset definitions are based on standardized metadata description of the data structure and content. With growing data sizes, this is often not enough and the ESG also offers remote analysis capabilities, whereby a copy of the required data nearest to a suitable computing resource is identified and efficiently moved with special protocols; metadata records help to identify suitable data replicates worldwide. The results of climate simulations are automatically annotated and archived where desired. The infrastructure has been successfully used for a number of international climate intercomparison studies, because of the accessibility and value of the results. In result of the extensive metadata, the climate community has been able to analyze the data effectively, resulting in many hundreds of peer reviewed scientific papers and contributing to the Nobel Prize-winning IPCC Fourth Assessment Report (AR4).

4.4.2 Support for Data Analysis and Exploitation in Data-Intensive Environments

The analysis of extreme scale data has many challenges. The key is moving large amounts of data and the identification of relevant information in large volumes of data. Metadata can be of essential help in addressing both of these challenges through support of: efficient search and retrieval, capture of key parameters, feature identification and extraction, and inference support. As the significant reduction of search effort through descriptive provenance metadata and availability of key parameters for data files has already been described, this discussion focuses on feature identification and inference support, which are of particular benefit for the data-intensive analysis of extreme scale data.

Feature identification and cataloguing: When assessing and analyzing the output of application runs or experimental/observational studies, researchers often are not so much interested in the data as a whole (statistical analysis) or the developments of particular variables over time or space, but are aiming to identify particular complex phenomena such as features within the data like a dying star, tornado, or group of suspect individuals communicating. Currently, much of this identification work has to be done by visually tracing through large amounts of data. In data-intensive computing environments, this task can no longer be accomplished by a single researcher or group. Instead, some are exploiting social data analysis [18, 19], where the general public is encouraged to look through visualizations or run small analysis on their systems to identify particular phenomena in the data and contribute results back to the repository. To make the most of the effort expended in identifying the various features in the data, researchers want to catalogue these described by metadata, so that they and others such as collaborators can quickly find and access them again for further analysis. Formalizing such metadata descriptions of phenomena and features will allow the identification, extraction, and comparison of such events across different sources and systems found in biology, astronomy, climate, and earth systems communities [23, 66].

Next to quantitative and qualitative analysis of events enabled through advanced access to features in the data, this also supports ongoing work further characterizing such events, and eventually enabling the automated detection of such features in the data – a development which, if it can be used with confidence in its accuracy, would speed up research processes in data rich environments tremendously. Again, metadata is instrumental here in providing efficient access to the relevant data, increasing the accuracy of methods through access to more complete data.

Inference support: Given the volume of data generated in data-rich environments, it is important to develop efficient analysis methods to enable researchers to explore the information and knowledge contained in the raw data. Advanced analysis methods and their support through metadata and provenance data are essential to identify features and patterns of interest in the data, semantic inference support builds on these and aims to draw new conclusions from data that have not been explicitly expressed in the data itself. Deductive inference can be supported using existing reasoners providing standard inference rule chaining. Biology is a key scientific discipline that utilizes this technique, such as the discovery of regulatory gene networks, which encode gene function, and can be aided by using prior biological knowledge captured through ontologies to infer likely function in combination with the analysis of experimental results [54]. In the latter, the meaning contained in the metadata is encoded in mathematical terms (vectors in highly dimensional space), a closeness of concepts can be deduced through distance calculations (between vectors), and probabilities through analysis of clustering of concepts (vectors).

4.4.3 Particular Metadata Challenges in Data-Intensive Computing Environments

Just as access and management of data presents specific challenges in data-intensive computing environments, metadata faces its own set of hurdles. These include the rate at which metadata needs to be created and captured, the appropriate granularity for metadata annotation, the volume of metadata potentially created, and the overhead that the creation of metadata might introduce into an application. As data is produced at ever faster rates and volumes, the rate and volume of the metadata increases too, requiring the optimization and intelligent design of the underlying metadata systems to keep a pace with the increased demand. The emphasis will be placed on efficient metadata systems, which may mean compact metadata formats (such as non-XML), efficient syntax (capturing as much information as required in the least verbose way), optimized access options, and/or partitioning strategies. In some cases, where the volume of metadata grows significantly, it might also be necessary to review if the level of detail captured is still appropriate or if reduced summary information, along with optional follow-up systems that may gather more provenance information only when requested, would be better. Finally, optimized database structures and connection mechanisms (such as connection pooling) may need to be employed to provide both the necessary speed and volume.

As the world is becoming more data rich and connected, the ability to focus quickly not only on the relevant data, but particular features within them becomes crucial. As more data is being processed by ever more complex processes, it is essential that is possible to verify these workflows, so that the resulting outcomes can be used with confidence. Without metadata and provenance, none of this could be accomplished, making it a fundamental enabling technology for data-intensive computing.

References

1. Altintas, I. "Lifecycle of Scientific Workflows and Their Provenance: A Usage Perspective." *IEEE Congress on Services – Part I*. 474–75, Honolulu, HI, July 2008.
2. Altintas, I., Bhagwanani, S., Buttler, D., Chandra, S., Cheng, Z., Coleman, M., Critchlow, T., Gupta, A., Han, W., Liu, L., Ludaescher, B., Pu, C., Moore, R., Shoshani, A., and Vouk, M. "A Modeling and Execution Environment for Distributed Scientific Workflows." *Proceedings of the 15th IEEE International Conference on Scientific and Statistical Database Management (SSDBM)*, Cambridge, MA, July 2003.
3. Adabi, D. J., Boncz, P. A., and Harizopoulos, S. "Column-Oriented Database Systems." Proceedings of the VLDB Endowment 2, no. 2 (August 2009): 1664–65. Available: http://cs-www.cs.yale.edu/homes/dna/papers/columnstore-tutorial.pdf.
4. Ali, N., Carns, P., Iskra, K., Kimpe, D., Lang, S., Latham, R., Ross, R., Ward, L., and Sadayappan, P. "Scalable I/O Forwarding Framework for High-Performance Computing Systems." *IEEE International Conference on Cluster Computing (Cluster 2009)*, New Orleans, LA, September 2009.
5. Agrawal, R., Gupta, A., and Sarawagi, S. "Modeling Multidimensional Databases." *Proceedings of the 13th International Conference on Data Engineering*, Birmingham, U.K., April 1997.

6. Becla, J., Lim, K.-T., Monkewitz, S., Nieto-Santisteban, M., and Thakar, A. "Orga-
    nizing the Extremely Large LSST Database for Real-Time Astronomical Process-
    ing." *17th Annual Astronomical Data Analysis Software and Systems Conference
    (ADASS 2007)*, London, England, September 2007.

7. Benedict, J. L., McGuinness, D. L., and Fox, P. "A Semantic Web-based Method-
    ology for Building Conceptual Models of Scientific Information." *American Geo-
    physical Union, Fall Meeting (AGU2006)*, San Francisco, CA, December 2007.

8. Chang, F., Dean, J., Ghemawat, S., Hsieh, W. C., Wallach, D. A., Burrows, M.,
    Chandra, T., Fikes, A., and Gruber, R. E. "Bigtable: A Distributed Storage System
    for Structured Data." *7th USENIX Symposium on Operating Systems Design and
    Implementation*, Boston, MA, May 2006.

9. Codd, E. F., Codd, S. B., and Salley, C. T. Providing OLAP (On-Line Analytical
    Processing) to User-Analysts: An IT Mandate. Report. Codd & Associates, 1993.

10. Carns, P., Harms, K., Allcock, W., Lang, S., Latham, R., and Ross, R. "Storage
    Access Characteristics of Computational Science Applications." *Proceedings of
    Supercomputing*, New Orleans, LA, November 2010.

11. Cudre-Mauroux, P., Kimura, H., Lim, K.-T., Rogers, J., Simakov, R., Soroush, E.,
    Velikhov, P., Wang, D. L., Balazinska, M., Becla, J., DeWitt, D., Heath, B., Maier,
    D., Madden, S., Patel, J., Stonebraker, M., and Zdonik, S. A Demonstration of
    SciDB: A Science-Oriented DBMS. VLDB'09 2, no. 1 (August 2009): 1534–37.
    Available: http://www.vldb.org/pvldb/2/vldb09–76.pdf.

12. Carns, P., Lang, S., Ross, R., Vilayannur, M., Kunkel, J., and Ludwig, T. "Small-
    File Access in Parallel File Systems." *Proceedings of the 23rd IEEE International
    Parallel and Distributed Processing Symposium*, Rome Italy, May 2009.

13. Codd, E. F. "A Relational Model for Large Shared Data Banks." *Communications
    of the ACM* 13, no. 6 (June 1970): 377–87.

14. Culler, D., Singh, J., and Gupta, A. *Parallel Computer Architecture: A Hardware/
    Software Approach*. San Francisco, CA: Morgan Kaufmann, 1999.

15. Chaudhuri, S., and Dayal, U. "An Overview of Data Warehousing and OLAP
    Technology." *ACM SIGMOD Record* 26, no. 1 (1997): 65–74.

16. Department of Defense. JASON Defense Advisory Panel Report. *Data Analysis
    Challenges*, JSR-08–142, December 2008.

17. Dehne, F., Eavis, T., and Rau-Chaplin, A. "The cgmCUBE Project: Optimizing
    Parallel Data Cube Generation for ROLAP." *Journal of Distributed and Parallel
    Databases* 19, no. 1 (2006): 29–62.

18. Freire, J., and Silva, C. "Towards Enabling Social Analysis of Scientific Data."
    Proceedings of CHI Social Data Analysis Workshop, Florence, Italy, April 2008.

19. Goodman, A. A., and Wong, C. G. 2009. "Bringing the Night Sky Closer: Dis-
    coveries in the Data Deluge." In *The Fourth Paradigm: Data-Intensive Scientific
    Discovery*, 39–44, edited by T. Hey, S. Tansley, K. Tolle. Microsoft Research.
    Redmond WA, 2006.

20. Gropp, W., Huss-Lederman, S. Lumsdaine, A. Lusk, E. Nitzberg, B. Saphir, W.,
    and Snir, M. *MPI – The Complete Reference, Volume 2, The MPI Extensions*.
    Cambridge, MA: The MIT Press, 1998.

21. Gopalkrishnan, V., Li, Q., and Karlapalem, K. "Star/Snow-Flake Schema Driven
    Object-Relational Data Warehouse Design and Query Processing Strategies." In
    Lecture Notes in Computer Science. Volume 1676/1999, 11–22. Berlin/Heidelberg:
    Springer, 1999.

22. Gray, J., Nieto-Santisteban, M. A., and Szalay, A. S. "The Zones Algorithm for Finding Points-Near-a-Point or Cross-Matching Spatial Datasets." In *The ACM Computing Research Repository* (CoRR). Vol abs/cs/0701171. Microsoft: 2007.

23. Hirschman, J. E., Balakrishnan, R., Christie, K. R., Costanzo, M. C., Dwight, S. S., Engel, S. R., Fisk, D. G., Hong, E. L., Livstone, M. S., Nash, R., Park, J., Oughtred, R., Skrzypek, M., Starr, B., Theesfeld, C. L., Williams, J., Andrada, R., Binkley, G., Dong, Q., Lane, C., Miyasato, S., Sethuraman, A., Schroeder, M., Thanawala, M. K., Weng, S., Dolinski, K., Botstein, D., and Cherry, J. M. "Genome Snapshot: A New Resource at the *Saccharomyces* Genome Database (SGD) Presenting an Overview of the *Saccharomyces cerevisiae* Genome." *Nucleic Acids Research* 34, no. 1: D442–D445.

24. The Hierarchical Data Format, Version 5 (HDF5). Available: http://www.hdfgroup.org/HDF5/doc/.

25. Hadjieleftheriou, M., Hoel, E., and Tsotras, V. J. "Sail: A Spatial Index Library for Efficient Application Integration." *GeoInformatica* 9, no. 4 (2005): 367–89.

26. Hey, T., Tansley, S., and Tolle, K. *The Fourth Paradigm, Data-Intensive Scientific Discovery*. Redmond, Washington: Microsoft Research, October 2009.

27. Joslyn, C., Burke, J., Critchlow, T., Hengartner, N., and Hogan, E. "View Discovery in OLAP Databases through Statistical Combinatorial Optimization." *Proceedings of the 21st International Conference on Scientific and Statistical Database Management*. New Orleans, LA, June 2009.

28. Kogge, P., Bergman, K., Borkar, S., Campbell, D., Carlson, W., Dally, W., Denneau, M., Franzon, P., Harrod, W., Hill, K., Hiller, J., Karp, S., Keckler, S., Klein, D., Lucas, R., Richards, M., Scarpelli, A., Scott, S., Snavely, A., Sterling, T., Williams, R. S., and Yelick, K. *Exascale Computing Study: Technology Challenges in Achieving Exascale Systems*. Technical Report DARPA, 2008.

29. Kleese van Dam, K., James, M., and Walker, A. "Integrating Data Management and Collaborative Sharing with Computational Science Research Processes." In *Handbook of Research on Computational Science and Engineering: Theory and Practice*, edited by J. Leng and W. Sharrock. 506–38, Hershey, PAIGI Global, September 2011.

30. Kumar, V. S., Kurc, T., Abdulla, G., Kohn, S. R., Saltz, J., and Matarazzo, C. "Architectural Implications for Spatial Object Association Algorithms." *Proceedings of the IEEE International Parallel and Distributed Processing Symposium*, Rome, Italy, IPDPS, May 2009.

31. Ludaescher, B., Altintas, I., Berkley, C., Higgins, D., Jaeger, E., Jones, M., Lee, E. A., Tao, J., and Zhao, Y. Scientific Workflow Management and the Kepler System. *Concurrency and Computation: Practice & Experience* 18, no 10: (August 2006) 1039–65.

32. Lang, S., Carns, P., Latham, R., Ross, R., Harms, K., and Allcock, W. "I/O Performance Challenges at Leadership Scale." *SC '09: Proceedings of the Conference on High Performance Computing Networking, Storage and Analysis*, New York, NY, November 2009.

33. Li, J., Liao, W.-K., Choudhary, A., Ross, R., Thakur, R., Gropp, W., and Latham, R. "Parallel netCDF: A Scientific High-Performance I/O Interface." Technical Report ANL/MCS-P1048–0503, Mathematics and Computer Science Division, Argonne National Laboratory, May 2003.

34. Ludaescher, B., and Goble, C. A., eds. "ACM SIGMOD Record." *Special Section on Scientific Workflows* 34, no. 3: September 2005.
35. Lofstead, J. F., Klasky, S., Schwan, K., Podhorszki, N., and Jin, C. "Flexible IO and Integration for Scientific Codes Through the Adaptable IO System." *Proceedings of the International Workshop on Challenges of Large Applications in Distributed Environments.* 15–24, Boston, MA, June 2008.
36. Lawrence, B. N., Lowry, R., Miller, P., Snaith, H., and Woolf, A. "Information in Environmental Data Grids." *Phil Trans R Soc A* 367 (2009): 1003–14.
37. http://www.lsst.org/lsst/science/concept_data.
38. Mokbel, M. F., and Aref, W. G. "PLACE: A Scalable Location-Aware Database Server for Spatio-Temporal Data Streams." *Data Engineering Bulletin* 28, no. 3 (2005): 3–10.
39. Musick, R., and Critchlow, T. "Practical Lessons in Supporting Large Scale Computational Science." *SIGMOD Record* 28, no. 4 (December 1999): 49–57.
40. McGuinness, D., Fox, P., Cinquini, L., West, P., Garcia, J., Benedict, J. L., and Middleton, D. "The Virtual Solar-Terrestrial Observatory: A Deployed Semantic Web Application Case Study for Scientific Research." *Proceedings of the Nineteenth Conference on Innovative Applications of Artificial Intelligence (IAAI-07).* Vancouver, British Columbia, Canada, July 22–26, 2007. Available: http://www.ksl.stanford.edu/KSL_Abstracts/KSL-07–01.html.
41. Mokbel, M. F., Ghanem, T. M., and Aref, W. G. Spatio-Temporal Access Methods. *IEEE Data Engineering Bulletin* 26, no. 2 (2003): 40–49.
42. Matthews, B., Sufi, S., Flannery, D., Lerusse, L., Griffin, T., Gleaves, M., and Kleese van Dam, K. "Using a Core Scientific Metadata Model in Large-Scale Facilities." *5th International Digital Curation Conference (IDCC 2009),* London, U.K., December 2009.
43. Maceachren, A. M., Robinson, A., Gardner, S., Murray, R., Gahegan, M., and Hetzler, E. "Visualizing Geospatial Information Uncertainty: What We Know and What We Need to Know." *Cartography and Geographic Information Science* 32, no. 3 (2005): 139–60.
44. http://www.netezza.com/.
45. Nanni, M., Kuijpers, B., Korner, C., May, M., and Pedreschi, D. Spatiotemporal Data Mining. In Giannotti, F., and Pedreschi, D., eds. *Mobility, Data Mining, and Privacy: Geographic Knowledge Discovery.* Berlin, Germany: Springer-Verlag, 2008.
46. Oracle Times Ten. In-Memory Database Architectural Overview. Release 6.0. Available: http://www.oracle.com/us/products/database/timesten/overview/index.html.
47. IEEE/ANSI Standard. 1003.1 Portable Operating System Interface (POSIX) – Part 1: System Application Program Interface (API) [C Language], 1996.
48. Werstein, P. "A Performance Benchmark for Spatio-Temporal Databases." *Proceedings of the 10th Annual Colloquium of the Spatial Information Research Centre,* The University of Otago, Dunedin, New Zealand. 365–73, December 1998.
49. Roddick, J. F., Hornsby, K. and Spiliopoulou, M "An Updated Bibliography of Temporal, Spatial and Spatio-Temporal Data Mining Research." In *Post-Workshop Proceedings of the International Workshop on Temporal, Spatial and Spatio-Temporal Data Mining. Lecture Notes in Artificial Intelligence.* Roddick, J. F. and Hornsby, K., eds. 147–63. Berlin: Springer, 2001.

50. Sellis, T. "Research Issues in Spatio-Temporal Database Systems." In Güting, R. H., Papadias, D., and Lochovsky, F., eds., *SSD'99, LNCS 1651.* 5–11, Berlin, Heidelberg: Springer-Verlag, 1999.

51. Schwan, P. "Lustre: Building a File System for 1000-Node Clusters." *Proceedings of the 2003 Linux Symposium*, Ottawa, Canada, July 2004.

52. Schneider, M. "Fuzzy Spatial Data Types for Spatial Uncertainty Management in Databases." *Handbook of Research on Fuzzy Information Processing in Databases.* Edited by J. Galindo Ed. 490–515. Hershey, PA: IGI Global, 2008.

53. Siebenlist, F., Ananthakrishnan, R., Bernholdt, D. E., Cinquini, L., Foster, I. T., Middleton, D. E., Miller, N., and Williams, D. N. "Enhancing the Earth System Grid Security Infrastructure Through Single Sign-on and Autoprovisioning." *Proceedings of the 5th Grid Computing Environments Workshop*, Portland, Oregon, November 14–20, 2009. GCE '09. ACM, New York, NY, 1–8. Available: http://doi.acm.org/10.1145/1658260.1658278.

54. Sanfilippo, A., Baddeley, B., Beagley, N., McDermott, J., Riensche, R., Taylor, R., and Gopalan, B. "Using the Gene Ontology to Enrich Biological Pathways. *International Journal of computational Biology and Drug design* 2, no. 3 (2009): 221–35.

55. Stonebraker, M., Becla, J., DeWitt, D., Lim, K-T., Maier, D., Ratzesberger, O., and Zdonik, S. "Requirements for Science Data Bases and SciDB." CIDR 2009 Conference, Asilomar, CA, January 2009. Available: http://www-db.cs.wisc.edu/cidr/cidr2009/Paper_26.pdf.

56. Shepler, S., Eisler, M., and Noveck, D. Network File System (NFS) Version 4 Minor Version 1 Protocol. January 2010. Available: http://datatracker.ietf.org/doc/rfc5661/.

57. Schmuck, F., and Haskin, R. "GPFS: A Shared-Disk File System for Large Computing Clusters." Proceedings of the FAST 2002 Conference on File and Storage Technologies, Monterey, CA, January 2002.

58. Silberschatz, A., Korth, H., and Sudarshan, S. *Database Systems Concepts.* New York: McGraw-Hill Publishing, January 2010.

59. Szalay, A. S., Gray, J., Thakar, A., Kunszt, P. Z., Malik, T., Raddick, J., Stoughton, C., and vandenBerg, J. "The SDSS SkyServer: Public Access to the Sloan Digital Sky Server Data." SIGMOD Conference, Madison, WI, June 2002: 570–81.

60. Shi, W., Wang, S., Li, D., and Wang, X. "Uncertainty-Based Spatial Datamining." ASIAGIS, Wuhan, China, October 2003.

61. Thakur, R., Gropp, W., and Lusk, E. "Data Sieving and Collective I/O in ROMIO." Proceedings of the Seventh Symposium on the Frontiers of Massively Parallel Computation, Los Alamitos CA, Feb.1999.

62. Thakur, R., Gropp, W., and Lusk, E. "On Implementing MPI-IO Portably and with High Performance." *Proceedings of the 6th Workshop on I/O in Parallel and Distributed Systems.* Atlanta, GA: ACM Press, May 1999.

63. Top500 List, November 2009. Available: http://www.top500.org/list/2009/11/100.

64. Twa, M., Parthasarathy, S., Rosche, T., and Bullmer, M. "Decision Tree Classification of Spatial Data Patterns." From Videokeratography Using Zernike Polynomials. *SIAM International Conference on Data Mining*, San Francisco, CA, May 2003.

65. Walker, A. M., Bruin, R. P., Dove, M. T., White, T. O. H., Kleese van Dam, K., and Tyer, R. P. Integrating Computing, Data and Collaboration Grids: The

RMCS Tool. *Phil Trans R Soc A* 367, no. 1890 (March 13, 2009): 1047–50; DOI: 10.1098/rsta.2008.0159.

66. Woolf, A., Lawrence, B., Lowry, R., Kleese van Dam, K., Cramer, R., Gutierrez, M., Kondapalli, S., Latham, S., Lowe, D., O'Neill, K., and Stephens, A. Data Integration with the Climate Science Modeling Language. *Adv Geosci* 8 (2006): 83–90. Available: www.adv-geosci.net/8/83/2006/.

67. Welch, B., Unangst, M., Abbasi, Z., Gibson, G., Mueller, B., Small, J., Zelenka, J., and Zhou, B. "Scalable Performance of the Panasas Parallel File System." *Proceedings of the 6th USENIX Conference on File and Storage Technologies*, San Jose, CA, February 2008.

68. Xu, X., Han, J., and Lu, W. "RT-Tree: An Improved R-Tree Index Structure for Spatiotemporal Databases." *Proceedings of the 4th International Symposium on Spatial Data Handling (SDH)*, Zurich Switzerland, July 1990.

5

Large-Scale Data Management Techniques in Cloud Computing Platforms

Sherif Sakr and Anna Liu

5.1 Introduction

In the last two decades, the continuous increase of computational power has produced an overwhelming flow of data, which called for a paradigm shift in the computing architecture and large scale data processing mechanisms. In a speech given just a few weeks before he was lost at sea off the California coast in January 2007, Jim Gray, a database software pioneer and a Microsoft researcher, called the shift a *"fourth paradigm"* [32]. The first three paradigms were experimental, theoretical and, more recently, computational science. Gray argued that the only way to cope with this paradigm is to develop a new generation of computing tools to manage, visualize, and analyze the data flood. In general, the current computer architectures are increasingly imbalanced where the latency gap between multicore CPUs and mechanical hard disks is growing every year, which makes the challenges of data-intensive computing harder to overcome [6]. Therefore, there is a crucial need for a systematic and generic approach to tackle these problems with an architecture that can also scale into the foreseeable future. In response, Gray argued that the new trend should instead focus on supporting cheaper clusters of computers to manage and process all this data instead of focusing on having the biggest and fastest single computer. Figure 5.1 illustrates an example of the explosion in scientific data, which creates major challenges for cutting-edge scientific projects. For example, modern high-energy physics experiments, such as *DZero*,[1] typically generate more than one terabyte of data per day. With data sets growing beyond a few hundreds of terabytes, scientists have no off-the-shelf solutions that they can readily use to manage and analyze these data [32]. Thus, significant

---

[1] http://www-d0.fnal.gov/.

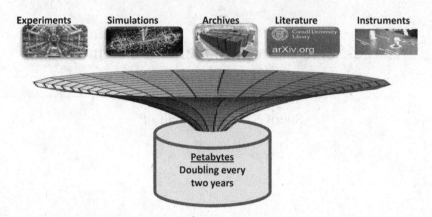

Figure 5.1. Data explosion in scientific computing [32].

human and material resources were allocated to support these data-intensive operations, which lead to high storage and management costs.

Additionally, the recent advances in Web technology have made it easy for any user to provide and consume content of any form. For example, building a personal Web page (such as Google Sites[2]), starting a blog (such as WordPress,[3] Blogger,[4] LiveJournal[5]), and making both searchable for the public have now become a commodity. Therefore, one of the main goals of the next wave is to facilitate the job of implementing every application as a *distributed*, *scalable*, and *widely-accessible* service on the Web. For example, it has been recently reported that the famous social network Web site, Facebook,[6] serves 570 billion page views per month, stores 3 billion new photos every month, manages 25 billion pieces of content (such as status updates and comments) every month, and runs its services to over thirty thousand servers. Although services such as Facebook, YouTube,[7] and LinkedIn[8] are currently leading this approach, it becomes an ultimate goal to make it easy for everybody to achieve these goals with the minimum amount of effort.

Recently, there has been a great deal of hype about cloud computing. Cloud computing is on the top of Gartners list of the ten most disruptive technologies of the next years [27]. Cloud computing is associated with a new paradigm for the provision of computing infrastructure. This paradigm shifts the location of this

---

[2] http://sites.google.com/.
[3] http://wordpress.org/.
[4] http://www.blogger.com/.
[5] http://www.livejournal.com/.
[6] http://www.facebook.com/.
[7] http://www.youtube.com/.
[8] http://www.linkedin.com/.

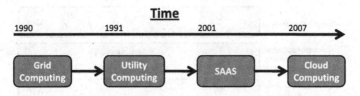

Figure 5.2. Technology evolution towards cloud computing.

infrastructure to the network to reduce the costs associated with the management of hardware and software resources [31]. Therefore, businesses and users are now able to access application services from anywhere in the world on demand. This represents the long-held dream of envisioning computing as a utility [4] where the economy of scale principles help to drive the cost of computing infrastructure effectively down. For example, Amazon Web Services (AWS)[9] offer Amazon Elastic Compute Cloud (EC2)[10] as a commodity that can be purchased and utilized. In principle, the concept of renting computing power goes back decades to the days when companies would share space on a single mainframe with big spinning tape drives. The technology industry has matured to the point where there is now an emerging mass market for this rental model. Therefore, cloud computing is not a revolutionary new development. However, it is an evolution that has taken place over several decades. As illustrated in Figure 5.2, the trend toward cloud computing started in the early 1990s with the concepts of grid computing [25] when the idea of using the resources of many computers in a network to solve a single problem (usually scientific) at the same time was introduced. Over the years, the research community has developed a wide spectrum of funding and usage models to address the ever growing need for computing resources. From locally owned clusters to national centers and from campus grids to national grids, researchers combine campus and federal funding with competitive and opportunistic compute time allocations to support their research [23]. This approach follows the principle that not all of the computing resources are needed at the same time, and when a project does not need their own resources, these resources can be made available to others in the broader collaboration.

In practice, the main goal of cloud computing is to provide the basic ingredients such as storage, CPUs, and network bandwidth as a commodity by specialized service providers at low unit cost. Therefore, users of cloud services should not need to worry about scalability because the storage provided is

---

[9] http://aws.amazon.com/.
[10] http://aws.amazon.com/ec2/.

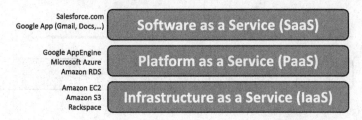

Figure 5.3. Layers of cloud services.

virtually infinite. In addition, cloud computing provides full availability where:
1) Users can read and write data at any time without ever being blocked.
2) The response times are (virtually) constant and do not depend on the number
of concurrent users, the size of the database or any other system parameter.
Furthermore, users do not need to worry about backups. If components fail,
it is the responsibility of the service provider to replace them and make the
data available using replicas in the meantime. Another important reason to
build new services based on cloud computing is that no investments are needed
upfront and the cost grows linearly and predictably with the increase of usage
(*pay-as-you-go*). For example, if a company is launching a new product that
requires a large database, it does not need to go out and buy one. However, it
can use one hosted by a cloud provider such as Amazon or Google. Therefore,
all of these advantages allow companies to focus on their business innovation
rather than focusing on building larger data centers to achieve scalability goals.
Figure 5.3 illustrates the three layers of cloud services, which are described as
follows [8].

1. *Infrastructure as a Service (IaaS)*: Provision resources such as servers (often
   in the form of virtual machines), network bandwidth, storage, and related
   tools necessary to build an application environment from scratch (such as
   Amazon EC2).
2. *Platform as a Service (PaaS)*: Provides a higher-level environment where
   developers can write customized applications (such as Microsoft Azure[11]
   and Google AppEngine[12]). The service provider is responsible for the
   maintenance, load-balancing, and scale-out of the platform such that the
   developer can concentrate on implementing the main functionalities of his
   application.

---

[11] http://www.microsoft.com/windowsazure/.
[12] http://code.google.com/appengine/.

3. *Software as a Service (SaaS)*: Refers to special-purpose software that are made available through the Internet (such as SalesForce[13]). Therefore, it does not require each end-user to manually download, install, configure, run, or use the software applications on their own computing environments.

This chapter gives an overview of numerous approaches and mechanisms of deploying data-intensive applications in the cloud, which are gaining a lot of momentum in both research and industrial communities. We discuss the advantages and the disadvantages of each approach and its suitability to support certain classes of applications and end-users. The remainder of this chapter is organized as follows. The following section gives an overview of the main goals and challenges of deploying data-intensive applications in cloud environments. The chapter then surveys the state-of-the-art of cloud data management systems before turning to a discussion of the different programming models for cloud applications. Finally, several real-world case studies are discussed before we conclude the chapter.

5.2 Cloud Data Management: Goals and Challenges

This section gives an overview of the main goals and challenges for deploying data-intensive computing application in cloud environments.

5.2.1 Goals

In general, successful cloud data management systems are designed to satisfy key items in the following *wish list* [2,17]:

- *Availability*: They must be always accessible even on the occasions where there is a network failure or a whole datacenter has gone offline.
- *Multitenancy*: They must be able to support many applications (tenants) on the same hardware and software infrastructure. However, the performance of these tenants must be isolated from each another. Adding a new tenant should require little or no effort beyond ensuring that enough system capacity has been provisioned for the new load.
- *Scalability*: They must be able to support very large databases with very high request rates at very low latency. They should be able to take on new tenants or handle growing tenants without much effort beyond that of adding more hardware. In particular, the system must be able to automatically redistribute data to take advantage of the new hardware.

---

[13] http://www.salesforce.com/.

- *Elasticity*: They must be able to satisfy changing application requirements in both directions (scaling up or scaling down). Moreover, the system must be able to gracefully respond to these changing requirements and quickly recover to its steady state.
- *Performance*: On public cloud computing platforms, pricing is structured in a way such that one pays only for what one uses, so the vendor price increases linearly with the requisite storage, network bandwidth, and compute power. Therefore, the system performance has a direct effect on its costs. Moreover efficient system performance is a crucial requirement to save money.
- *Load and tenant balancing*: They must be able to automatically move load between servers so that most of the hardware resources are effectively utilized and to avoid any resource overloading situations.
- *Fault tolerance*: For transactional workloads, a fault tolerant cloud data management system needs to be able to recover from a failure without losing any data or updates from recently committed transactions. Moreover, it needs to successfully commit transactions and make progress on a workload even in the face of worker node failures. For analytical workloads, a fault tolerant cloud data management system should not need to restart a query if one of the nodes involved in query processing fails.
- *Ability to run in a heterogeneous environment*: On cloud computing platforms, there is a strong trend towards increasing the number of nodes that participate in query execution. It is nearly impossible to get homogeneous performance across hundreds or thousands of compute nodes. Part failures that do not cause complete node failure, but result in degraded hardware performance become more common at scale. A cloud data management system should be designed to run in a heterogeneous environment and must take appropriate measures to prevent its performance from degrading because of parallel processing on distributed nodes.
- *Flexible query interface*: They should support both SQL and non-SQL interface languages (such as MapReduce). Moreover, they should provide mechanism for allowing the user to write user defined functions (UDFs) and queries that utilize these UDFs and should be automatically parallelized during their processing.

5.2.2 Challenges

Deploying data-intensive applications on cloud environment is not a trivial or straightforward task. Armbrust et al. [4] and Abadi [1] argued a list of obstacles to the growth of cloud computing applications as follows.

- *Availability of a service*: Organizations worry about whether cloud computing services will have adequate availability. High availability is one of the most challenging goals because even the slightest outage can have significant financial consequences and impacts customer trust.
- *Data confidentiality*: In general, moving data off premises increases the number of potential security risks and appropriate precautions must be made. Transactional databases typically contain the complete set of operational data needed to power mission-critical business processes. This data includes detail at the lowest granularity, and often includes sensitive information such as customer data or credit card numbers. Therefore, unless such sensitive data is encrypted using a key that is not located at the host, the data may be accessed by a third party without the customers knowledge.
- *Data lock-in*: APIs for cloud computing have not yet been a subject of active standardization. Thus, customers cannot easily extract their data and programs from one site to run on another. The concerns about the difficulties of extracting data from the cloud is preventing some organizations from adopting cloud computing. Customer lock-in may be attractive to cloud computing providers but cloud computing users are vulnerable to price increases, reliability problems, or even providers going out of business.
- *Data transfer bottlenecks*: Various vendors deploy varying technology, data writing systems, and protocols to render their services at different rates. Cloud users and cloud providers have to think about the implications of placement and traffic at every level of the system if they want to minimize costs because of the data transfer restrictions (such as limits on volume of data).
- *Application parallelization*: Computing power is elastic but only if workload is parallelizable. Getting additional computational resources is not as simple as a magic upgrade to a bigger and more powerful machine on the fly. However, the additional resources are typically obtained by allocating additional server instances to a task.
- *Shared-nothing architecture*: Data management applications designed to run on top of cloud environment should follow a shared-nothing architecture [41] where each node is independent and self-sufficient and there is no single point of contention across the system. Most of transactional data management systems do not typically use a shared-nothing architecture.
- *Application debugging in large-scale distributed systems*: A challenging aspect in cloud computing programming is the removal of errors in these very large-scale distributed systems. A common occurrence is that these bugs cannot be reproduced in smaller configurations, so the debugging must occur at the same scale as that in the production datacenters.

5.3 Cloud Data Management Systems: State of the Art

The task of storing data persistently has been traditionally achieved through filesystems or relational databases. In recent years, this task is increasingly achieved through simpler storage systems that are easier to build and maintain at large scale while achieving reliability and availability as primary goals. This section provides a survey of state-of-the-art large-scale data management systems in the cloud environments organized by their source service provider (such as Google, Yahoo!, Microsoft, and open source projects).

5.3.1 Google: Bigtable

5.3.1.1 Bigtable

Bigtable is a distributed storage system for managing structured data that is designed to scale to a very large size (petabytes of data) across thousands of commodity servers [15]. It has been used by more than sixty Google products and projects such as Google search engine,[14] Google Finance,[15] Orkut,[16] Google Docs,[17] and Google Earth.[18] These products use Bigtable for a variety of demanding workloads, which range from throughput-oriented batch-processing jobs to latency-sensitive serving of data to end users. The Bigtable clusters used by these products span a wide range of configurations, from a handful to thousands of servers, and store up to several hundred terabytes of data.

Bigtable does not support a full relational data model. However, it provides clients with a simple data model that supports dynamic control over the data layout and format. In particular, a Bigtable is a sparse, distributed, persistent, multidimensional, and sorted map. The map is indexed by a row key, column key, and a timestamp. Each value in the map is an uninterpreted array of bytes. Thus, clients usually need to serialize various forms of structured and semi-structured data into these strings. A concrete example that reflects some of the main design decisions of Bigtable is the scenario of storing a copy of a large collection of web pages into a single table. Figure 5.4 illustrates an example of this table where *URLs* are used as row keys and various aspects of web pages as column names. The contents of the web pages are stored in a single column, which stores multiple versions of the page under the timestamps when they were fetched.

[14] http://www.google.com/.
[15] http://www.google.com/finance.
[16] http://www.orkut.com/.
[17] http://docs.google.com/.
[18] http://earth.google.com/.

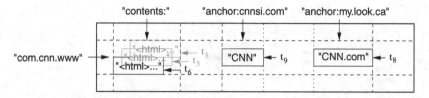

Figure 5.4. Sample BigTable Structure [15].

The row keys in a table are arbitrary strings where every read or write of data under a single row key is atomic. Bigtable maintains the data in lexicographic order by row key where the row range for a table is dynamically partitioned. Each row range is called a *tablet*, which represents the unit of distribution and load balancing. Thus, reads of short row ranges are efficient and typically require communication with only a small number of machines. Bigtables can have an unbounded number of columns, which are grouped into sets called *column families*. These column families represent the basic unit of access control. Each cell in a Bigtable can contain multiple versions of the same data, which are indexed by their timestamps. Each client can flexibly decide the number of n versions of a cell that need to be kept. These versions are stored in decreasing timestamp order so that the most recent versions can be always read first.

The Bigtable API provides functions for creating and deleting tables and column families. It also provides functions for changing cluster, table, and column family metadata such as access control rights. Client applications can write or delete values in Bigtable, look up values from individual rows, or iterate over a subset of the data in a table. On the transaction level, Bigtable supports only *single-row* transactions, which can be used to perform atomic read-modify-write sequences on data stored under a single row key (such as no general transactions across row keys).

On the physical level, Bigtable uses the distributed Google File System (GFS) [29] to store log and data files. The Google *SSTable* file format is used internally to store Bigtable data. An SSTable provides a persistent, ordered immutable map from keys to values, where both keys and values are arbitrary byte strings. Bigtable relies on a distributed lock service called *Chubby* [12] that consists of five active replicas, one of which is elected to be the *master* and actively serve requests. The service is live when a majority of the replicas are running and can communicate with each other. Bigtable uses Chubby for a variety of tasks such as: 1) Ensuring that there is at most one active master at any time. 2) Storing the bootstrap location of Bigtable data. 3) Storing Bigtable schema information and the access control lists. The main limitation of this

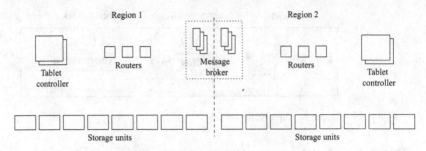

Figure 5.5. PNUTS system architecture [18].

design is that if Chubby becomes unavailable for an extended period of time, the whole Bigtable becomes unavailable.

On the runtime, each Bigtable is allocated to one master server and many tablet servers, which can be dynamically added (or removed) from a cluster based on the changes in workloads. The master server is responsible for assigning tablets to tablet servers, balancing tablet-server load, and garbage collection of files in GFS. In addition, it handles schema changes such as table and column family creations. Each tablet server manages a set of tablets. The tablet server handles read and write requests to the tablets that it has loaded, and also splits tablets that have grown too large.

5.3.2 Yahoo!: PNUTS/Sherpa

The *PNUTS* system (renamed later to Sherpa) is a massive-scale hosted database system that is designed to support Yahoo!s web applications [18]. The main focus of the system is on data serving for web applications, rather than complex queries. It relies on a simple relational model where data is organized into tables of records with attributes. In addition to typical data types, *blob* is a main valid data type, which allows storing arbitrary structures inside a record, but not necessarily large binary objects such as images or audio. The PNUTS system does not enforce constraints such as referential integrity on the underlying data. Therefore, the schema of these tables are flexible where new attributes can be added at any time without halting any query or update activity. In addition, it is not required that each record have values for all attributes.

Figure 5.5 illustrates the system architecture of PNUTS. The system is divided into regions where each region contains a full complement of system components and a complete copy of each table. Regions are typically, but not necessarily, geographically distributed. Therefore, on the physical level, data tables are horizontally partitioned into groups of records called *tablets*.

These tablets are scattered across many servers where each server might have hundreds or thousands of tablets. The assignment of tablets to servers is flexible in a way that allows balancing the workloads by moving a few tablets from an overloaded server to an underloaded server.

The query language of PNUTS supports selection and projection from a single table. Operations for updating or deleting existing record must specify the primary key. The system is designed primarily for online serving workloads that consist mostly of queries that read and write single records or small groups of records. Thus, it provides a *multiget* operation, which supports retrieving multiple records in parallel by specifying a set of primary keys and an optional predicate. The *router* component (Figure 5.5) is responsible for determining which storage unit need to be accessed for a given record to be read or written by the client. Therefore, the primary-key space of a table is divided into intervals where each interval corresponds to one tablet. The router stores an interval mapping, which defines the boundaries of each tablet and maps each tablet to a storage unit. The query model of PNUTS does not support join operations, which are too expensive in such massive scale systems.

The PNUTS system does not have a traditional database log or archive data. However, it relies on a pub/sub mechanism that acts as a redo log for replaying updates that are lost before being applied to disk because of failure. In particular, PNUTS provides a consistency model that is between the two extremes of general serializability and eventual consistency [47]. The design of this model is derived from the observation that web applications typically manipulate one record at a time whereas different records may have activity with different geographic locality. Thus, it provides *per-record timeline* consistency where all replicas of a given record apply all updates to the record in the same order. In particular, for each record, one of the replicas (independently) is designated as the master where all updates to that record are forwarded to the master. The master replica for a record is adaptively changed to suit the workload where the replica receiving the majority of write requests for a particular record is selected to be the master for that record. Relying on the per-record timeline consistency model, the PNUTS system supports the following range of API calls with varying levels of consistency guarantees:

- *Read-any*: This call has the lower latency as it returns a possibly stale version of the record.
- *Read-critical (required version)*: It returns a version of the record that is strictly newer than, or the same as the *required version*.
- *Read-latest*: This call returns the latest copy of the record that reflects all writes that have succeeded. It is expected that the *read-critical* and *read-latest*

can have a higher latency than read-any if the local copy is too stale and the system needs to locate a newer version at a remote replica.

- *Write*: This call gives the same ACID guarantees as a transaction with a single write operation in it (such as blind writes).
- *Test-and-set-write (required version)*: This call performs the requested write to the record, if and only if the present version of the record is the same as the required version. This call can be used to implement transactions that first read a record and then do a write to the record based on the read such as incrementing the value of a counter.

Because the system is designed to scale to cover several worldwide replicas, automated failover and load balancing is the only way to manage the operations load. Therefore, for any failed server, the system automatically recovers by copying data from a replica to other live servers.

5.3.3 *Amazon: Dynamo / S3 / SimpleDB / RDS*

Amazon runs a worldwide e-commerce platform that serves tens of millions customers at peak times using tens of thousands of servers located in many data centers around the world. In this environment, there are strict operational requirements on Amazons platform in terms of performance, reliability and efficiency, and to be able to support continuous growth the platform needs to be highly scalable. Reliability is one of the most important requirements because even the slightest outage has significant financial consequences and impacts customer trust. To meet these needs, Amazon has developed a number of storage technologies such as Dynamo System [22], Simple Storage Service (S3),[19] Sim-pleDB,[20] and Relational Database Service (RDS).[21]

5.3.3.1 Dynamo

The Dynamo system [22] is a highly available and scalable distributed key/value based datastore built for supporting Amazon's *internal* applications. Dynamo is used to manage the state of services that have very high reliability requirements and need tight control over the tradeoffs between availability, consistency, cost-effectiveness, and performance. There are many services on Amazons platform that only need primary-key access to a data store. The common pattern of using a relational database would lead to inefficiencies and limit scale and availability. Thus, Dynamo provides a simple primary-key only interface to

[19] https://s3.amazonaws.com/.
[20] http://aws.amazon.com/simpledb/.
[21] http://aws.amazon.com/rds/.

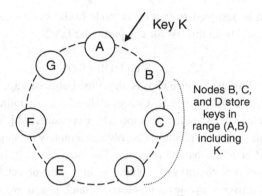

Figure 5.6. Partitioning and replication of keys in Dynamo ring [22].

meet the requirements of these applications. The query model of the Dynamo system relies on simple read and write operations to a data item that is uniquely identified by a key. State is stored as binary objects (blobs) identified by unique keys. No operations span multiple data items.

Dynamo's partitioning scheme relies on a variant of consistent hashing mechanism [33] to distribute the load across multiple storage hosts. In this mechanism, the output range of a hash function is treated as a fixed circular space or ring (for example, the largest hash value wraps around to the smallest hash value). Each node in the system is assigned a random value within this space, which represents its position on the ring. Each data item identified by a key is assigned to a node by hashing the data items key to yield its position on the ring, and then walking the ring clockwise to find the first node with a position larger than the items position. Thus, each node becomes responsible for the region in the ring between it and its predecessor node on the ring. The principle advantage of consistent hashing is that the departure or arrival of a node only affects its immediate neighbors whereas other nodes remain unaffected.

In the Dynamo system, each data item is replicated at N hosts where N is a parameter configured per-instance. Each key k is assigned to a coordinator node. The coordinator is in charge of the replication of the data items that fall within its range. In addition to locally storing each key within its range, the coordinator replicates these keys at the $N - 1$ clockwise successor nodes in the ring. This results in a system where each node is responsible for the region of the ring between it and its Nth predecessor. As illustrated in Figure 5.6, node B replicates the key k at nodes C and D in addition to storing it locally. Node D will store the keys that fall in the ranges $(A, B]$, $(B, C]$, and $(C, D]$. The list of nodes that is responsible for storing a particular key is called the preference list. The system is designed so that every node in the system can determine which nodes should be in this list for any particular key.

5.3.3.2 S3 / SimpleDB / RDS

Amazon Simple Storage Service (S3) is an online public storage web service offered by Amazon Web Services. Conceptually, S3 is an infinite store for objects of variable sizes. An object is simply a byte container, which is identified by a URI. Clients can read and update S3 objects remotely using a simple web services (SOAP or REST-based) interface. For example, *get(uri)* returns an object and *put(uri, bytestream)* writes a new version of the object. In S3, stored data is organized over a two-level namespace: *buckets* and *objects*. Buckets are similar to folders or containers that can store an unlimited number of data objects. Objects are composed from two parts: an opaque blob (of up to 5 GB in size) and metadata, which includes user-specified key/value pairs for each object (up to 2 KB) and a small number of predefined HTTP metadata entries (e.g., Last-Modified). In S3, search function is limited to a single bucket and is based on the object name only. Metadata or content-based search capabilities are not provided. Thus, S3 can be considered as an online backup solution for storing large objects that are not frequently updated.

Brantner et al. [9] present initial efforts of building Web-based database applications on top of S3. They describe various protocols in order to store, read, and update objects and indexes using S3. For example, the *record manager* component is designed to manage records where each record is composed of a key and payload data. Both key and payload are bytestreams of arbitrary length where the only constraint is that the size of the whole record must be smaller than the page size. Physically, each record is stored in exactly one page, which in turn is stored as a single object in S3. Logically, each record is part of a *collection* (such as a table). The record manager provides functions to create new objects, read objects, update objects, and scan collections. The *page manager* component implements a buffer pool for S3 pages. It supports the reading of pages from S3, pinning the pages in the buffer pool, updating the pages in the buffer pool, and marking the pages as updated. All these functionalities are implemented in a straightforward way just as in any standard database system. Furthermore, the page manager implements the commit and abort methods where it is assumed that the write set of a transaction (for example, a set of updated and newly created pages) fits into the clients main memory or secondary storage (flash or disk). If an application commits, all the updates are propagated to S3 and all the affected pages are marked as unmodified in the clients' buffer pool. Moreover, they implemented standard B-tree indexes on top of the page manager and basic redo log records. On the other side, there are many database-specific issues that have not yet been addressed by this work. For example, DB-style strict consistency and transactions mechanisms. Furthermore, query processing techniques (such as join algorithms and query optimization techniques) and traditional database functionalities such as bulk-load a database, create indexes, and drop a whole collection need to be devised.

Similar to S3, Amazon has not published the details of its other two products: SimpleDB and RDS. Generally, SimpleDB is designed for running queries on structured data. In SimpleDB, data is organized into *domains* (such as tables) within which we can put data, get data, or run queries. Each domains consist of *items* (such as records), which are described by *attribute* name/value pairs. It is not necessary to predefine all of the schema information as new attributes can be added to the stored dataset when needed. Thus, the approach is similar to that of a spreadsheet and does not follow the traditional relational model. SimpleDB provides a small group of API calls that enables the core functionality to build client applications such as *CreateDomain*, *DeleteDomain*, *PutAttributes*, *DeleteAttributes*, *GetAttributes*, and *Select*. The main focus of SimpleDB is fast reading. Therefore, query operations are designed to run on a single domain. SimpleDB keeps multiple copies of each domain where a successful write operation guarantees that all copies of the domain will durably persist. In particular, SimpleDB supports two read consistency options: eventually consistent read [47] and consistent read.

Amazon Relational Database Service (RDS) is another recent service that gives access to the full capabilities of a familiar MySQL database. Therefore, the code, applications, and tools which are already designed on existing MySQL databases can work seamlessly with Amazon RDS. Once the database instance is running, Amazon RDS can automate common administrative tasks such as performing backups or patching the database software. Amazon RDS can also manage synchronous data replication and automatic failover management. Recently, RDS announced the availability of using Oracle Database 11g via the Amazon Relational Database Service.[22]

5.3.4 Microsoft SQL Azure

Microsoft has recently released the Microsoft SQL Azure Database system.[23] It has been announced as a cloud-based relational database service which has been built on Microsoft SQL Server technologies. It provides a highly available, scalable, multitenant database service hosted by Microsoft in the

---

[22] http://aws.amazon.com/rds/oracle/.
[23] http://www.microsoft.com/windowsazure/sqlazure/.

cloud. Applications can create, access, and manipulate tables, views, indexes, roles, stored procedures, triggers, and functions. The SQL Azure Database system can also execute complex queries and joins across multiple tables where support is available for Transact-SQL (T-SQL), native ODBC, and ADO.NET data access.[24] In particular, the SQL Azure service can be seen as running an instance of SQL server in a cloud hosted server, which is automatically managed by Microsoft instead of running it on an on-premise managed server. In SQL Azure, the size of each hosted database cannot exceed the 50 GB limit. An important capability of Cloud SQL Server is its support of ACID transactions. The transaction commitment protocol requires that only a quorum of the replicas be up. A Paxos-like [14] consensus algorithm is used to maintain a set of replicas to deal with replica failures and recoveries. Dynamic quorums are used to improve availability in the face of multiple failures. SQL Azure is currently used as the storage system for two large-scale web services: Exchange Hosted Archive[25] and an e-mail and instant messaging repository.

In Microsoft SQL Azure, a logical database is called a *table group* [7]. A table group can be *keyless* or *keyed*. If a table group is keyed then all of its tables must have a common column called the *partitioning key*. SQL Azure requires that each transaction executes on *one* table group. The *consistency unit* of an object is the set of data that can be read and written by ACID transaction. Each copy of consistency unit is fully contained in a single instance of SQL server running on one machine. Hence, there is no need for a two-phase commit. A query can execute on multiple partitions of a keyed table group with an isolation level of read-committed. Thus, data that the query reads from different partitions may reflect the execution of different transactions. Transactionally consistent read beyond a consistency unit are not supported.

At the physical level, a keyed table group is split into *partitions* based on ranges of its partitioning key. Replicas of each partition are scattered across servers such that no two copies reside in the same *failure domain* (such as under the same network switch or in the same rack). Replicas of each partition are assigned to servers independently of the assignment of other partitions to servers, even if the partitions are from the same table group. For each partition, at each point in time one replica is designated to be the *primary*. The primary replica is responsible of processing all queries and update operations. The system currently does not allow any reads to be executed on the *secondary* replicas.

---

[24] http://msdn.microsoft.com/en-us/library/h43ks021(VS.71).aspx.
[25] http://www.microsoft.com/online/exchange-hosted-services.mspx.

5.3.5 Open Source Projects

In practice, most of the cloud data management systems provided by the major suppliers (such as BigTable, Dynamo, PNUTS) are designed for their internal use and are not available for public use. Therefore, many open source projects have been built to implement the concepts of these systems and are made available for public users. Some of these systems have started to gain a lot of interest from the research community. There are not much details that have been published about the implementation most of these systems yet. Therefore, we give a brief introduction about some of these projects. However, for the full list, refer to the NoSQL database Web site.[26]

Cassandra[27] is presented as a highly scalable, eventually consistent, distributed, structured key-value store [35]. It has been open sourced by Facebook in 2008. It is designed by Avinash Lakshman (one of the authors of Amazon's Dynamo) and Prashant Malik (Facebook Engineer). Cassandra brings together the distributed systems technologies from Dynamo and the data model from Google's Bigtable. Like Dynamo, Cassandra is eventually consistent. Like Bigtable, Cassandra provides a ColumnFamily-based data model that is richer than typical key/value systems. In Cassandra's data model, the *column* is the lowest/smallest increment of data. It's a tuple (triplet) that contains a name, a value and a timestamp. A *column family* is a container for columns, which is analogous to the table in a relational system. It contains multiple columns, each of which has a name, value, and a timestamp, and are referenced by row keys. A *keyspace* is the first dimension of the Cassandra hash, and is the container for column families. Keyspaces are of roughly the same granularity as a schema or database (such as a logical collection of tables) in RDBMS. They can be seen as a namespace for ColumnFamilies and is typically allocated as one per application. *SuperColumns* represent columns that themselves have subcolumns (such as Maps).

The HyperTable[28] project is designed to achieve a high performance, scalable, distributed storage, and processing system for structured and unstructured data. It is designed to manage the storage and processing of information on a large cluster of commodity servers, providing resilience to machine and component failures. In HyperTable, data is represented in the system as a multi-dimensional table of information. The HyperTable systems provides a

---

[26] http://nosql-database.org/.
[27] http://cassandra.apache.org/.
[28] http://hypertable.org/.

low-level API and Hypertable Query Language (HQL) that allows the user to create, modify, and query the underlying tables. The data in a table can be transformed and organized at high speed by performing computations in parallel and pushing them to where the data is physically stored.

Voldemort[29] is an open-source Java-based database, which is created by LinkedIn based on Amazon Dynamo concepts. It provides client-tunable consistency where applications can choose the read and write quorum sizes as required for specific operations. It supports sophisticated conflict detection using vector clocks when data inconsistencies occur because of network partitions or concurrent updates. This allows application-specific data conflict resolution instead of simple last timestamp wins solutions, and means less reliance on accurate clock synchronisation between all nodes. Voldemort has a pluggable architecture that allows the underlying storage engine to be specifically selected for an application. Supported storage engines include MySQL, BerkeleyDB, Hadoop, and in-memory storage.

CouchDB[30] is a document-oriented database that can be queried and indexed in a MapReduce fashion using JavaScript. In CouchDB, documents are the primary unit of data. A CouchDB document is an object that consists of named fields. Field values may be strings, numbers, dates, or even ordered lists and associative maps. Therefore, a CouchDB database is a flat collection of documents where each document is identified by a unique ID. CouchDB provides a RESTful HTTP API for reading and updating (add, edit, or delete) database documents. The CouchDB document update model is lockless and optimistic. Document edits are made by client applications. If another client was editing the same document at the same time, the client gets an edit conflict error on save. To resolve the update conflict, the latest document version can be opened, the edits reapplied and the update retried again. Document updates are all or nothing, either succeeding entirely or failing completely. The database never contains partially saved or edited documents.

Many other variant projects have recently started to follow the NoSQL movement and support different types of data stores such as key-value stores (for example, Redis[31] and Dynomite[32]), document stores (for example, MongoDB[33] and Riak[34]) and graph stores (for example, Neo4j[35] and DEX[36]).

---

[29] http://project-voldemort.com/.
[30] http://couchdb.apache.org/.
[31] http://redis.io/.
[32] http://wiki.github.com/cliffmoon/dynomite/dynomite-framework.
[33] http://www.mongodb.org/.
[34] http://wiki.basho.com/display/RIAK/Riak.
[35] http://neo4j.org/.
[36] http://www.dama.upc.edu/technology-transfer/dex.

Table 5.1. *Design decisions of cloud storage systems*

System	Data Model	Consistency	Query Interface
BigTable	Column families	Eventually consistent	Low-level API
Google AppEng	Objects store	Strictly consistent	Python API – GQL
PNUTS	Key-value store	Timeline consistent	Low-level API
Dynamo	Key-value store	Eventually consistent	Low-level API
S3	Large objects store	Eventually consistent	Low-level API
SimpleDB	Key-value store	Eventually consistent	Low-level API
RDS	Relational store	Strictly consistent	SQL
SQL Azure	Relational store	Strictly consistent	SQL
Cassandra	Column families	Eventually consistent	Low-level API
Hypertable	Multi-dimensional table	Eventually consistent	Low-level API, HQL
Voldemort	Key-value store	Eventually consistent	Low-level API
CouchDB	Document-oriented store	Optimistically consistent	Low-level API

5.3.6 Cloud Data Management: Trade-Offs

An important issue in designing large-scale data management applications is to avoid the mistake of trying to be "*everything for everyone.*" As with many types of computer systems, no one system can be best for all workloads and different systems make different tradeoffs in order to optimize for different applications. Therefore, the most challenging aspects in these application is to identify the most important features of the target application domain and to decide about the various design trade-offs, which immediately lead to performance trade-offs. To tackle this problem, Jim Gray came up with the heuristic rule of "*20 queries*" [32]. The main idea of this heuristic is that on each project, we need to identify the twenty most important questions the user wanted the data system to answer. He said that five questions are not enough to see a broader pattern and a hundred questions would result in a shortage of focus. Table 5.1 summarizes the design decisions of our surveyed systems.

In general, it is hard to maintain ACID guarantees in the face of data replication over large geographic distances. The CAP theorem [10, 30] shows that a shared-data system can only choose at most two out of three properties: *Consistency* (all records are the same in all replicas), *Availability* (all replicas can accept updates or inserts), and *tolerance to Partitions* (the system still functions when distributed replicas cannot talk to each other). When data is replicated over a wide area, this essentially leaves just consistency and availability for a system to choose between. Thus, the '*C*' (consistency) part of ACID is typically compromised to yield reasonable system availability [1]. Therefore, most of the cloud data management overcome the difficulties of distributed replication by relaxing the ACID guarantees of the system. In particular, they implement various forms of weaker consistency models (such as eventual consistency, timeline consistency, and session consistency [44]) so that all replicas do not have to agree on the same value of a data item at every moment of time. Therefore, transactional data management applications (such as banking, stock trading, and supply chain management), which rely on the ACID guarantees that databases provide, tend to be fairly write-intensive or require microsecond precision are less obvious candidates for the cloud environment until the cost and latency of wide-area data transfer decrease significantly. Cooper et al. [5] discusses the tradeoffs facing cloud data management systems as follows:

- *Read performance versus write performance*: On the one hand, log structured systems that only store update deltas can be very inefficient for reads if the data is modified over time. On the other hand, writing the complete record to the log on each update avoids the cost of reconstruction at read time but there is a correspondingly higher cost on update. Unless all data fits in memory, random I/O to the disk is needed to serve reads (such as opposed to scans). However, for write operations, much higher throughput can be achieved by appending all updates to a sequential disk-based log.
- *Latency versus durability*: Writes may be synched to disk before the system returns a success result to the user or they may be stored in memory at write time and synchronized later. The advantages of the latter approach are that avoiding disk operations greatly improves write latency, and potentially improves throughput. The disadvantage is the risk of data loss if a server crashes and loses unsynchronized updates.
- *Synchronous versus asynchronous replication*: Synchronous replication ensures all copies are up to date but potentially incurs high latency on updates.

Furthermore, availability may be impacted if synchronously replicated updates cannot complete whereas some replicas are offline. Asynchronous replication avoids high-write latency but allows replicas to be stale. Furthermore, data loss may occur if an update is lost due to failure before it can be replicated.

- *Data partitioning*: Systems may be strictly row-based or allow for column storage. Row-based storage supports efficient access to an entire record and is ideal if we typically access a few records in their entirety. Column-based storage is more efficient for accessing a subset of the columns, particularly when multiple records are accessed.

Kossmann et al. [34] conducted an end-to-end experimental evaluation on the performance and cost of running enterprise web applications with OLTP workloads on alternative cloud services (such as RDS, SimpleDB, S3, Google AppEngine, and Azure). The results of the experiments showed that the alternative services varied greatly both in cost and performance. Most services had significant scalability issues. They confirmed the observation that public clouds lack the ability to support the upload of large data volumes. It was difficult for them to upload 1 TB or more of raw data through the APIs provided by the providers. With regard to cost, they concluded that Google seems to be more interested in small applications with light workloads, whereas Azure is currently the most affordable service for medium to large services.

With the goal of facilitating performance comparisons of the trade-offs on cloud data management systems, Cooper et al. [5] have presented the Yahoo! Cloud Serving Benchmark (YCSB) framework and a core set of benchmarks. The benchmark tool has been made available via open source[37] in order to allow extensible development of additional cloud benchmark suites that represent different classes of applications and to allow evaluating different cloud data management systems.

5.4 Cloud Applications: Programming Models

This section provides a survey of state-of-the-art alternative programming models which have been proposed to implement the application logics over cloud data storage systems.

---

[37] http://wiki.github.com/brianfrankcooper/YCSB/.

```
map(String key, String value):
// key: document name
// value: document contents
for each word w in value:
        EmitIntermediate(w, "1");
```

```
reduce(String key, Iterator values):
// key: a word
// values: a list of counts
int result = 0;
for each v in values:
        result += ParseInt(v);
Emit(AsString(result));
```

Figure 5.7. An Example MapReduce program [20].

5.4.1 MapReduce

MapReduce is a simple and powerful programming model that enables easy development of scalable parallel applications to process vast amounts of data on large clusters of commodity machines [20, 21]. It isolates the application from the details of running a distributed program such as issues on data distribution, scheduling, and fault tolerance. In this model, the computation takes a set of input key/value pairs and produces a set of output key/value pairs. The user of the MapReduce framework expresses the computation using two functions: *Map* and *Reduce*. The Map function takes an input pair and produces a set of intermediate key/value pairs. The MapReduce framework groups together all intermediate values associated with the same intermediate key I and passes them to the Reduce function. The Reduce function receives an intermediate key I with its set of values and merges them together. Typically just zero or one output value is produced per Reduce invocation. The main advantage of this models is that it allows large computations to be easily parallelized and re-execution to be used as the primary mechanism for fault tolerance. Figure 5.7 illustrates an example MapReduce program expressed in pseudo-code for counting the number of occurrences of each word in a collection of documents. In this example, the map function emits each word plus an associated mark of occurrences while the reduce function sums together all marks emitted for a particular word.

The MapReduce framework has been designed according to the following main principles [50]:

• *Low-cost unreliable commodity hardware*: Instead of using expensive, high-performance, reliable symmetric multiprocessing (SMP) or massively parallel processing (MPP) machines equipped with high-end network and storage subsystems, the MapReduce framework is designed to run on large clusters of commodity hardware. This hardware is managed and powered by open-source operating systems and utilities so that the cost is low.

- *Extremely scalable RAIN cluster*: Instead of using centralized RAID-based SAN or NAS storage systems, every MapReduce node has its own local off-the-shelf hard drives. These nodes are loosely coupled in rackable systems connected with generic LAN switches. These nodes can be taken out of service with almost no impact to still-running MapReduce jobs. These clusters are called Redundant Array of Independent (and Inexpensive) Nodes (RAIN).
- *Fault-tolerant yet easy to administer*: MapReduce jobs can run on clusters with thousands of nodes or even more. These nodes are not very reliable as at any point in time, a certain percentage of these commodity nodes or hard drives will be out of order. Therefore, the MapReduce framework applies straightforward mechanisms to replicate data and launch backup tasks so as to keep still-running processes going. To handle crashed nodes, system administrators simply take crashed hardware offline. New nodes can be plugged in at any time without much administrative hassle. There is no complicated backup, restore and recovery configurations like the ones that can be seen in many DBMS.
- *Highly parallel yet abstracted*: The most important contribution of the MapReduce framework is its ability to automatically support the parallelization of task executions. Hence, it allows developers to focus mainly on the problem at hand rather than worrying about the low-level implementation details such as memory management, file allocation, parallel, multi-threaded or network programming. Moreover, MapReduce's shared-nothing architecture [41] makes it much more scalable and ready for parallelization.

Hadoop[38] is an open source Java software that supports data-intensive distributed applications by realizing the implementation of the MapReduce framework. On the implementation level, the Map invocations are distributed across multiple machines by automatically partitioning the input data into a set of *M* splits. The input splits can be processed in parallel by different machines. Reduce invocations are distributed by partitioning the intermediate key space into *R* pieces using a partitioning function (such as hash(key) mod R). The number of partitions (R) and the partitioning function are specified by the user. Figure 5.8 illustrates an example of the overall flow of a MapReduce operation, which goes through the following sequence of actions:

1. The input files of the MapReduce program is split into *M* pieces and starts up many copies of the program on a cluster of machines.

---

[38] http://hadoop.apache.org/.

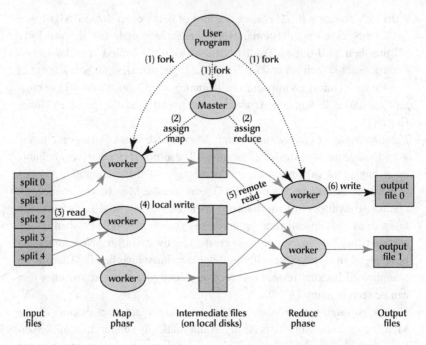

Figure 5.8. An overview of the flow of execution a MapReduce operation [20].

2. One of the copies of the program is elected to be the *master* copy whereas the rest are considered as *workers* that are assigned their work by the master copy. In particular, there are M map tasks and R reduce tasks to assign. The master picks idle workers and assigns each one a map task or a reduce task.

3. A worker who is assigned a map task reads the contents of the corresponding input split and parses key/value pairs out of the input data and passes each pair to the user-defined Map function. The intermediate key/value pairs produced by the Map function are buffered in memory.

4. Periodically, the buffered pairs are written to local disk, partitioned into R regions by the partitioning function. The locations of these buffered pairs on the local disk are passed back to the master, who is responsible for forwarding these locations to the reduce workers.

5. When a reduce worker is notified by the master about these locations, it reads the buffered data from the local disks of the map workers, which is then sorted by the intermediate keys so that all occurrences of the same key are grouped together. The sorting operation is needed because typically many different keys map to the same reduce task.

6. The reduce worker passes the key and the corresponding set of intermediate values to the user's Reduce function. The output of the Reduce function is appended to a final output file for this reduce partition.
7. When all map tasks and reduce tasks have been completed, the master program wakes up the user program. At this point, the MapReduce invocation in the user program returns back to the user code.

During the execution process, the master pings every worker periodically. If no response is received from a worker in a certain amount of time, the master marks the worker as failed. Any map tasks marked completed or in progress by the worker are reset back to their initial idle state and therefore become eligible for scheduling on other workers. Completed map tasks are re-executed on a failure because their output is stored on the local disk(s) of the failed machine and is therefore inaccessible. Completed reduce tasks do not need to be re-executed because their output is stored in a global file system.

The original implementation of the MapReduce framework had some limitations that have been tackled by many research efforts in following up work. For example, Yang et al. [50] have proposed the *Map-Reduce-Merge* model that enables processing of multiple datasets in one pass. Condie et al. [43] proposed a modified architecture in which intermediate data is *pipelined* between operators while preserving the programming interfaces and fault tolerance models of previous MapReduce frameworks. Nykiel et al. [38] propose *MRShare* as a sharing framework, which is tailored to transform a batch of queries into a new batch that will be executed more efficiently by merging jobs into groups and evaluating each group as a single query. Based on a defined cost model, they describe an optimization problem that aims of deriving the optimal grouping of queries in order to avoid performing redundant work and save processing time and money. Dittrich et al. [24] present the *Hadoop++* system, which aims of boosting the query performance of the Hadoop project (the open source implementation of the MapReduce framework) without changing any of the system internals. They achieve this goal by injecting *trojan indices* and *trojan joins* through user-defined function (UDFs), which only affect the Hadoop system from inside without any external effect. Bu et al. [11] present the *HaLoop* system, which is designed to efficiently support iterative computations. In particular, HaLoop extends the basic MapReduce framework with two main functionalities: 1) Caching the invariant data in the first iteration and then reuse them in later iterations. 2) Caching the reducer outputs, which makes checking for a fixpoint more efficient, without an extra MapReduce job.

Recently, several research efforts have reported about applying the Map-Reduce framework for solving challenging data processing problems on large-scale datasets in different domains. For example, Wang et al. [48] present the *MapDupReducer* system for detecting near duplicates over massive datasets. *Surfer* [16] and *Pregel* [37] systems have been designed to achieve efficient distributed processing of large-scale graphs. Mahout[39] is an apache project, which is designed with the aim of building scalable machine learning libraries by using the MapReduce framework. *Ricardo* [19] is a scalable platform for applying sophisticated statistical methods over huge data repositories. It is designed to facilitate the *trading* between R (a famous statistical software packages) and Hadoop where each trading partner performs the tasks that it does best. Cary et al. [13] present an approach for applying the MapReduce model in the domain of spatial data management. In particular, they focus on the bulk-construction of R-Trees and aerial image quality computation, which involves vector and raster data.

5.4.2 SQL-Like

For programmers, a key appealing feature in the MapReduce framework is that there are only two high-level declarative primitives (*map* and *reduce*) that can be written in any programming language of choice and without worrying about the details of their parallel execution. However, the MapReduce programming model has its own limitations such as:

- Its one-input and two-stage data flow is extremely rigid. As we previously discussed, to perform tasks having a different data flow (such as joins or *n* stages), inelegant workarounds have to be devised.
- Custom code has to be written for even the most common operations (such as projection and filtering), which leads to the fact that the code is usually difficult to reuse and maintain.
- The opaque nature of the map and reduce functions impedes the ability of the system to perform optimizations.

Moreover, many programmers could be unfamiliar with the MapReduce framework and they would prefer to use SQL (because they are more proficient in the language) as a high level declarative language to express their task while leaving all of the execution optimization details to the backend engine. In the following subsection discusses research efforts that have been proposed to tackle these problems and add the SQL flavor on top of the MapReduce framework.

---

[39] http://mahout.apache.org/.

SQL	Pig Latin

SELECT category, **AVG**(pagerank)
 FROM urls
 WHERE pagerank > 0.2
 GROUP BY category
 HAVING COUNT(*) > 10^6
	good_urls = **FILTER** urls **BY** pagerank > 0.2;
	 groups = **GROUP** good_urls **BY** category;
	 big_groups = **FILTER** groups **BY** COUNT(good_urls)>10^6;
	 output = **FOREACH** big_groups **GENERATE**
	 category, **AVG**(good_urls.pagerank);

Figure 5.9. An Example SQL query and its equivalent pig Latin program [28].

5.4.2.1 Pig Latin

Olston et al. [28] present a language called *Pig Latin* that takes a *middle* position between expressing task using high-level declarative querying model in the spirit of SQL and low-level/procedural programming using MapReduce. Pig Latin is implemented in the scope of *Pig* project[40] and is used by programmers at Yahoo! for developing data analysis tasks.

Writing a Pig Latin program is similar to specifying a query execution plan (such as a data flow graph). To experienced programmers, this method is more appealing than encoding their task as an SQL query and then coercing the system to choose the desired plan through optimizer hints. In general, automatic query optimization has its limits especially with uncataloged data, prevalent user-defined functions, and parallel execution, which are all features of the data analysis tasks targeted by MapReduce framework. Figure 5.9 shows an example SQL query and its equivalent Pig Latin program. Given a *URL* table with the structure (*url*, *category*, *pagerank*), the task of the SQL query is to find each large category and its average pagerank of high-pagerank urls (> 0.2). A Pig Latin program is a sequence of steps where each step represents a single data transformation. This characteristic is appealing to many programmers. At the same time, the transformation steps are described using high-level primitives (such as filtering, and grouping, and aggregation) much like in SQL.

Pig Latin has several other features that are important for casual ad-hoc data analysis tasks. These features include support for a flexible, fully nested data model, extensive support for user-defined functions, and the ability to operate over plain input files without any schema information. In particular, Pig Latin has a simple data model consisting of the following four types:

1. *Atom*: An atom contains a simple atomic value such as a string or a number, like "alice".
2. *Tuple*: A tuple is a sequence of fields, each of which can be any of the data types such as ("alice", "lakers").

---

[40] http://incubator.apache.org/pig.

3. *Bag*: A bag is a collection of tuples with possible duplicates. The schema of the constituent tuples is flexible whereas not all tuples in a bag need to have the same number and type of fields. For example, the following

$$\left\{ \begin{array}{l} (\text{"alice", "lakers"}) \\ (\text{"alice", ("iPod", "apple")}) \end{array} \right\}$$

4. *Map*: A map is a collection of data items, where each item has an associated key through which it can be looked up. As with bags, the schema of the constituent data items is flexible. However, the keys are required to be data atoms, such as $\left\{ \begin{array}{l} \text{"k1"} \rightarrow (\text{"alice", "lakers"}) \\ \text{"k2"} \rightarrow \text{"20"} \end{array} \right\}$

To accommodate specialized data processing tasks, Pig Latin has extensive support for UDFs. The input and output of UDFs in Pig Latin follow its fully nested data model. Pig Latin is architected such that the parsing of the Pig Latin program and the logical plan construction is independent of the execution platform. Only the compilation of the logical plan into a physical plan depends on the specific execution platform chosen. Currently, Pig Latin programs are compiled into sequences of MapReduce jobs, which are executed using the Hadoop MapReduce environment. In particular, a Pig Latin program goes through a series of transformation steps [39] before being executed. The parsing steps verifies that the program is syntactically correct and that all referenced variables are defined. The output of the parser is a canonical logical plan with a one-to-one correspondence between Pig Latin statements and logical operators, which are arranged in a directed acyclic graph (DAG). The logical plan generated by the parser is passed through a logical optimizer. In this stage, logical optimizations such as projection pushdown are carried out. The optimized logical plan is then compiled into a series of MapReduce jobs, which are then passed through another optimization phase. The DAG of optimized MapReduce jobs is then topologically sorted and jobs are submitted to Hadoop for execution.

5.4.2.2 SQL/MapReduce

In general, a UDF is a powerful database feature that allows users to customize database functionality. Friedman et al. [26] introduces the SQL/MapReduce (SQL/MR) UDF framework, which is designed to facilitate parallel computation of procedural functions across hundreds of servers working together as a single relational database. The framework is implemented as part of the *Aster Data Systems*[41] nCluster shared-nothing relational database.

The framework leverage ideas from the MapReduce programming paradigm to provide users with a straightforward API through which they can implement

---

[41] http://www.asterdata.com/.

```
SELECT ...
FROM functionname(
    ON table-or-query
    [PARTITION BY expr, ...]
    [ORDER BY expr, ...]
    [clausename(arg, ...) ...]
    )
```

Figure 5.10. Basic syntax of SQL/MR query function [26].

a UDF in the language of their choice. Moreover, it allows maximum flexibility as the output schema of the UDF is specified by the function itself at query plan-time. This means that a SQL/MR function is polymorphic as it can process arbitrary input because its behavior as well as output schema are dynamically determined by information available at query plan-time. This also increases reusability as the same SQL/MR function can be used on inputs with many different schemas or with different user-specified parameters. In particular, SQL/MR allows the user to write custom-defined functions in any programming language and insert them into queries that otherwise leverage traditional SQL functionality. A SQL/MR function is defined in a manner similar to Map-Reduce's map and reduce functions.

The syntax for using a SQL/MR function is depicted in Figure 5.10 where the SQL/MR function invocation appears in the SQL *FROM* clause and consists of the function name followed by a parenthetically enclosed set of clauses. The *ON* clause specifies the input to the invocation of the SQL/MR function. It is important to note that the input schema to the SQL/MR function is specified implicitly at query plan-time in the form of the output schema for the query used in the ON clause.

In practice, a SQL/MR function can be either a mapper (*Row* function) or a reducer (*Partition* function). The definitions of row and partition functions ensure that they can be executed in parallel in a scalable manner. In the *Row Function*, each row from the input table or query will be operated on by exactly one instance of the SQL/MR function. Semantically, each row is processed independently, allowing the execution engine to control parallelism. For each input row, the row function may emit zero or more rows. In the *Partition Function*, each group of rows as defined by the *PARTITION BY* clause will be operated on by exactly one instance of the SQL/MR function. If the *ORDER BY* clause is provided, the rows within each partition are provided to the function instance in the specified sort order. Semantically, each partition is processed independently, allowing parallelization by the execution engine at the level of a partition. For each input partition, the SQL/MR partition function may output zero or more rows.

5.4.3 Hybrid Systems

5.4.3.1 Hive

The *Hive* project[42] is an open-source data warehousing solution, which has been built by the Facebook Data Infrastructure Team on top of the Hadoop environment [45]. The main goal of this project is to bring the familiar relational database concepts (such as tables, columns, and partitions) and a subset of SQL to the unstructured world of Hadoop while still maintaining the extensibility and flexibility that Hadoop enjoyed. Thus, it supports all the major primitive types (such as integers, floats, doubles, and strings) as well as complex types (such as maps, lists, and structs). Hive supports queries expressed in a SQL-like declarative language, *HiveQL*,[43] and therefore can be easily understood by anyone who is familiar with SQL. These queries are compiled into MapReduce jobs that are executed using Hadoop. In addition, HiveQL enables users to plug in custom MapReduce scripts into queries. HiveQL supports data definition language (DDL) statements, which can be used to create, drop, and alter tables in a database [46]. It allows users to load data from external sources and insert query results into Hive tables via the load and insert data manipulation language (DML) statements respectively. However, HiveQL currently does not support the update and deletion of rows in existing tables (in particular, INSERT INTO, UPDATE, and DELETE statements), which allows the use of very simple mechanisms to deal with concurrent read and write operations without implementing complex locking protocols.

The metastore component is the Hive's system catalog, which stores metadata about the underlying table. This metadata is specified during table creation and reused every time the table is referenced in HiveQL. The metastore distinguishes Hive as a traditional warehousing solution when compared with similar data processing systems that are built on top of MapReduce-like architectures such as Pig Latin [39].

5.4.3.2 HadoopDB

Parallel database systems have been commercially available for nearly two decades and there are now about a dozen of different implementations in the marketplace (such as Teradata,[44] Aster Data,[45] Netezza,[46] Vertica,[47]

---

[42] http://hadoop.apache.org/hive/.
[43] http://wiki.apache.org/hadoop/Hive/LanguageManual.
[44] http://www.teradata.com/.
[45] http://www.asterdata.com/.
[46] http://www.netezza.com/.
[47] http://www.vertica.com/.

ParAccel,[48] Greenplum).[49] The main aim of these systems is to improve performance through the parallelization of various operations such as loading data, building indexes, and evaluating queries. These systems are usually designed to run on top of a shared-nothing architecture [41] where data may be stored in a distributed fashion and input/output speeds are improved by using multiple CPUs and disks in parallel.

Pavlo et al. [40] conducted a large-scale comparison between the Hadoop implementation of MapReduce framework and parallel SQL database management systems in terms of performance and development complexity. On the one hand, the results of this comparison show that parallel database systems displayed a significant performance advantage over MapReduce in executing a variety of data-intensive analysis tasks. On the other hand, the Hadoop implementation was much easier and straightforward to set up and use in comparison to that of parallel database systems. MapReduce has also shown to have superior performance in minimizing the amount of work that is lost when a hardware failure occurs. In addition, MapReduce (with its open source implementations) represents a very cheap solution in comparison to the very financially expensive parallel DBMS solutions (the price of an installation of a parallel DBMS cluster usually consists of seven figures of U.S. dollars)[42].

The *HadoopDB* project[50] is a hybrid system that tries to combine the scalability advantages of MapReduce with the performance and efficiency advantages of parallel databases [2]. The basic idea behind HadoopDB is to connect multiple single node database systems (PostgreSQL) using Hadoop as the task coordinator and network communication layer. Queries are expressed in SQL but their execution are parallelized across nodes using the MapReduce framework, however, as much of the single node query work as possible is pushed inside of the corresponding node databases. Thus, HadoopDB tries to achieve fault tolerance and the ability to operate in heterogeneous environments by inheriting the scheduling and job tracking implementation from Hadoop. Parallely, it tries to achieve the performance of parallel databases by doing most of the query processing inside the database engine.

Figure 5.11 illustrates the architecture of HadoopDB, which consists of two layers: 1) A data storage layer or the Hadoop Distributed File System[51] (HDFS). 2) A data processing layer or the MapReduce Framework. In this architecture, HDFS is a block-structured file system managed by a central *NameNode*. Individual files are broken into blocks of a fixed size and distributed across

---

[48] http://www.paraccel.com/.
[49] http://www.greenplum.com/.
[50] http://db.cs.yale.edu/hadoopdb/hadoopdb.html.
[51] http://hadoop.apache.org/hdfs/.

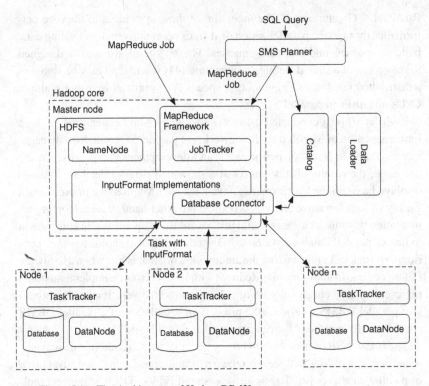

Figure 5.11. The Architecture of HadoopDB [2].

multiple *DataNodes* in the cluster. The NameNode maintains metadata about
the size and location of blocks and their replicas. The MapReduce Framework
follows a simple master-slave architecture. The master is a single *JobTracker*
and the slaves or worker nodes are *TaskTrackers*. The JobTracker handles the
runtime scheduling of MapReduce jobs and maintains information on each
TaskTracker's load and available resources. The *Database Connector* is the
interface between independent database systems residing on nodes in the cluster and TaskTrackers. The Connector connects to the database, executes the
SQL query, and returns results as key-value pairs. The *Catalog* component
maintains metadata about the databases, their location, replica locations, and
data partitioning properties. The *Data Loader* component is responsible for
globally repartitioning data on a given partition key upon loading and break-
ing apart single node data into multiple smaller partitions or chunks. The
SMS planner extends the HiveQL translator [45] and transforms SQL into
MapReduce jobs that connect to tables stored as files in HDFS. Abouzeid
et al. [3] demonstrate HadoopDB in action by running two different application

types: 1) A semantic web application that provides biological data analysis of protein sequences and 2) a classical business data warehouse.

Teradata [49] has recently started to follow the same approach of integrating Hadoop and parallel databases. It provides a fully parallel load utility for loading Hadoop data to its datawarehouse store. Moreover, it provides a database connector for Hadoop, which allows MapReduce programs to directly access Teradata datawarehouses data via JDBC drivers without the need of any external steps of exporting (from DBMS) and loading data to Hadoop. It also provides a *Table* UDF, which can be called from any standard SQL query to retrieve Hadoop data directly from Hadoop nodes in parallel. This means that any relational tables can be joined with the Hadoop data that are retrieved by the Table UDF and any complex business intelligence capability provided by Teradata's SQL engine can be applied to both Hadoop data and relational data. Therefore, no extra steps of exporting/importing Hadoop data to/from Teradata datawarehouse are required.

5.5 Real-World Case Studies

In principle, many Cloud providers (such as Amazon, Microsoft, Google, VMWare,[52] Rackspace,[53] Terremark,[54] GoGrid)[55] are currently working hard to convince companies to give up building and managing their own data centers and to utilize the computing computing that is supplied by the Cloud providers instead. Recently, many businesses have started to rethink their strategy for managing their computing resources.

Given the falling costs of transferring data over the Internet and companies' realization that managing complicated hardware and software building blocks is often a losing proposition, many are willing to outsource some of the job. Therefore, one of the things that Amazon concluded was that cloud computing can allow having access to a workforce that is based around the world and is able to do things that computer algorithms are not really good for. Therefore, Amazon has launched the Mechanical Turk (MTurk) system[56] as a crowdsourcing Internet marketplace where computer programmers (Requesters) are able to pose tasks known as HITs (Human Intelligence Tasks) such as choosing the best among several photographs of a storefront, writing product descriptions, or identifying performers on music CDs. Workers (Providers) can then browse

---

[52] http://www.vmware.com/.
[53] http://www.rackspace.com/.
[54] http://www.terremark.com/.
[55] http://www.gogrid.com/.
[56] https://www.mturk.com/mturk/.

among existing tasks and complete them for a monetary payment set by the
Requester. Requesters can ask that workers fulfill the required qualifications
before engaging a task and they can set up a test in order to verify these
qualifications. They can also accept or reject the result sent by the Worker, which
reflects on the Worker's reputation. Recently, Amazon has announced that the
MTurk system has over two hundred thousand workers in hundred different
countries.

In practice, many companies have used the cloud services for different purposes such as *application hosting* (99designs,[57] the Guardian News, and Media,[58] ftopia)[59] *data backup and storage* (ElephantDrive[60] and Jungle Disk),[61]
media hosting (fotopedia,[62] SmugMug[63]), and Web hosting (Digitaria[64] and
ShareThis).[65] Moreover, more than eighty companies and organizations (such
as AOL, LinkedIn, Twitter, and Adobe) are listed as users of Hadoop for processing their large scale data sources.[66] On one hand, most cloud services
have largely been aimed at start-ups, like the legion of Facebook and iPhone
applications developers who found that they could rent a first-class computing
infrastructure on the fly. In addition, some venture capital firms have made it
almost a precondition of investing in startups that they use Amazon's cloud
software. On the other hand, the U.S Federal Government has announced the
moving of Recovery.gov,[67] which specializes in tracking economic recovery,
to Amazon's EC2 platform. It is considered as the first federal government
production system to run on Amazon EC2. However, it seems that many other
federal agencies are also planning to be shifting aggressively into full-scale
adoption of the cloud services model.[68]

Webmail.us[69] uses Amazon S3 to host more than 350,000 paid mailboxes
with 10GB of mail per user. Netflix,[70] a company that offers online services for
a flat rate fee on DVD rental-by-mail and video streaming in the United States,
has decided to move most of its Web technology (such as customer movie
queues and search tools) to Amazon. Netflix has recently announced that it has
more than ten million subscribers, over 100,000 DVD titles, fifty distribution

[57] http://99designs.com/.
[58] http://www.guardian.co.uk/iphone.
[59] http://www.ftopia.com/.
[60] http://www.elephantdrive.com/.
[61] https://www.jungledisk.com/.
[62] http://www.fotopedia.com/.
[63] http://www.smugmug.com/.
[64] http://www.digitaria.com/.
[65] http://sharethis.com/.
[66] http://wiki.apache.org/hadoop/PoweredBy.
[67] http://www.recovery.gov/.
[68] http://www.informationweek.com/blog/main/archives/2010/06/federal_agencie.html.
[69] http://webmail.us/.
[70] http://www.netflix.com/.

centers, and attracts over 12,000 instant titles. VISA[71] has also announced that they are using the Hadoop framework for analyzing its massive volumes of data and for applying analytic models to individual clients and not only for client segments.

In 2007, the New York Times launched a project named *TimesMachine*.[72] The aim of this project is to build a service that provides access to any New York Times issue since 1851. Therefore, the bulk of 11 million articles had to be served in the form of PDF files. To tackle the challenge of converting 4 Terabyte of source data into PDF, the project members decided to make use of Amazon's Web Services Elastic Compute Cloud (EC2) and Simple Storage Service (S3). They uploaded the source data to S3 and started a Hadoop cluster of customized EC2 Amazon Machine Images (AMIs). With one hundred EC2 AMIs running in parallel, it was possible to complete the task of reading the source data from S3, converting it to PDF and storing it back to S3 within a total time of thirty-six hours.

AzureBlast [36] is a system that is designed to show the applicability of cloud platforms for science applications. *BLAST* is one of the most widely used bioinformatics algorithms in life science applications. It is designed to discover the similarities between the two bio-sequences (such as Protein). AzureBlast is a parallel BLAST engine that runs on the Windows Azure cloud fabric. Instead of using some high-level programming models or runtimes such as MapReduce, AzureBlast is built directly on the fundamental services of Windows Azure.

5.6 Conclusion

In the last two decades, the continuous increase of computational power has produced an overwhelming flow of data. The result of this is the appearance of a clear gap between the amount of data that is being produced and the capacity of traditional systems to store, analyze, and make the best use of this data. Cloud computing has gained much momentum in recent years because of its economic advantages. In particular, cloud computing has promised a number of advantages for its ability to host the deployments of data-intensive applications such as:

- Reduced time-to-market by removing or simplifying the time-consuming hardware provisioning, purchasing, and deployment processes.
- Reduced cost by following a pay-as-you-go business model.

---

[71] http://www.slideshare.net/cloudera/hw09-large-scale-transaction-analysis.
[72] http://timesmachine.nytimes.com/.

- Reduced operational cost and pain by automating IT tasks such as security patches and fail-over.
- Unlimited (virtually) throughput by adding servers if the workload increases.

In this chapter, we highlighted the main goals and basic challenges of deploying data-intensive applications in cloud environments. We provided a survey on numerous approaches and mechanisms of tackling these challenges and achieving the required goals. We analyzed the various design decisions of each approach and its suitability to support certain class of applications and end-users. A discussion of open issues pertaining to finding the right balance between scalability, consistency, and economical aspects of the trade-off design decisions was then provided. Finally, we reported about some real-world applications and case studies that started to realize the momentum of cloud technology.

In general, there are several important classes of existing applications that seems to be more compelling with cloud environments and contribute further to its momentum in the near future [4].

1. *Mobile interactive applications*: Such applications will be attracted to the cloud not only because they must be highly available but also because these services generally rely on large data sets, which are difficult to be stored on small devices with limited computing resources. Hence, these large data sets are most conveniently hosted in large data centers and accessed through the cloud on demand.
2. *Parallel batch processing*: Cloud computing presents a unique opportunity for batch-processing and analytics jobs that analyze terabytes of data and may take many hours to finish. If there is enough data parallelism in the application, users can take advantage of the cloud's reduced cost model to use hundreds of computers for a short-time cost instead of achieving the same result by using a few computers for a longer time cost.
3. *The rise of analytical applications*: While the large database industry was originally dominated by transaction processing, this fact is currently changing. A growing share of companies' resources is now directed to large-scale data analysis applications such as understanding customers behavior, efficient supply chains management, and recognizing buying habits. Therefore, decision support systems are growing rapidly, shifting the resource balance in database processing from online transaction processing (OLTP) systems to business analytics.
4. *Backend-support for compute-intensive desktop applications*: In general, CPU-intensive applications (for example multimedia applications) are

among the best candidates for successful deployment on cloud environments. The latest versions of the mathematics software packages Matlab and Mathematica are capable of using cloud computing to perform expensive evaluations. Therefore, an interesting alternative model might be to keep the data in the cloud and rely on having sufficient bandwidth to enable suitable visualization and a responsive GUI back to the human user (such as offline image rendering or 3D animation applications).

Recently, Amazon's chief executive predicted that its cloud computing division will one day generate as much revenue as its retail business does now. However, Amazon and other cloud providers need to advance their technology to the level that they can convince big companies to rely on using cloud services so as to achieve this goal.

References

1. Abadi D. "Data Management in the Cloud: Limitations and Opportunities." *IEEE Data Eng. Bull.* 32, no. 1 (2009): 3–12.
2. Abouzeid A., Bajda-Pawlikowski K., Abadi D., Rasin A., and Silberschatz A. "Hadoopdb: An Architectural Hybrid of Mapreduce and Dbms Technologies for Analytical Workloads." *PVLDB* 2, no. 1 (2009): 922–33.
3. Abouzeid A., K. Bajda-Pawlikowski, Huang J., Abadi D., and Silberschatz A. "HadoopDB in Action: Building Real World Applications." In *SIGMOD*, 2010.
4. Armbrust M., Fox A., Rean G., Joseph A., Katz R., Konwinski A., Gunho L., David P., Rabkin A., Stoica I., and Zaharia M. *Above the Clouds: A Berkeley View of Cloud Computing.* Feb. 2009.
5. Tam E., Ramakrishnan R., Cooper B., Silberstein A., and Sears R. "Benchmarking Cloud Serving Systems with YCSB." In *ACM SoCC*, 2010.
6. Bell G., Gray J., and Szalay A. "Petascale Computational Systems." *IEEE Computer* 39, no. 1 (2006): 110–12.
7. Bernstein P., Cseri I., Dani N., N. Ellis, Kalhan A., Kakivaya G., Lomet D., Manne R., Novik L., and Talius T. "Adapting Microsoft SQL Server for Cloud Computing." In *ICDE*, pages 1255–1263, 2011.
8. Binnig C., Kossmann D., Kraska T., and Loesing S. "How is the Weather Tomorrow?: Towards a Benchmark for the Cloud." In *DBTest*, 2009.
9. Brantner M., Florescu D., Graf D., Kossmann D., and Kraska T. "Building a Database on S3." In *SIGMOD*, pages 251–264, 2008.
10. Brewer E. Towards Robust Distributed Systems (abstract). In *PODC*, page 7, 2000.
11. Bu Y., Howe B., Balazinska M., and Ernst M. HaLoop: Efficient Iterative Data Processing on Large Clusters. *PVLDB* 3, no. 1 (2010): 285–96.
12. Burrows M. The Chubby Lock Service for Loosely-Coupled Distributed Systems. In *OSD*, pages 335–350, 2006.
13. Cary A., Sun Z., Hristidis V., and Rishe N. "Experiences on Processing Spatial Data with MapReduce." In *SSDBM*, pages 302–319, 2009.

14. Deepak T. Chandra, Griesemer R., and Redstone J. Paxos made live: an engineering perspective. In *PODC*, pages 398–407, 2007.
15. Chang F., Dean J., Ghemawat S., Hsieh W., Wallach D., Burrows M., Chandra T., Fikes A., and Gruber R. "Bigtable: A Distributed Storage System for Structured Data." *ACM Trans. Comput. Syst.* 26, no. 2 (2008).
16. Chen R., Weng X., He B., and Yang M. "Large Graph Processing in the Cloud." In *SIGMOD*, pages 1123–1126, 2010.
17. Cooper B., Baldeschwieler E., Fonseca R., Kistler J., Narayan P., Neerdaels C., Negrin T., Ramakrishnan R., Silberstein A., Srivastava U., and Stata R. Building a Cloud for Yahoo! *IEEE Data Eng. Bull.* 32, no. 1 (2009): 36–43.
18. Cooper B., Ramakrishnan R., Srivastava U., Silberstein A., Bohannon P., H. Jacobsen, Puz N., Weaver D., and Yerneni R. "Pnuts: Yahoo!'s Hosted Data Serving Platform." *PVLDB* 1, no. 2 (2008): 1277–88.
19. Das S., Sismanis Y., Beyer K., Gemulla R., Haas P., and McPherson J. "Ricardo: Integrating R and Hadoop." In *SIGMOD*, pages 987–998, 2010.
20. Dean J., and Ghemawat S. "Mapreduce: Simplified Data Processing on Large Clusters." In *OSDI*, pages 137–150, 2004.
21. Dean J., and Ghemawat S. Mapreduce: Simplified Data Processing on Large Clusters. *Commun. ACM* 51, no. 1 (2008): 107–13.
22. DeCandia G., Hastorun D., Jampani M., Kakulapati G., Lakshman A., Pilchin A., Sivasubramanian S., Vosshall P., and Vogels W. "Dynamo: Amazon's Highly Available Key-Value Store." In *SOSP*, pages 205–220, 2007.
23. Deelman E., Singh G., Livny M., Berriman G., and Good J. "The Cost of Doing Science on the Cloud: The Montage Example." In *SC*, page 50, 2008.
24. Dittrich J., Quiané-Ruiz J., Jindal A., Kargin Y., Setty V., and Schad J. Hadoop++: Making a Yellow Elephant Run Like a Cheetah (Without It Even Noticing). *PVLDB*, 3, no. 1 (2010): 518–29.
25. Foster I. and Kesselman C. *The Grid: Blueprint for a New Computing Infrastructure*. Morgan Kaufmann, 1999.
26. Friedman E., Pawlowski P., and Cieslewicz J. Sql/mapreduce: A Practical Approach to Self-Describing, Polymorphic, and Parallelizable User-defined Functions. *PVLDB* 2, no. 2 (2009): 1402–13.
27. Gartner. Gartner top ten disruptive technologies for 2008 to 2012. Emerging trends and technologies roadshow, 2008.
28. Gates A., Natkovich O., Chopra S., Kamath P., Narayanam S., Olston C., Reed B., Srinivasan S., and Srivastava U. "Building a Highlevel Dataflow System on Top of Mapreduce: The Pig Experience." *PVLDB* 2, no. 2 (2009): 1414–25.
29. Ghemawat S., Gobioff H., and Leung S. The Google File System. In *SOSP*, pages 29–43, 2003.
30. Gilbert S. and Lynch N. Brewer's Conjecture and the Feasibility of Consistent, available, partition-tolerant web services. *SIGACT News*, 33(2): 51–59, 2002.
31. Gonzalez L., Merino L., Caceres J., and Lindner M. "A Break in the Clouds: Towards a Cloud Definition." *Computer Communication Review* 39, no. 1 (2009): 50–5.
32. Hey T., Tansly S., and Tolle K., eds. *The Fourth Paradigm: Data-Intensive Scientific Discovery*. Microsoft Research, October 2009.

33. Karger D., Lehman E., Leighton F., Panigrahy R., Levine M., and Lewin D. "Consistent Hashing and Random Trees: Distributed Caching Protocols for Relieving Hot Spots on the World Wide Web." In *STOC*, pages 654–663, 1997.

34. Kossmann D., Kraska T., and Loesing S. "An Evaluation of Alternative Architectures for Transaction Processing in the Cloud." In *SIGMOD*, 2010.

35. Lakshman A., and Malik P. "Cassandra: Structured Storage System on a p2p Network." In *PODC*, page 5, 2009.

36. Lu W., Jackson J., and Barga R. "AzureBlast: a case study of developing science Applications on the Cloud." In *HPDC*, pages 413–420, 2010.

37. Malewicz G., Austern M., Bik A., Dehnert J., Horn I., Leiser N., and Czajkowski G. Pregel: A System for Large-Scale Graph Processing. In *SIGMOD*, pages 135–146, 2010.

38. Nykiel T., Potamias M., Mishra C., Kollios G., and Koudas N. "MRShare: Sharing Across Multiple Queries in MapReduce." *PVLDB* 3, no. 1 (2010): 494–505.

39. Olston C., Reed B., Srivastava U., Kumar R., and Tomkins A. "Pig Latin: A Not-So-Foreign Language for Data Processing." In *SIGMOD*, pages 1099–1110, 2008.

40. Pavlo A., Paulson E., Rasin A., Abadi D., DeWitt D., Madden S., and M. Stonebraker. "A Comparison of Approaches to Large-Scale Data Analysis." In *SIGMOD*, pages 165–178, 2009.

41. Stonebraker M. "The Case for Shared Nothing." *IEEE Database Eng. Bull.* 9, no. 1 (1986): 4–9.

42. Stonebraker M., Abadi D., DeWitt D., Madden S., Paulson E., Pavlo A., and Rasin A. "MapReduce and Parallel DBMSs: Friends or Foes?" *Commun. ACM* 53, no. 1 (2010): 64–71.

43. Alvaro P., Hellerstein J., Elmeleegy K., Condie T., Conway N., and Sears R. "Mapre-duce Online." In *NSDI*, 2010.

44. Tanenbaum A., and Steen M., eds. *Distributed Systems: Principles and Paradigms.* Prentice Hall, 2002.

45. Thusoo A., Sarma J., Jain N., Shao Z., Chakka P., Anthony S., Liu H., Wyckoff P., and Murthy R. "Hive – A Warehousing Solution Over a Map-reduce Framework." *PVLDB* 2, no. 2 (2009): 1626–29.

46. Thusoo A., Sarma J., Jain N., Shao Z., Chakka P., Zhang N., Anthony S., Liu H., and Murthy R. "Hive – A Petabyte Scale Data Warehouse Using Hadoop." In *ICDE*, pages 996–1005, 2010.

47. Vogels W. Eventually consistent. *Commun. ACM* 52, no. 1 (2009): 40–44.

48. Wang C., Wang J., Lin X., Wang W., Wang H., Li H., Tian W., Xu J., and R. Li. "MapDupReducer: Detecting Near Duplicates Over Massive Datasets." In *SIGMOD*, pages 1119–1122, 2010.

49. Xu Y., Kostamaa P., and Gao L. "Integrating Hadoop and Parallel Dbms." In *SIGMOD*, pages 969–974, 2010.

50. Yang H., Dasdan A., Hsiao R., and Parker D. "Map-Reduce-Merge: Simplified Relational Data Processing on Large Clusters." In *SIGMOD*, pages 1029–1040, 2007.

6

Dimension Reduction for Streaming Data

Chandrika Kamath

6.1 Introduction

With sensors becoming ubiquitous, there is an increasing interest in mining the data from these sensors as the data are being collected. This analysis of streaming data, or data streams, is presenting new challenges to analysis algorithms. The size of the data can be massive, especially when the sensors number in the thousands and the data are sampled at a high frequency. The data can be non-stationary, with statistics that vary over time. Real-time analysis is often required, either to avoid untoward incidents or to understand an interesting phenomenon better. These factors make the analysis of streaming data, whether from sensors or other sources, very data- and compute-intensive. One possible approach to making this analysis tractable is to identify the important data streams to focus on them. This chapter describes the different ways in which this can be done, given that what makes a stream important varies from problem to problem and can often change with time in a single problem. The following illustrate these techniques by applying them to data from a real problem and discuss the challenges faced in this emerging field of streaming data analysis.

This chapter is organized as follows: first, I define what is meant by streaming data and use examples from practical problems to discuss the challenges in the analysis of these data. Next, I describe the two main approaches used to handle the streaming nature of the data – the sliding window approach and the forgetting factor approach. I discuss how these can be incorporated into commonly-used dimension reduction methods such as identification of correlated features, random projections, principal component analysis, and sub-space trackers. Next, I present the results obtained by applying these techniques to streaming data from a simulator, which models a network of sensors monitoring the chlorine concentration in a water distribution piping system. The chapter

124

concludes by suggesting areas of research in this emerging field of streaming data analysis, in particular the task of identifying important data streams.

6.2 Background and Motivation

The traditional focus of data analysis endeavors has been on data that have been collected over time and which are analyzed as a whole, after the data collection has been completed. However, more recently, there has been an increasing interest in analyzing data as they are being collected. There are several factors driving this. The first is the advances in sensor technology, which have enabled sensors to be deployed in various locations ranging from physics experiments to the power grid and the Internet. The second is the all pervasiveness of the Internet, which has enabled easy access to multiple streams of data in fields as diverse as finance and weather prediction. The third is the increase in computational power, which has made possible the analysis of these massive amounts of data. Finally, there is the realization that by analyzing data as they are being collected, we have the opportunity to prevent untoward incidents, assign additional resources to investigate interesting events, and improve the monitoring and running of complex systems, ranging from the power grid to physics experiments.

This new modality of data is referred to as streaming data, data streams, or semiinfinite time series data. There are several application domains where such data arise. Consider, for example, sensors monitoring a physics experiment. The physicist may be interested in identifying when the experiment transitions from one normal operating state to another, so the controls can be changed appropriately. Or, they may want to know when the experiment is about to get into an anomalous state, which may cause damage to the experimental set up. Sometimes they may want to mine the data from the sensors so subsets of the data representing interesting events can be sent to remote researchers for further investigation or used to determine the parameter settings for the next set of experiments.

As another example, consider the problem of integration of wind energy into the power grid. Wind is an intermittent resource and can be difficult to manage as the forecasts of power generation are often inaccurate and a control room operator in a power utility may not know how much wind energy to schedule when the forecasts do not match the actual generation. In addition, there are ramp events, where the energy can increase or decrease by a large amount in a small time interval, making it difficult to keep the load balanced. In such cases, it may be helpful to consider weather data in the local area near the wind farm to see if they can help guide the scheduling. For example, a storm brewing near the region of the wind farm may indicate a higher chance of observing ramp events in the near future.

There are several other applications where monitoring of data streams is important. For example, with multi-core systems becoming the norm, massively parallel computers at the peta-scale have hundreds of thousands of cores. The health of such systems is monitored using hardware and software monitors, which detect bottlenecks in the system or the failure of a component that may require a task to be migrated to another component. Other examples of health monitoring systems include the sensors monitoring the space shuttle or the power grid, as well as the problem of network intrusion detection, where the network traffic is monitored to detect anomalous events such as break-ins or denial of service attacks. In the case of the Internet, the incoming packets on a computer can be examined to detect suspicious patterns. In other problems, the properties of the network, such as the number of links between nodes, may change, indicating an anomaly.

Figures 6.1 and 6.2 show examples of data from two problems – the first is wind-generation weather data and the second is data from four sensors monitoring the DIII-D experiment [12]. These illustrate several of the challenges faced in the analysis of streaming data. The data sizes can be very large, especially if there are a large number of streams and the data are being sampled at a high frequency. The different sensors may sample the different streams at different rates, for example, newer sensors monitoring a physics experiment may collect samples more frequently than older sensors on the same experiment as they have larger memories to store the data. Often, the number of sensors can be very large, for example, thousands of phasor measurement units or synchrophasors are being deployed to convert the power grid into the smart grid. In some problems, the different streams may measure very different quantities, for example, a finance application may monitor various stocks, the price of gold, the interest rate, and so on. Frequently, the data are of poor quality, with noise or missing values due to faulty or inoperable sensors. There may be a spatial aspect to the data if the spatial locations of the sensors are also relevant to the analysis.

Although these challenges are prevalent in nonstreaming data as well, streaming data present some unique issues [3, 14, 15]. Often, the data are nonstationary, that is, their statistical properties change over time. Thus, any models built to represent the data must also evolve with time. As the data are analyzed during the collection process, the analysis typically focuses on a small window around the current time interval, and past data, which lie outside this time window, are ignored. If the data are used in decision making, it introduces a real-time aspect to the analysis, which can aggravate the computational requirements to process the data. This can be addressed by using fast, but less accurate, algorithms.

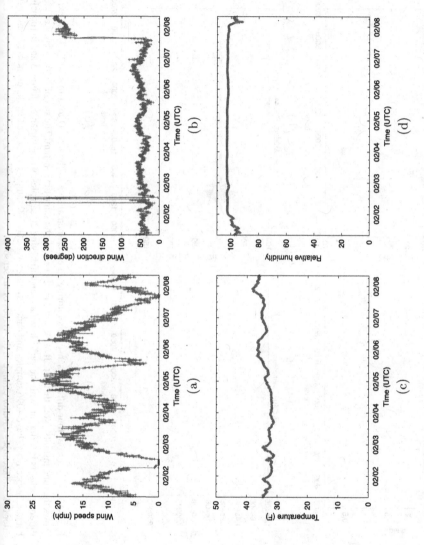

Figure 6.1. Wind-generation weather data for the first week of February 2010 from a meteorological station in the vicinity of wind farms in the Columbia Basin region near the Oregon-Washington border. (a) wind speed in miles per hour; (b) wind direction in degrees; (c) temperature in degrees Farenheit; and (d) percentage relative humidity.

127

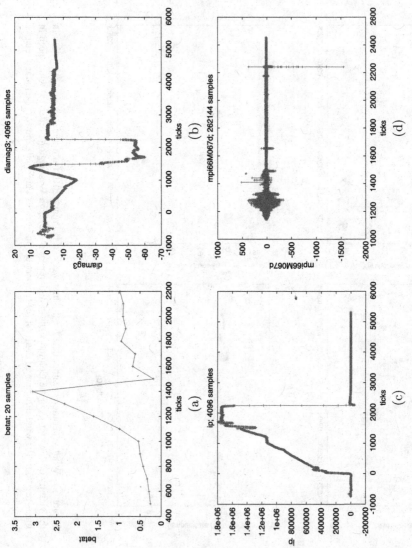

Figure 6.2. Data from four different sensors monitoring an experimental shot of the DIII-D toka-mak [12]. The x-axis shows the time instants. Note that not all the sensors start or end at the same time instant. The sampling frequency of the different sensors is different, with the variable betat (panel a) having 20 samples, while variables diamag3 and ip (panels b and c, respectively) have 4096 samples and panel (d) have over 260,000 samples. Observe that the event occurring just after tick 2,200 causes a major change in the values of all sensors.

However, it can result in a high rate of false positives in tasks such as anomaly detection.

A typical approach to analysis of streaming data is composed of three phases. First, the *preprocessing* of the data to address issues such as noise in the data and a mismatch of sampling frequencies; second, *dimension reduction*, or the identification of the important data streams; and, third, the actual *analysis*, which depending on the problem may constitute detection of concept drift anomalies, or interesting events. This chapter focuses on one aspect of the analysis of streaming data, namely dimension reduction or the selection of key data streams. I start by describing the need for dimension reduction in streaming data, and then discuss ways in which the streaming nature of the data can be accommodated in the algorithms.

6.3 Dimension Reduction Techniques

In the context of streaming data, we can consider each time instant to be represented by a vector of floating-point values, one from each of the data streams. These values can be considered as a representation of the state of the system, as seen by the sensors, at that time instant. The time instant could be every minute, or every second, depending on the problem. In some cases, where the exact time is less important, these time instants could just be an increasing sequence of consecutive integer values.

This chapter assumes that issues such as noise in the data streams or the different sampling rates for the different data streams have already been addressed. These are usually problem-dependent issues and their solutions vary, with problem-specific approaches often yielding better results than more general approaches.

Our goal in dimension reduction is to reduce the number of data streams, d. This is referred to as the dimension of the problem as each instant, represented by d values, can be considered as a point in a d–dimensional space. The idea of reducing the dimension of a data analysis problem is not new. Many of the reasons why we want to reduce the number of dimensions in streaming data are the same as for nonstreaming data. Some of the data streams may be correlated with others, or may be irrelevant to the problem. By keeping and monitoring only the more important data streams, we can reduce the memory requirements and computational time for the analysis algorithms. Fewer data streams may also lead to simpler and more interpretable models, say for anomaly detection. These models may also be more accurate, especially if the data streams being ignored were mainly noise. A large number of streams also leads to the "curse of dimensionality" – for problems in classification, a data set with high dimensionality can require a large number of training samples, whereas clustering can be a challenge as it is difficult to interpret distances between two points in the high-dimensional space.

Dimension reduction, in the context of data streams, where there is a temporal component to the data presents an interesting challenge. It is possible that either the number, or the set, of streams, which are considered important, vary with time. This is especially true if the data have concept drift, that is, the underlying statistical distributions of the data change over time. This means that we need to monitor all the data streams at all times. It also implies that dimension reduction algorithms must accommodate this nonstationarity of the data, making them more complex than the algorithms used for non-streaming data. At the same time, when the number or set of important data streams changes, it can provide insights into the data as such changes could indicate anomalies or a change point in the data.

Because data streams are considered semiinfinite, any analysis is done using data from just the recent past, with data that are older than some time period being ignored. This is especially important in the case of nonstationary data as old data, with different statistics from recent data, should not influence the decisions made based on the recent data. There are two ways in which we can "forget" the old data:

- **Sliding window approach:** In this approach, only the data from the recent past are considered in the analysis. The more commonly used option considers a fixed-sized time window and the data that fall within this window are used in the analysis. Thus, for a window length of l_w, if the current time instant is t, we consider only the values at time instants from $(t - l_w + 1)$ through t, with both end points included. At the next time instant, $t + 1$, the oldest set of values in the window, corresponding to time instant $(t - l_w + 1)$, are removed and the values at the new time instant $(t + 1)$ are added.

  The fixed-size sliding window approach requires that we select a window size at the start of the analysis; this is usually done by trial and error or by exploiting any information we might know about the data. It is also possible to use a landmark-based window, where a new window starts when a certain landmark occurs in the data. This typically grows until the landmark occurs again or the window size become too large and the oldest data values are dropped from the window.

- **Forgetting factor approach:** The idea behind the forgetting factor (also called the damping factor) is to incorporate a multiplicative factor $0 < \alpha < 1.0$ into the analysis, which essentially acts as a way of reducing the contribution of older values. For example, to calculate the mean of the values in a data stream, we could keep a running sum of the values seen until a time instant, and multiply this by α before adding the value at the new time instant. Because α is typically chosen to be a bit smaller than 1.0, repeated multiplications by α over time will progressively reduce the contributions of the oldest values. A value of α close to 1.0 (say 0.99) will reduce the contributions of past values slower than a value farther from 1.0 (say 0.96). α is typically chosen to be greater than 0.95, with the choice depending on how fast we want the older values to be forgotten. For time instants $t \gg 1$, the use of a forgetting factor α results in an effective window length of $1/(1 - \alpha)$.

When algorithms used for analyzing nonstreaming data are extended to work on streaming data, they can be extended using either the sliding window or the forgetting factor approach. In the case of the sliding window, the idea is to exploit as much as possible the computation that has already been done on the previous window, while incorporating the newest data and removing the oldest data. Although it is possible to redo the analysis using the data in the new window, this is often time consuming, and an incremental approach is required to meet the real-time requirements of many streaming data problems. When an algorithm is modified using a forgetting factor, the idea is to suitably incorporate α into the analysis so that it has the desired effect of appropriately reducing the contributions of the older data values. Note that the two approaches do not give identical results as they treat the current and past data values differently. Also, the sliding window approach, unlike the use of the forgetting factor, requires additional memory to store the values in the window.

The preceding assumes that the updates to the data streams are done synchronously, that is, the latest values for all sensor streams are available at the same time. This may not be true in all problems. In some problems, each of the sensors may be sampled at a fixed, known frequency, but the frequency may differ from sensor to sensor. This sampling mismatch must be addressed first, prior to the dimension reduction step. We may also have situations where a sensor may provide a measurement at nonperiodic intervals, for example, when it takes a reading only when certain conditions are satisfied.

Underlying the discussion so far is the idea that we are monitoring a set of sensors that provide data samples over time. Thus, if we look at the data over a time window, we can treat them as a matrix where the rows (or columns) are the time instants and the columns (or rows) are the sensor values. This matrix is dense as there is a sensor value corresponding to each instant and the number of sensors is assumed fixed. There are also streaming data problems where the time aspect is implicit. For example, recommender systems use a small sample of customer preferences to predict likes and dislikes over a wider set of products. The matrix is then formed using the customer × product scores. This matrix is sparse, with many of the scores unknown. In addition, the number of rows and columns can change over time with products and customers being added and removed, and the value for a specific customer and product can change as the customer revises and updates their score for a product.

The next section describes streaming variants of some of the commonly used dimension reduction techniques. First, a note about terminology, the vector of sensor values describing each instant is also referred to as a *feature vector*, where each variable measured by a sensor is a *feature*. Dimension reduction techniques consist of feature selection methods, where a subset of the original features are selected and feature transform methods, where the original features are transformed into a different space of a lower dimension.

6.3.1 Correlation-Based Techniques

In the case of classification and regression problems in nonstreaming data, we can identify key features by considering how correlated the features are to each other and to the target output variable [16]. Given two vectors, **x** and **y**, each of length n, the Pearson correlation coefficient between them is given by

$$\frac{1}{n} \frac{\sum_{i=1}^{n} (x_i - \bar{x})(y_i - \bar{y})}{\sigma(x)\sigma(y)} \tag{6.1}$$

where x_i is the i-th element of the vector **x**, $\bar{x}$ is its mean value, and $\sigma(x)$ is its standard deviation.

In the case of streaming data, we rarely have an output or class label assigned to each time instant as the data are being analyzed as they are being collected. So, one approach to reducing the dimension is to identify the correlated data streams and monitor or display only the uncorrelated ones. It may also be possible to detect concept drift or anomalies by considering how the correlations among the data streams change over time.

To accomplish this, we need to incrementally calculate the correlation coefficient between two data streams. By expanding the product in the numerator of Equation 6.1, and substituting

$$\sigma(x) = \sqrt{\frac{\sum_{i=1}^{n} x_i^2}{n} - \left\{\frac{\sum_{i=1}^{n} x_i}{n}\right\}^2} \tag{6.2}$$

for the standard deviation in the denominator, we can rewrite the correlation coefficient between vectors x and y as:

$$\frac{n \sum_{i=1}^{n} (x_i y_i) - \sum_{i=1}^{n} x_i \sum_{i=1}^{n} y_i}{\sqrt{n \sum_{i=1}^{n} x_i^2 - \left\{\sum_{i=1}^{n} x_i\right\}^2} \sqrt{n \sum_{i=1}^{n} y_i^2 - \left\{\sum_{i=1}^{n} y_i\right\}^2}} \tag{6.3}$$

So, to calculate the correlation between two vectors, we need to keep track of five quantities: the sum of the values for each of the vectors, the sum of the values squared for each vector, and the sum of the element-wise product of the values of the two vectors. In the case of d features, the sufficient statistics are the d values each for the sum and sum squared of each feature as well as a $d \times d$ matrix of the sum of element wise product of the features taken two as a time. Because this matrix is symmetric, only half of it can be calculated, stored, and updated.

The calculation of correlation coefficients is simple in the case of the sliding window as we can update each of these terms by removing the contributions of the oldest time instant and adding the contribution of the newest time instant. However, observe that floating point errors are likely to accumulate over time in the three sums because of the additions and subtractions. After a while, this will result in a difference between the sums calculated incrementally over time and over just the values in the current window. One option may be to periodically recalculate these terms using the most recent data in the current window.

In the case of the forgetting factor approach, an approximation to the correlations is a bit more complex as the forgetting factor has to be incorporated appropriately into Equation 6.3 for the correlation coefficient. By reducing the contribution of each term in Equation 6.3 by the forgetting factor α, we obtain

$$\frac{1}{n} \frac{\sum_{i=1}^{n} \alpha^{(n-i)}(x_i - \bar{x}_\alpha)\alpha^{(n-i)}(y_i - \bar{y}_\alpha)}{\sigma_\alpha(x)\sigma_\alpha(y)} \tag{6.4}$$

where the mean and standard deviation are defined as

$$\bar{x}_\alpha = \frac{1}{1/(1-\alpha)} \sum_{i=1}^{n} \alpha^{(n-i)} x_i \tag{6.5}$$

and

$$\sigma_\alpha(x) = \sqrt{\frac{1}{1/(1-\alpha)} \sum_{i=1}^{n} \alpha^{2(n-i)}(x_i - \bar{x}_\alpha)^2}, \tag{6.6}$$

respectively. Note that the $1/(1-\alpha)$ term acts as an equivalent window length for a forgetting factor of α. The inclusion of the $\alpha < 1.0$ term in the summation progressively reduces the contribution of the oldest values. The sufficient statistics to obtain the correlation coefficients using the forgetting factor are:

$$\sum_{i=1}^{n} \alpha^{2(n-i)}, \ \sum_{i=1}^{n} \alpha^{(n-i)} x_i, \ \sum_{i=1}^{n} \alpha^{2(n-i)} x_i, \ \sum_{i=1}^{n} \alpha^{2(n-i)} x_i^2 \ \text{and} \ \sum_{i=1}^{n} \alpha^{2(n-i)} x_i y_i.$$

(6.7)

The idea of using correlation functions to identify correlated data streams and observe only one, but not all of them is particularly useful in problems where the sensors are homogeneous and placed spatially close to each other so that the quantities they measure are often correlated. The method is also appealing as we are working with the original features and can thus identify the specific sensors that must be monitored. However, correlation coefficients may not be the best approach for determining concept drift as they do not detect changes in amplitude or phase if the streams remain correlated.

6.3.2 Random Projections

Random projections is a recent approach to dimension reduction that is gaining popularity because of its simplicity, ease of implementation, and low computational cost. It projects data, which are originally in a high-dimensional space of dimension d, onto a lower dimensional space of dimension $k < d$ such that all pairwise distances are approximately preserved. More formally, it is based on the Johnson-Lindenstrauss lemma [2], which asserts that any set of n points in a d–dimensional Euclidean space can be embedded into k–dimensional Euclidean space, where k is logarithmic in n and independent of d, so that all pairwise distances are maintained within an arbitrarily small factor. The projection in the lower dimensional space can then be used in algorithms, which utilize the distance between two points, with the assurance that the result will be a good approximation to the same algorithm applied in the original, higher-dimensional space.

Practically, a random projection is obtained by multiplying the input matrix A, of order $n \times d$, which represents the n d–dimensional data points, by a dense matrix, R, of order $d \times k$ of real numbers. Achlioptas [2] shows that if the elements r_{ij} of R are chosen from either one of the following two very simple probability distributions

$$r_{ij} = \begin{cases} +1 & \text{with probability } 1/2 \\ -1 & \text{with probability } 1/2 \end{cases}$$

(6.8)

$$r_{ij} = \sqrt{3} \begin{cases} +1 & \text{with probability } 1/6 \\ 0 & \text{with probability } 2/3 \\ -1 & \text{with probability } 1/6 \end{cases}$$

(6.9)

then the projections of the original data matrix A onto R will be a k–dimensional dataset where the distances between the data points are preserved in accordance with the Johnson-Lindenstrauss lemma.

Random projections have been used in several practical applications involving nonstreaming data, including image and text analysis [6], optical character recognition [11], cluster ensemble methods [13], and assessing the stability of gene expression clustering [5].

The extension of random projections to streaming data is very simple, with the reduced dimension representation of the new data obtained by projecting it onto the random matrix. If the random matrix has a large size, then it is possible to generate it on the fly by storing only the seeds used to generate the random numbers for each row or by considering the row number as the seed itself [20].

Unlike the correlation approach described in earlier, random projections would be used not to identify the important features, but to transform the original data into a lower dimensional space so that the transformed data can be used in distance-based techniques such as clustering and nearest neighbor algorithms.

6.3.3 Incremental Singular Value Decomposition

A commonly used technique for dimension reduction in nonstreaming data is Principal Component Analysis (PCA) [17]. This starts with a data set consisting of a large number of possibly interrelated features and transforms it into a new set of features, which are uncorrelated and ordered so that the first few transformed features contain most of the variation present in the original data. These few features can be used to represent the original data in the reduced dimension space. A practical way of performing PCA is using the Singular Value Decomposition (SVD) [26]. Suppose we have a real matrix $\mathbf{M}$ of r rows and c columns. Then, the SVD decomposition of $\mathbf{M}$ can be written as

$$\mathbf{M} = \mathbf{U}\boldsymbol{\Sigma}\mathbf{V}^T \tag{6.10}$$

where $\mathbf{U}$ is an $r \times r$ orthogonal matrix, $\mathbf{V}$ is a $c \times c$ orthogonal matrix, and $\boldsymbol{\Sigma}$ is an $r \times c$ diagonal matrix with entries $(\sigma_1, \sigma_2, \ldots, \sigma_p)$, where $p = \min(r, c)$ and $\sigma_1 \geq \sigma_2 \geq \ldots \geq \sigma_p \geq 0$). The σ are the singular values of $\mathbf{M}$ and the columns of $\mathbf{U}$ and $\mathbf{V}$ are the left and right singular vectors, respectively, of $\mathbf{M}$. A reduced dimensional representation $\mathbf{M}_k$ of $\mathbf{M}$ can then be obtained by considering only the top largest k singular values (also called the principal singular values) and the corresponding column vectors of $\mathbf{U}$ and $\mathbf{V}$, which form the submatrices $\mathbf{U}_k$ and $\mathbf{V}_k$, respectively:

$$\mathbf{M}_k = \mathbf{U}_k\boldsymbol{\Sigma}_k\mathbf{V}_k^T.$$

In the signal processing domain, this reduced dimensional space is often called the signal space as k is chosen so that the singular values that are excluded are small and form the noise in the data.

A naive approach to extending PCA to streaming data using the windowing concept would be to implement the SVD decomposition from scratch each time the values in the window were updated. If the streaming data have concept drift, that is, their statistics vary over time, it would then be very easy to keep track of the changing rank of the signal space over time. However, the operation count to obtain an SVD of an $r \times c$ matrix is $O(rc^2)$, assuming that $r \gg c$. This can be an issue when real-time response is required, which is often the case in streaming data applications.

To address this, SVD algorithms for streaming data often consider approximations to the singular values and vectors. These approximations keep just the information in the lower dimensional signal space, discarding the noise component. As new data arrive, this information in the signal subspace is updated appropriately, along with any changes in the rank of the signal subspace.

The following describes a fast algorithm for tracking the singular values and singular vectors of streaming data, called Fast Approximate Subspace Tracking (FAST), that was proposed by Real, Tufts and Cooley in 1997 [22, 30]. It considers the sliding window as a sequence of overlapping matrices. Suppose at a given time instant, the data in the window are represented by the $r \times c$ matrix $\mathbf{M}_{old}$, which can be considered to be the sum of a reduced-rank signal matrix $\mathbf{S}_{old}$ of rank k and a full-rank noise matrix $\mathbf{N}_{old}$:

$$\mathbf{M}_{old} = \mathbf{S}_{old} + \mathbf{N}_{old}$$

The rows of $\mathbf{M}_{old}$ represent the data streams and the columns represent the time instants in the window. Representing $\mathbf{M}_{old}$ in terms of its column vectors $\mathbf{m}_i$, $i = 1, \ldots, c$, we have

$$\mathbf{M}_{old} = \begin{bmatrix} \mathbf{m}_1 & \mathbf{m}_2 & \ldots & \mathbf{m}_c \end{bmatrix}$$

Because the data at each time instant are in the form of a column of the matrix representing the sliding window, we are interested in the left singular values of the matrix. If we had represented the data as row vectors, we would consider the right singular values.

When the data at the new time instant arrive, the data in the sliding window can be represented as:

$$\mathbf{M}_{new} = \begin{bmatrix} \mathbf{m}_2 & \mathbf{m}_2 & \ldots & \mathbf{m}_{(c+1)} \end{bmatrix}$$

where the oldest values are removed from one end of the matrix and the new ones added at the other end. Our goal is to track the k singular values and vectors of the signal subspace as the matrix representing the data in the sliding window transitions from $\mathbf{M}_{old}$ to $\mathbf{M}_{new}$.

Suppose that we have a sufficiently accurate approximation to the k principal singular values and the corresponding left singular vectors of $\mathbf{M}_{old}$. Let these k orthonormal approximate left singular vectors be represented as the columns of an $r \times k$ matrix $\mathbf{U}_{old}$ as

$$\mathbf{U}_{old} = \begin{bmatrix} \mathbf{u}_1 & \mathbf{u}_2 & \dots & \mathbf{u}_k \end{bmatrix}$$

where $\mathbf{u}_i$ is associated with the i-th largest approximate singular value. These column vectors form the basis for the signal space corresponding to $\mathbf{M}_{old}$. By definition, the error in reconstruction resulting from the use of only the largest k singular values and their corresponding vectors is given by the squared Frobenius norm of the difference between the original matrix $\mathbf{M}_{old}$ and its projection onto the reduced dimension space spanned by the columns of $\mathbf{U}_{old}$:

$$\epsilon_{old} = ||\mathbf{M}_{old} - \mathbf{U}_{old}\mathbf{U}_{old}^T\mathbf{M}_{old}||_F^2.$$

The FAST algorithm updates the approximate singular values and vectors in two steps. First, it creates a low-rank approximation $\mathbf{A}$, of r rows and c columns, to $\mathbf{M}_{new}$ such that

$$||\mathbf{M}_{new} - \mathbf{A}||_F^2 \leq \epsilon_{old}.$$

Thus, if the error ϵ_{old} was acceptable in the prior step, the error in the new approximation will be no greater, and therefore, should be acceptable as well. The second step uses the information in the matrix $\mathbf{A}$ to construct a smaller matrix $\mathbf{F}$, which is then used to obtain the approximate singular values and vectors of $\mathbf{M}_{new}$.

Let the approximation to $\mathbf{M}_{old}$ be written as:

$$\mathbf{M}_{old} \approx \mathbf{U}_{old}\,\mathbf{U}_{old}^T\,\mathbf{M}_{old}$$
$$= \mathbf{U}_{old}\begin{bmatrix} \mathbf{a}_1 & \mathbf{a}_2 & \dots & \mathbf{a}_c \end{bmatrix}$$
$$= \begin{bmatrix} \mathbf{g}_1 & \mathbf{g}_2 & \dots & \mathbf{g}_c \end{bmatrix}$$

where $\mathbf{a}_j = \mathbf{U}_{old}^T\,\mathbf{m}_j$ is a $k \times 1$ column vector, $\mathbf{m}_j$ is the j-th column of $\mathbf{M}_{old}$, and $\mathbf{g}_j$ is the j-th column of $\mathbf{U}_{old}\,\mathbf{U}_{old}^T\,\mathbf{M}_{old}$. Because $\mathbf{M}_{new}$ differs from $\mathbf{M}_{old}$ in two columns, we can exploit the existing decomposition of the approximation to

M_{old} to create the matrix A, which is the rank $(k + 1)$ approximation to M_{new}, as follows:

$$A = \begin{bmatrix} U_{old} & q \end{bmatrix} \begin{bmatrix} a_2 & a_3 & \cdots & a_c & a_{(c+1)} \\ 0 & 0 & \cdots & 0 & b \end{bmatrix} \quad (6.11)$$

$$= \begin{bmatrix} U_{old} & q \end{bmatrix} E.$$

The first matrix on the right-hand side is an $r \times (k + 1)$ matrix, while the second matrix, E, is a $(k + 1) \times c$ matrix. The $r \times 1$ column vector q and the scalar b are obtained by decomposing the new column $m_{(c+1)}$ into two components – one (that is, $U_{old}\, a_{(c+1)}$), which is in the column space of U_{old} and one (that is, bq), which is in the space orthogonal to U_{old}:

$$a_{(c+1)} = U_{old}^T m_{(c+1)}$$

$$z = m_{(c+1)} - U_{old} a_{(c+1)}$$

$$b = ||z||$$

$$q = \frac{z}{b}$$

By expanding the right-hand side of Equation 6.11, we can write A as:

$$A = \begin{bmatrix} g_2 & g_3 & \cdots & g_c & m_{(c+1)} \end{bmatrix}.$$

and the resulting error in approximating M_{new} by A is given by:

$$||M_{new} - A||_F^2 = \sum_{i=2}^{c} \{||m_i - g_i||^2\} + ||m_{(c+1)} - m_{(c+1)}||^2$$

with the second term on the right-hand side being zero. When compared with the error at the prior step:

$$\epsilon_{old} = ||M_{old} - U_{old} U_{old}^T M_{old}||_F^2$$

$$= \sum_{i=1}^{c} ||m_i - g_i||^2,$$

we see that the new error is less than or equal to the old error (as the sum goes from 2 to c instead of 1 to c), making A an acceptable rank $(k + 1)$ approximation to M_{new}.

However, A is the same size as M_{new}. So, the next step in the FAST algorithm is to reduce the amount of computations required to update U_{old} by working with a matrix of a smaller size than M_{new}. We first observe that the first matrix on the right-hand side of Equation 6.11 has, by definition, $(k + 1)$ orthonormal columns. Therefore, if we construct the singular value decomposition of the second matrix, $\mathbf{E}$, of size $(k + 1) \times c$, as follows:

$$\mathbf{E} = \mathbf{U}_E \mathbf{\Sigma}_E \mathbf{V}_E^T$$

then, we can generate the singular value decomposition of $\mathbf{A}$ as:

$$\mathbf{A} = \left([\, \mathbf{U}_{old} \quad \mathbf{q}\,] \mathbf{U}_E \right) \mathbf{\Sigma}_E \mathbf{V}_E^T$$
$$= \mathbf{U}_A \mathbf{\Sigma}_A \mathbf{V}_A^T$$

where

$$\mathbf{U}_A = [\, \mathbf{U}_{old} \quad \mathbf{q}\,] \mathbf{U}_E \qquad (6.12)$$
$$\mathbf{\Sigma}_A = \mathbf{\Sigma}_E \qquad .$$
$$\mathbf{V}_A = \mathbf{V}_E.$$

This allows us to obtain the $(k + 1)$ principal left singular vectors of $\mathbf{A}$ as the columns of the $r \times (k + 1)$ matrix $\mathbf{U}_A$ by calculating the singular value decomposition of the smaller matrix $\mathbf{E}$. Because $\mathbf{A}$ is an approximation to $\mathbf{M}_{new}$, this gives us the approximation to the left singular values of $\mathbf{M}_{new}$. The approximation to the singular values of $\mathbf{M}_{new}$ can be obtained by considering the $(k + 1)$ elements from the main diagonal of $\mathbf{\Sigma}_E$.

It is possible to reduce the computations even further by considering the matrix $\mathbf{F}$ defined as:

$$\mathbf{F} = \mathbf{E}\mathbf{E}^T \qquad (6.13)$$
$$= \left(\mathbf{U}_E \mathbf{\Sigma}_E \mathbf{V}_E^T \right) \left(\mathbf{V}_E \mathbf{\Sigma}_E \mathbf{U}_E^T \right)$$
$$= \mathbf{U}_E \mathbf{\Sigma}_E \mathbf{\Sigma}_E \mathbf{U}_E^T \qquad (6.14)$$
$$= \mathbf{U}_E \mathbf{\Sigma}_E \mathbf{V}_F^T.$$

The matrix $\mathbf{F}$ is a smaller $(k + 1) \times (k + 1)$ matrix and its singular value decomposition can be obtained more easily than that of $\mathbf{E}$, which is a $(k + 1) \times c$ matrix.

From the preceding, we see that the singular value decomposition of $\mathbf{F}$ gives us the information we need to obtain the singular values and vectors of $\mathbf{A}$. The singular vectors of $\mathbf{F}$ are the columns of $\mathbf{U}_F$. Because these are also the columns of $\mathbf{U}_E$, we can use Equation 6.12 to calculate the left singular vectors of $\mathbf{A}$. In addition, from Equation 6.14, it follows that the singular values of $\mathbf{A}$ are the square-root of the singular values of $\mathbf{F}$.

In summary, using the FAST algorithm, we can obtain an approximation to the singular values and vectors of $\mathbf{M}_{new}$ by calculating the singular values and vectors of $\mathbf{F}$ and combining them with $\mathbf{U}_{old}$ from the previous step and the vector $\mathbf{q}$, which is obtained using $\mathbf{U}_{old}$ and the vector $\mathbf{m}_{(c+1)}$ representing the new values in $\mathbf{M}_{new}$. The steps in the FAST method are summarized in Algorithm 6.1.

Algorithm 6.1 *FAST algorithm.*

Obtain initial estimate of k principal singular values and left singular vectors $\mathbf{U}_{old}$ of the initial matrix $\mathbf{M}$
while new data arrive **do**
    Obtain new data vector $\mathbf{m}_{(c+1)}$
    $\mathbf{a}_i = \mathbf{U}_{old}^T \mathbf{m}_i, i = 2, 3, \ldots, (c+1)$
    $\mathbf{z} = \mathbf{m}_{(c+1)} - \mathbf{U}_{old} \mathbf{a}_{(c+1)}$
    $b = \|\mathbf{z}\|$
    $\mathbf{q} = \mathbf{z}/b$
    $\mathbf{E} = \begin{bmatrix} \mathbf{a}_2 & \mathbf{a}_3 & \cdots & \mathbf{a}_c & \mathbf{a}_{(c+1)} \\ 0 & 0 & \cdots & 0 & b \end{bmatrix}$
    $\mathbf{F} = \mathbf{E}\mathbf{E}^T$
    Compute SVD: $\mathbf{F} = \mathbf{U}_F \mathbf{\Sigma}_F \mathbf{V}^F$
    Replace columns of $\mathbf{U}_{old}$ with columns of $[\mathbf{U}_{old} \quad \mathbf{q}]\mathbf{U}_F$
    Replace old singular values with square root of singular values of $\mathbf{\Sigma}_F$
    Update data vectors: $\mathbf{m}_i \leftarrow \mathbf{m}_{(i+1)}, i = 1, 2, \ldots, c$
end while

We observe that the FAST algorithm tracks the change in approximate singular values and vectors as the matrix of observations changes from $\mathbf{M}_{old}$ to $\mathbf{M}_{new}$. It can also be used to detect any changes in the dimension of the signal subspace [22].

The typical approach to identifying the dimension of the signal subspace is to consider the top k singular values and vectors such that a reconstruction using them explains most of the energy in the data. The energy of the data is the sum of the squares of the singular values of the matrix. A threshold is therefore assumed and starting with $k = 1$, partial sums of squares of the largest k singular values obtained for increasing k, until the sum exceeds the threshold. The contribution of the remaining singular values can be considered to correspond to the noise component of the data. Alternatively, the threshold could be placed on the noise component and the partial sums created starting with the smallest singular value.

Because the FAST algorithm tracks only the largest singular values, the energy in the data, which is the sum of squares of all the singular values, can be obtained by calculating the square of the Frobenius norm of the matrix. Given the Frobenius norm of $\mathbf{M}_{old}$ from the previous step, the norm of $\mathbf{M}_{new}$ can be obtained easily as:

$$||\mathbf{M}_{new}||_F^2 = ||\mathbf{M}_{old}||_F^2 - ||\mathbf{m}_1||_2^2 + ||\mathbf{m}_{(c+1)}||_2^2$$

Suppose $\mathbf{M}_{old}$ was represented using k approximate singular values and vectors. If the energy calculation for $\mathbf{M}_{new}$ indicates that the signal subspace dimension has increased, we can keep all the $(k + 1)$ approximate singular values and vectors calculated using Algorithm 6.1. However, if the energy calculation for $\mathbf{M}_{new}$ indicates that the signal subspace dimension has reduced or remained at k, the corresponding number of approximate singular values and vectors can be retained at the end of the processing of $\mathbf{M}_{new}$.

The FAST algorithm stores the data for the previous decomposition and thus requires a memory of at least dc to store $\mathbf{U}_{old}$, where d (which is r in the preceding discussion) is the dimension of the original data. Its computational cost is $O(dk^2)$ [22].

6.3.3.1 Extensions to the FAST Algorithm

In their paper [22], Real, Tufts and Cooley describe two extensions to the FAST algorithm. The first is an approximation to improve the speed of the algorithm, which replaces the matrix $\mathbf{E}$ in Equation 6.11 by an approximation, which is easier to compute. The second enhancement to FAST is to consider the addition and deletion of more than a single column of data, enabling the rank of the new matrix to increase by the number of new columns instead of just one.

Interestingly, an approach for incremental singular value decomposition, which is very similar to the FAST algorithm was proposed independently by Matthew Brand. He first considers a case where the original matrix is updated with another matrix whose columns represent the newly arrived data [7]. As in the case of the FAST algorithm, the singular value decomposition of the original matrix is updated by decomposing the matrix of new values into components within and orthogonal to the SVD-derived subspace of the original matrix. A follow-on paper [8, 9] extends the algorithm to low rank updates of the original matrix. This includes the recentering of the original matrix as well as revisions, additions, and deletions to it. The low-time complexity of the algorithm allows it to be used in lightweight recommender systems where users can make changes to their recommendations of movies, books, and so on.

6.3.4 Subspace Tracking Methods

This section describes another approach to incrementally maintaining the reduced dimension subspace, which is based on the use of a forgetting factor.

Like the FAST algorithm described earlier, the Projection Approximation Subspace Tracking (PAST) algorithm is motivated by applications where we need to estimate the signal subspace recursively. This is especially true for problems where the subspace changes over time, as in the estimation of the direction of arrival of plane waves impinging on an antenna array.

The PAST algorithm [31] is one of the earliest representatives of fast subspace trackers, a class of algorithms where the principal subspace (corresponding to the signal) is tracked using $O(dk)$ computations, where k is the dimension of the signal subspace and d is the dimension of the original data. PAST interprets the signal subspace as the solution of a projection-like unconstrained minimization problem. Given a sequence of vectors $\mathbf{x}_i$, it attempts to find a projection matrix

$$\mathbf{W} = \begin{bmatrix} \mathbf{w}_1 & \mathbf{w}_2 & \dots & \mathbf{w}_t \end{bmatrix}, \tag{6.15}$$

which minimizes the exponentially weighted sum

$$\sum_{i=1}^{t} \alpha^{t-i} ||\mathbf{x}_i - \mathbf{W}(t)\mathbf{W}^T(t)\mathbf{x}_i||^2. \tag{6.16}$$

This is essentially the error between the original vectors and their projection onto the subspace spanned by $\mathbf{W}(t)$, with the forgetting factor α included to reduce the contributions of the older values. Note that if we do not include the forgetting factor, then the solution to Equation 6.16 are the first k principal directions and the projection of $\mathbf{x}$, onto $\mathbf{W}_j$

$$y_{ij} = \mathbf{w}_j^T \mathbf{x}_i, \quad i = 1, \dots, t \tag{6.17}$$

is the j-th principal component.

The sum in Equation 6.16 is a fourth-order function of the elements of $\mathbf{W}(t)$. The PAST algorithm simplifies this function by using the approximation

$$\mathbf{W}^T(t)\mathbf{x}_i \approx \mathbf{W}^T(i-1)\mathbf{x}_i = \mathbf{y}_i \tag{6.18}$$

resulting in a cost function

$$\sum_{i=1}^{t} \alpha^{t-i} ||\mathbf{x}_i - \mathbf{W}(t)\mathbf{y}_i||^2 \tag{6.19}$$

which is quadratic in the elements of $\mathbf{W}(t)$. This projection approximation, which gives the algorithm its name, results in a small error for stationary or slowly varying signals as the difference between $\mathbf{W}^T(t)\mathbf{x}$, and $\mathbf{W}^T(i-1)\mathbf{x}_i$ in such cases would be small for i close to t. For i far from t, the forgetting factor would reduce the contributions of any errors to the sum resulting from the approximation.

The solution to Equation 6.19 is well studied in adaptive filtering [25] and can be solved using various recursive least square approaches, which is the approach used in the PAST algorithm. Yang [31] also proposed a modification of the PAST algorithm, called PASTd, which incorporates deflation, an idea used in eigenanalysis to sequentially estimate the eigenvalues and eigenvectors of a matrix [23, 24]. Algorithm 6.2 describes the PASTd method. The vector $\mathbf{x}(t)$ is the vector of new values at each time instant. The vector $\mathbf{w}_i(t)$ is the estimate of the i-th eigenvector of the damped sample correlation matrix

$$C(t) = \sum_{i=1}^{t} \alpha^{t-i} \mathbf{x}_i \mathbf{x}_i^T \qquad (6.20)$$

and $d_i(t)$ is an exponentially weighted estimate of the corresponding eigenvalue. The algorithm assumes that we keep k of the eigencomponents. The initial $\mathbf{w}_i(0)$ is set to all zeros, except for a 1 in the i-th position and the d_i are set to a small positive value. The forgetting factor, α, is set to a value close to, but less than, 1.0.

Algorithm 6.2 *PASTd algorithm.*

Select $d_i(0)$ and $\mathbf{w}_i(0)$ appropriately for $i = 1, \ldots, k$
for $t = 1, 2, \ldots$ **do**
  $\mathbf{x}_1(t) = \mathbf{x}(t)$
  for $i = 1, 2, \ldots, k$ **do**
    $y_i(t) = \mathbf{w}_i^T(t - 1)\mathbf{x}_i(t)$
    $d_i(t) = \alpha d_i(t - 1) + |y_i(t)|^2$
    $e_i(t) = \mathbf{x}_i(t) - \mathbf{w}_i(t - 1)y_i(t)$
    $\mathbf{w}_i(t) = \mathbf{w}_i(t - 1) + \{y_i(t)/d_i(t)\}\, e_i(t)$
    $\mathbf{x}_{i+1}(t) = \mathbf{x}_i(t) - y_i(t)\mathbf{w}_i(t)$
  end for
end for

The PASTd algorithm requires $4dk + O(k)$ operations per update, where d is the original dimension and k is the reduced dimension. Because it uses a forgetting factor, the original data do not have to be stored, though storage of $O(dk)$ is required for storing the $\mathbf{w}_i$.

6.3.4.1 Variations of the Fast Subspace Trackers
There have been several variations of the fast subspace trackers proposed to address issues related to speed and stability [29]. All these algorithms track the principal subspace with a computational complexity of $O(dk)$. A good comparison of various algorithms proposed during the last decade is given by

Strobach [28]. In particular, he observes that algorithms such as PASTd, which are based on the matrix inversion lemma, can cause problems with fading signals. The PASTd algorithm implicitly involves the inversion of a correlation matrix, a task which is implemented recursively at each instant using the matrix inversion lemma, also referred to as the Sherman-Morrison-Woodbury formula or the Woodbury formula. This formula has known stability issues, with the correlation matrix losing its positive-definiteness and the inverse matrix "exploding" in case of fading signals. In contrast, low-rank adaptive filters, such as LORAF [27], do not calculate the inverse, and so are more stable. The LORAF techniques are similar to the FAST algorithm described earlier, where the new incoming data are decomposed into two components, one in the signal subspace and one orthogonal to it. However, because these techniques can be computationally expensive relative to PASTd, Strobach suggests using the row Householder approach [28], which is a LORAF-type of technique and therefore, does not have stability issues.

Another issue with the PASTd algorithm is the loss of orthogonality of the **w** vectors. Various ways of orthonormalizing these vectors have been proposed, with varying levels of computational complexity [1, 4, 31].

Although many of the extensions of the PAST and PASTd algorithms have come from the signal processing community, the algorithm has also received attention in the data mining community, especially in the context of streaming data analysis. The SPIRIT algorithm [21] combines PASTd with an approach to track the varying dimension of the reduced dimensional subspace. A common approach to determine the number of principal components to keep is to use the eigenvalues to estimate the energy in the reduced representation and compare it with the energy in the original data, represented by the Frobenius norm (as in the FAST algorithm). If we set a low and a high threshold for the percentage of energy we wish to maintain in the reduced representation, we can appropriately increase or decrease the number of principal components to keep whenever the percentage energy in the reduced representation is below the low threshold or above the high threshold.

6.4 Illustrative Experiments

To illustrate the dimension reduction techniques described earlier, the following uses a simple dataset from a practical problem. The Chlorine dataset [10] is generated by the EPANET simulator, which models water distribution piping systems. It performs an extended period simulation of the hydraulic and water quality behavior within pressurized pipe networks. The simulation tracks various quantities for each pipe such as the pressure at a node, the concentration of chemical species, and so on.

The Chlorine dataset tracks the chlorine concentration in the network shown in Figure 6.3. The data for 166 sensors are available for fifteen days of simulation. They are collected once every five minutes, for a total of 4,310 time instants. Figure 6.4 shows the data for a few of the sensors for five days. Note the daily periodicity, which reflects the fact that during certain times of the day, the water usage is high, resulting in higher concentration, which gradually drops as the usage goes down and the stationary water in the pipes loses its dissolved chlorine. We also observe that some of the streams are very similar, which is to be expected as the nodes close to each other on the network will have chlorine concentrations that are likely to be correlated.

6.4.1 Identifying Correlated Variables

This section considers three ways of calculating the correlation coefficients to identify the uncorrelated variables in the Chlorine dataset. The first is the sliding window approach, with the correlation coefficients for the data in the window at each instant calculated from scratch. The second is the faster incremental version of the sliding window approach and the third is the forgetting factor approach.

Once the correlation coefficients between the streams are obtained for each time instant, we use a threshold-based, greedy approach to select the uncorrelated variables. Given a fixed threshold, we consider two streams to be correlated if the correlation coefficient between them exceeds the threshold. For each time instant, starting with the first variable, we drop all other variables that are correlated to it. Then, we consider the second variable, and repeat the process. The variables left are uncorrelated and indicate the sensors that should be monitored. We observe that the list of uncorrelated variables will vary from instant to instant, especially if any of the correlation coefficients lie close to the threshold or if the statistics of the streams change over time.

Table 6.1 lists the count of data streams that are uncorrelated using the first 4,000 instants from the Chlorine data for three window sizes and two threshold values. We count streams, which are uncorrelated to the other streams during at least one instant out of the 4,000. For example, for a window length of 100 and a threshold of 0.80 using the forgetting factor approach, 62 of the data streams are considered as uncorrelated in at least one of the 4,000 instants. Interpreted a different way, it indicates that 104 ($=166 - 62$) of the streams are correlated to one of the other streams for each of the 4,000 instants considered. These results show that, as expected, several of the streams in the chlorine data are correlated and increasing the threshold leads to more uncorrelated variables. Also, increasing the window size leads to fewer uncorrelated variables as the

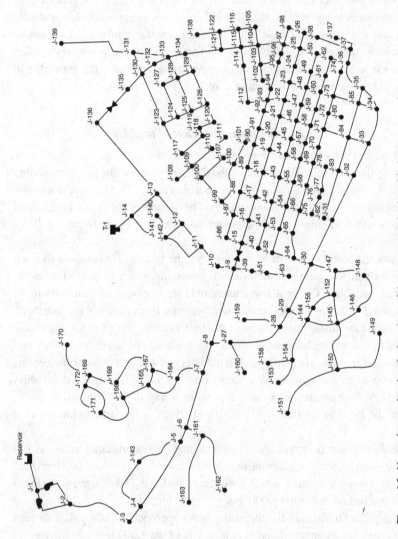

Figure 6.3. Network map showing the locations of the sensors monitoring chlorine concentrations.

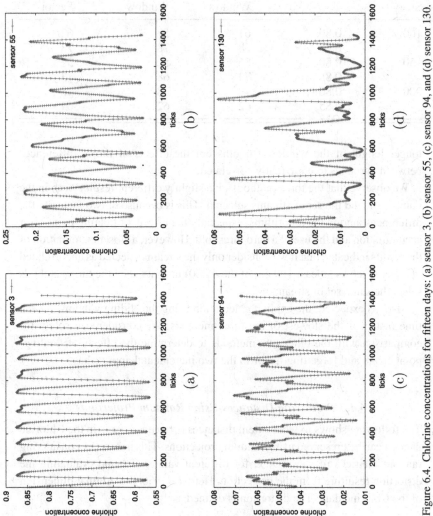

Figure 6.4. Chlorine concentrations for fifteen days: (a) sensor 3, (b) sensor 55, (c) sensor 94, and (d) sensor 130.

Table 6.1. *Number of variables identified as uncorrelated by the three different methods for various window sizes and thresholds. The forgetting factor is selected to have the equivalent window size*

Window Size	Threshold	Sliding Window	Incremental Window	Forgetting Factor
100	0.80	61	57	62
	0.85	78	78	78
150	0.80	56	52	57
	0.85	73	68	73
200	0.80	48	48	48
	0.85	62	62	64

longer length of the window smooths out the effects of minor differences between variables that are really correlated.

We observe that the three methods give slightly different results, both in the number of, and the set of streams selected. This is because of two factors – the differences among the algorithms, especially the effects of floating point error accumulation and the use of a hard threshold. However, a closer examination of the results indicated that if we consider only the streams selected as uncorrelated in many (such as at least 100 out of the 4,000) instants, then the three methods select the same set of streams.

Also, as expected, the explicit calculation using the sliding window at each time instant is the slowest of the three methods. We considered it solely for comparison with the other two methods to determine the effects of floating-point errors and forgetting factor in the two incremental approaches.

6.4.2 Preserving Distances Using Random Projections

The following shows to what extent distances between instants in the Chlorine data set can be preserved using random projections. This is done by considering random matrices of size $d \times k$, for different values of k and evaluating the distortion resulting from the projection. Here $d = 166$, the original dimension of the Chlorine data. The distortion is defined as:

$$\frac{1}{k} \frac{||\mu(x) - \mu(y)||_2}{||x - y||_2} \tag{6.21}$$

where $\mu(x)$ is the projection of the vector x. Figure 6.5 shows the results of the maximum, average, and minimum distortion as the value of k is increased from 10 to 166. The results are generated using the second matrix from Achlioptas

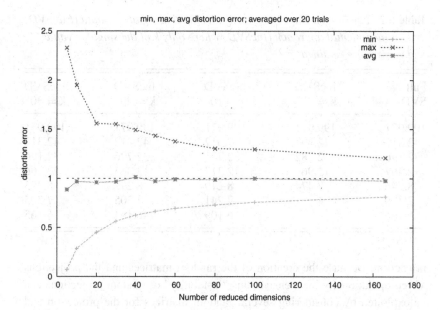

Figure 6.5. The distortion using random projection as the number of reduced dimensions is varied. The maximum, minimum, and average distortion are the average of these quantities over twenty tries.

(Equation 6.9). The result for each value of k is the average over twenty random matrices. A subset of the Chlorine data, representing five days (1,440 instants), was used in this experiment.

This plot shows that the average distortion, even when the number of reduced dimensions is small, is close to 1.0, indicating that on an average, the distances are preserved when the points are projected onto the lower dimensional space. The maximum and minimum distortions, averaged over twenty tries, can be quite far from 1.0 when the number of reduced dimensions is low, but reduce rapidly as this number increases. Also, the maximum and minimum distortion in an 80-dimensional space is close to the maximum and minimum distortion using all the 166 variables. Because the random projections can be easily obtained for streaming data, this preservation of distances implies that these projections provide a simple and cost-effective way of reducing the number of dimensions for problems involving analysis of data streams. The resulting reduced dimensional data can then be used in algorithms which are based solely on distances, such as nearest neighbor methods.

Figure 6.5 also indicates that if we consider a random projection onto a single matrix and use the reduced dimension data in further processing, we are likely to get very different results if we change the random matrix used in the

Table 6.2. *The top ten singular values calculated using all the data (FullSVD) and an incremental approach (IncSVD) where only k of the singular values and vectors are retained*

Full SVD	IncSVD $k = 5$	IncSVD $k = 10$	IncSVD $k = 20$	IncSVD $k = 30$
199.971	199.971	199.971	199.971	199.971
42.312	42.299	42.312	42.312	42.312
32.796	32.782	32.795	32.796	32.796
12.367	11.969	12.317	12.365	12.366
8.296	7.474	8.219	8.292	8.295
7.306	−	7.241	7.305	7.305
6.166	−	6.109	6.164	6.165

projection. Because the creation of the random matrices and the projections are computationally inexpensive, this "instability" of random projections can be exploited by considering several random matrices for the projection and using ensemble approaches in the analysis, such as ensemble clustering [13].

6.4.3 Reconstructing Original Data Using Reduced Dimensions

This section considers to what extent the projection onto the reduced dimension subspace, whether obtained through an incremental SVD approach (such as FAST) or a subspace tracking approach (such as PASTd), can be used to reconstruct the original data. The idea behind our experiments is to determine the error incurred when the data are represented in the lower dimensional space.

Starting with the full Chlorine dataset with $d = 166$ streams at 4310 instants, we incrementally build a reduced dimensional dataset keeping only k streams at any instant. Table 6.2 shows the top ten singular values of the original matrix (calculated using the LAPACK routine GESVD [19]) and the singular values obtained using the PAST algorithm, as the value of k is varied from 5 to 30. Figure 6.6 shows how the error in reconstructing the original data, defined as

$$\frac{||A - \tilde{A}||_F}{||A||_F} \tag{6.22}$$

changes as the number of singular values is changed. Here A is the original matrix and $\tilde{A}$ is the matrix reconstructed from the singular value decomposition using only the top k singular values and vectors. We compare the reconstruction error using the top k singular values and vectors from the full SVD versus the

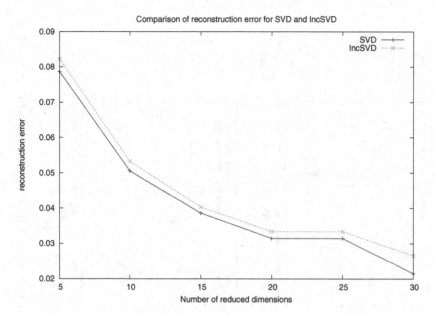

Figure 6.6. Comparison of the reconstruction error using k of the singular vectors and the full SVD method versus the incremental SVD method.

incremental approach, where the processing keeps only k singular values and vectors as the data arrive incrementally.

Table 6.2 indicates that as the number of singular values and vectors kept by the incremental approach increases, the quality of the approximation improves, with the largest singular values approaching the true singular values of the data matrix. In addition, if we reconstruct the original data using only the top k singular values and vectors, then the error between the reconstruction using the SVD of the full matrix and the incremental SVD is quite small. This indicates that techniques such as FAST and the incremental SVD approach of Brand are viable techniques to generate a low dimensional representation of streaming data.

The following considers the fast subspace trackers, in particular the PASTd algorithm. Results for two cases are presented – one where we explicitly set the dimension of the reduced subspace, and the other where we use the approach proposed by Papadimitriou [21] to adaptively select the dimension. Figure 6.7 shows the reconstructed version of 1,500 instants for 4 of the 166 sensors when we explicitly set the reduced dimension to $k = 10$. Figure 6.8 shows the corresponding results when we let the algorithm select the number of dimensions to keep. In this case, the minimum and maximum energy threshold

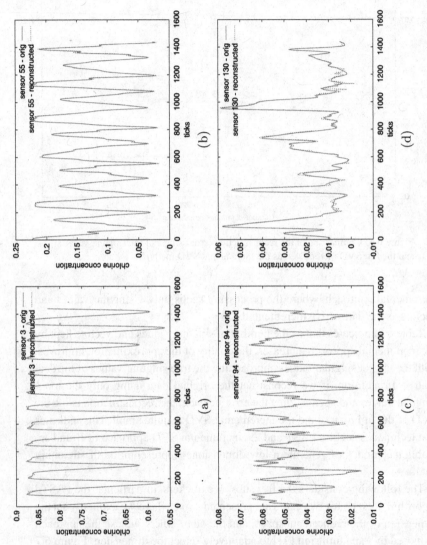

Figure 6.7. Original and reconstructed signals using PASTd with $k = 10$. (a) Sensor 3; (b) Sensor 55; (c) Sensor 94; and (d) Sensor 130.

152

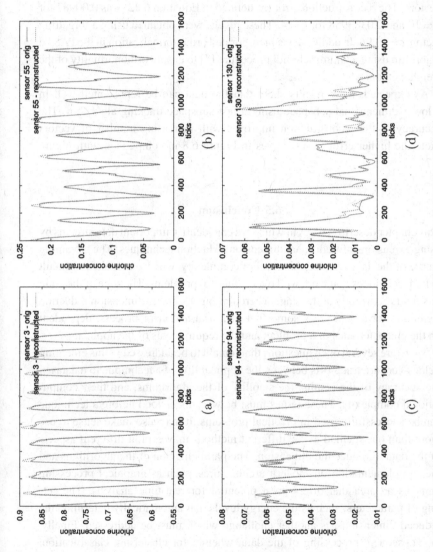

Figure 6.8. Original and reconstructed signals using PASTd with $k = 4$. (a) Sensor 3; (b) Sensor 55; (c) Sensor 94; and (d) Sensor 130.

was set to 0.98 and 0.999, respectively, indicating that the dimension was chosen so that the energy in the reduced dimensional data, as a percentage of the total energy in the data, did not fall below the lower threshold or exceed the higher threshold. The algorithm determined that this could be achieved using $k = 4$ vectors. The reconstruction error (as defined in Equation 6.22) was 0.00987 for $k = 10$ and 0.0383958 for $k = 4$. These results were obtained using a forgetting factors $\alpha = 0.96$. In addition, we incorporated orthonormalization in the PASTd algorithm using a Gram-Schmidt procedure [4] to ensure orthonormality of the weight vectors $\mathbf{w}$.

As expected, these results show that the data can be represented well in a lower dimensional subspace using a fast subspace tracking algorithm. The accuracy of the reconstruction improves with increasing number of vectors (note the higher error in the curves in Figure 6.8 in comparison with Figure 6.7).

6.5 Conclusion

This chapter describes ways in which we can identify important data streams by using extensions of traditional dimension reduction techniques. The streaming nature of the data adds another level of complexity, which can make it difficult to find techniques that work well over a range of problems. The state of the art in this field is currently at the stage where finding a suitable dimension reduction technique for a data set is somewhat of a trial and error process, dependent on the characteristics of a problem and the requirements of the application.

There are several open questions that remain to be addressed in this emerging field. There are trade-offs between the applicability of a technique to a dataset, the accuracy of the results, the stability of the algorithms, and their computational complexity. These issues must be well understood before a technique can be successfully used in practical problems. It may also make sense to use more than one method as the different methods may exploit different aspects of the data to reduce the dimension. The parallelization of the algorithms and their implementation on modern architectures, such as graphical processing units, is an area that offers great potential for real-time analysis. The setting of parameters, such as the energy levels that automatically determine the reduced dimensions, is another challenge which must be addressed. Finally, the subsequent processing of the data, whether for clustering, classification, or anomaly detection, must be closely coupled with the dimension reduction so that an appropriate technique can be chosen to identify the important data streams.

Acknowledgments

I would like to thank Matthew Neel from Bonneville Power Administration for access to the wind energy weather data and Drs. David Humphreys and Alan Hyatt of General Atomics for access to the DIII-D data. This work is part of the SensorStreams effort supported by the Advanced Scientific Computing Research program at the Office of Science, U.S. Department of Energy.

LLNL-MI-462732: This work performed under the auspices of the U.S. Department of Energy by Lawrence Livermore National Laboratory under Contract DE-AC52–07NA27344.

References

1. Abed-Meraim, K., Chkeif, A., and Hua, Y. "Fast Orthonormal PAST Algorithm." *IEEE Signal Processing Letters 7* (2000): 60–62.
2. Achlioptas, D. "Database-Friendly Random Projections: Johnson-Lindenstrauss with Binary Coins." *Journal of Computer and System Sciences 66* (2003): 671–87.
3. Aggarwal, C. C., Ed. *Data Streams: Models and Algorithms*. New York: Springer, 2007.
4. Ali, I., Kim, D. N., and Jeong, T. T. "A New Subspace Tracking Algorithm Using Approximation of Gram-Schmidt Procedure." In *Proceedings, IEEE International Conference on Information and Multimedia Technology* (2009).
5. Bertoni, A., and Valentini, G. "Random Projections for Assessing Gene Expression Cluster Stability." In *IEEE International Joint Conference on Neural Networks* (2005), pp. 149–154.
6. Bingham, E., and Mannila, H. "Random Projection in Dimensionality Reduction: Applications to Image and Text Data." In *Proceedings, ACM International Conference on Know ledge Discovery and Data Mining* (2001), pp. 245–250.
7. Brand, M. "Incremental Singular Value Decomposition of Uncertain Data with Missing Value." In *Proceedings, European Conference on Computer Vision (ECCV), Lecture Notes in Computer Science*, Volume 2350 (2002), pp. 707–720.
8. Brand, M. "Fast Online SVD Revisions for Lightweight Recommender Systems." In *Proceedings, SIAM International Conference on Data Mining* (2003), pp. 37–46.
9. Brand, M. "Fast Low-Rank Modifications of the Thin Singular Value Decomposition." *Linear Algebra and its Applications 415* (2006), 20–30.
10. Chlorine data set. http://www.cs.cmu.edu/afs/cs/project/spirit-1/www/. Accessed June 1, 2012.
11. Dasgupta, S. "Experiments with Random Projection." In *Proceedings, Sixteenth Conference on Uncertainty in Artificial Intelligence* (2000), pp. 143–151.
12. DIII-D Website. https://fusion.gat.com/global/DIII-D. Accessed June 1, 2012.
13. Fern, X. Z., and Brodley, C. "Random Projection for High Dimensional Data Clustering: A Cluster Ensemble Approach." In *Proceedings of 20th International Conference on Machine Learning* (2003), pp. 186–193.

14. Gama, J. *Knowledge Discovery from Data Strams*. Boca Raton, FL: CRC Press, 2010.

15. Gama, J., and Gaber, M. M., Eds. *Learning from Data Strams*. New York: Springer, 2007.

16. Hall, M. A. *Correlation-Based Feature Selection for Machine Learning*. PhD thesis, Department of Computer Science, University of Waikato, New Zealand, 1998.

17. Jolliffe, I. T. *Principal Components Analysis*, second ed. New York: Springer, 2002.

18. Kamath, C. *Scientific Data Mining: A Practical Perspective*. Philadephia: SIAM, 2009.

19. LAPACK Website. http://www.netlib.org/lapack/. Accessed June 1, 2012.

20. Menon, A., Pham, G. V. A., Chawla, S., and Viglas, A. "An Incremental Data-Stream Sketch Using Sparse Random Projections." In *Proceedings, SIAM International Conference on Data Mining* (2007), pp. 563–568.

21. Papadimitriou, S., Sun, J., and Faloutsos, C. "Streaming Pattern Discovery in Multiple Time Series." In *Proceedings, 31st VLDB Conference* (2005).

22. Real, E. C., Tufts, D. W., and Cooley, J. "Two Algorithms for Fast Approximate Subspace Tracking." *IEEE Transactions on Signal Processing* 47, 7 (July 1999), 1936–1945.

23. Saad, Y. *Numerical Methods for Large Eigenvalue Problems*. Manchester, UK: Manchester University Press, 1992. Available online from http://www-users.cs.umn.edu/~saad/books.html.

24. Saad, Y. *Numerical Methods for Large Eigenvalue Problems*, second ed. Philadelphia: SIAM, 2011. Avaialble online from http://www-users.cs.umn.edu/~saad/books.html.

25. Sayed, A. *Fundamentals of Adaptive Filtering*. New York: John Wiley and Sons, 2003.

26. Stewart, G. W. "On the Early History of the Singular Vaue Decomposition." *SIAM Review* 35, no. 4 (1993): 551–66.

27. Strobach, P. Low Rank Adaptive Filters. *IEEE Trans. on Signal Processing* 44, no. 12 (1996): 2932–47.

28. Strobach, P. The Fast Recursive Row-Householder Subspace Tracking Algorithm. *Signal Processing* 89 (2009): 2514–28.

29. Teixeira, P. H. S. Data Stream Anomaly Detection Through Principal Subspace Tracking. Master's thesis, Pontifícia Universidade Católica do Rio de Janeiro, 2009.

30. Tufts, D. W., Real, E. C., and Cooley, J. "Fast Approximate Subspace Tracking (FAST)." In *Proceedings, IEEE Int. Conf. Acoust., Speech, Signal Processing* (1997), vol. 1 .

31. Yang, B. Projection Approximation Subspace Tracking. *IEEE Transactions on Signal Processing* 43, no. 1 (January 1995): 95–107.

7

Binary Classification with Support Vector Machines

Patrick Nichols, Bobbie-Jo Webb-Robertson, and Christopher Oehmen

7.1 Introduction

Support vector machines (SVM) are currently one of the most popular and accurate methods for binary data classification and prediction. They have been applied to a variety of data and situations such as cyber-security, bioinformatics, web searches, medical risk assessment, financial analysis, and other areas [1]. This type of machine learning is shown to be accurate and is able to generalize predictions based upon previously learned patterns. However, current implementations are limited in that they can only be trained accurately on examples numbering to the tens of thousands and usually run only on serial computers. There are exceptions. A prime example is the annual machine learning and classification competitions such as the International Conference on Artificial Neural Networks (ICANN), which present problems with more than 100,000 elements to be classified. However, in order to treat such large test cases the formalism of the support vector machines must be modified.

SVMs were first developed by Vapnik and collaborators [2] as an extension to neural networks. Assume that we can convert the data values associated with an entity into numerical values that form a vector in the mathematical sense. These vectors form a space. Also, assume that this space of vectors can be separated by a hyperplane into the vectors that belong to one class and those that form the opposing class. If this is the case, one can find the normal vector, w, and the bias, b, of the hyperplane (the distance from the origin) in a process known as training and the classification, which can be done by computing the value of the following function,

$$f(\vec{x}_i) = sign(\vec{w} \bullet \vec{x} - b)$$

where x denotes some vector formed from data we wish to classify and the sign function returns 1 for a result greater than zero and -1 otherwise. The

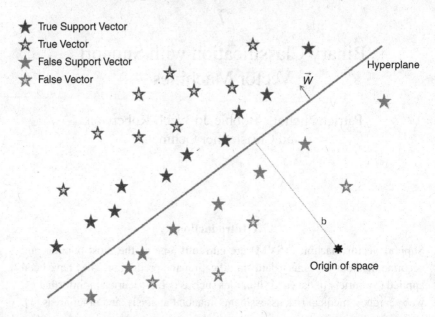

Figure 7.1. A simple illustration of the vector space for a two dimensional SVM problem. Each vector has 2 features.

dot product previously shown is not in general a conventional dot product, but instead represents a metric function that we explain later in this work. Figure 7.1 presents an example for a two-dimensional problem.

The normal vector and bias are found by solving a constrained optimization problem with some set of "test vectors" in a process known as training. These test vectors must represent "typical" data one would want to classify in the sense that any vector of the data, which we wish to classify is geometrically close to at least one of test vectors. This distance is determined by examining the inner product of this vector and a given test vector. The metric function used in this determination is called a kernel function. This function must satisfy the conditions to define a metric in this space, the Reproducing Kernel Hilbert Space (RKHS). Also, a related set of conditions known as the Mercer conditions must hold for this function. Examples of functions used in most support vector machines include the usual vector dot product or inner product, the polynomial function $(c_1 \vec{x} \bullet \vec{y} + c_2)^p$ where $\vec{x} \bullet \vec{y}$ is the usual vector dot product between vectors x and y and p is an integer. The most widely used kernel function is the radial basis function or Gaussian kernel $e^{-c|\vec{x}-\vec{y}|^2}$, where once again c is real constant. The popularity of this function comes from the fact it defines a space where vectors are the most separated and the return values are also normalized (returns values between 0 and 1).

Once one has a proper kernel function, one can solve for the bias, b, and normal vector, w, of the hyperplane using a set of labeled test vectors. The label denotes the expected value for the vectors, (1 or -1 for the sign function previously given). These are found by solving the following optimization problem with a Lagrange multiplier terms, α, to enforce the constraints.

$$\min L = \frac{1}{2}\vec{w} \bullet \vec{w} - \sum_{i=1}^{N} \alpha_i(y_i(\vec{w} \bullet \vec{x}_i - b) - 1)$$

Taking the derivative with respect to each of the free variable yields the following equations.

$$\frac{\delta L}{\delta \vec{w}} = \vec{w} - \sum_{i=1}^{N} \alpha_i y_i x_i = 0$$

$$\frac{\delta L}{\delta b} = -\sum_{i=1}^{N} \alpha_i y_i = 0$$

We have the condition that $0 \le \alpha_i$. Consequently, we have the following relations.

$$\vec{w} = \sum_{i} y_i \alpha_i \vec{x}_i$$

$$\sum_{i} \alpha_i y_i = 0$$

$$\vec{w} \bullet \vec{z} = \sum_{i} \alpha_i y_i K(\vec{x}_i, \vec{z}) \forall \vec{z} \in \Re^M$$

$$y_i(\vec{w} \bullet xi - b) \ge 1$$

Here y represents the label for the test vector x. This is usually solved using the dual Lagrangian,

$$\max L = -\frac{1}{2}\sum_{i=1}^{N}\sum_{j=1}^{N} y_i y_j K(\vec{x}_i, \vec{x}_j)\alpha_i \alpha_j + \sum_{i=1}^{N} \alpha_i$$

using one of the many developed optimization techniques, which we discuss later in this chapter. One should note that in the case, where $\alpha_i = 0$, the vector x_i has no influence on the solution and can be ignored. Those vectors in which alpha are nonzero are called support vectors because they determine the separating plane and the bias. Often one wants the margin, distance from the hyperplane to the support vectors, to vary from one region of the feature space to another. This is accomplished by adding a "slack" variable to Lagrangian, ξ.

$$\min L = \frac{1}{2}\vec{w} \bullet \vec{w} - \sum_{i=1}^{N} \alpha_i(y_i(\vec{w} \bullet \vec{x}_i - b) - 1 + \xi_i) - C\sum_{1}^{N} \xi_i + \sum \xi_i r_i$$

$$y_i(\vec{w} \bullet xi - b) \geq 1 - \xi_i$$

Note that this does not change to dual Lagrangian. But the condition for the Lagrange multiplier is changed to $0 \leq \alpha_i \leq C$.

Generally, it is assumed that the more test vectors provided during the training phase, the more accurate the predictions will be in the classification phase. However, this is not always the case. It is crucial that the test vectors span the entire space for which one wishes to make predictions, but an abundance of vectors in only one part of the RKHS is not usually helpful and leads to unnecessary amount of computation effort in dealing with these vectors.

7.2 Problems in Support Vector Machine Training

The first problem that arises in support vector machine training is the separability of the true and false training vectors. One can sometimes deal with this issue using a soft margin ($\xi > 0$) and an appropriate kernel function (such as the RBF kernel), though in some cases the assumption that a separating hyperplane exists for the set of data in question is wrong. For example, the domain of one class is not simply connected with itself or the two classes have appreciable overlap with each other (this state of affairs precludes any attempt at classification) [3].

The other issue is the condition number of the kernel matrix. Most formal methods in linear algebra such as quadratic programming require well conditioned matrices for numerically stability. When this is not the case, there are only a few methods that can be employed and good results are not always obtained. When such a catastrophe occurs, one cannot complete the optimization needed for finding the hyperplane and the training becomes impossible.

The third problem is that a prohibitive number of test vectors are needed for accurate predictions, but can overwhelm the computer's memory. First, one cannot say which vectors are crucial for training and which vectors are not. In other words, one cannot pick out support vectors. Thus, the only reliable approach would be to include them all. Because most current support vector machine training algorithms do not scale well either in memory or computational operations, one is either forced to include only a fraction of the vectors, which degrades the accuracy of the solution, or resort to caching strategies, which can degrade performance by several orders of magnitude. Previous methods of dealing with the latter problem have focused on first approximating the solution through several iterations over the entire set (still very expensive), then using the information gained from this to eliminate vectors that do not appear to be support vectors. In some methods, the vectors that are eliminated can be brought back into the set. However, the initial training set is still the entire set and although one can reduce the time to solution in this manner, there is no clear cut savings in memory. Another approach is to somehow eliminate test vectors before the training begins without sacrificing accuracy, which is still a subject undergoing intense research.

Assuming we have solved the training problem and have solved for the parameters needed to develop the classification function, the next step is, of course, validation in the case where we have known data to test against or classification if we have data with no known class. This step is trivially parallel and can be separated out to many different computers across the network. In fact, even the latency associated with international data transfers would not be a serious obstacle for this step, if there are plentiful amounts of data to classify or predict. For this reason, the next section focuses on this topic. These parts of the support vector machine methodology are trivially parallel and can be implemented using MPI, MapReduce, and many other approaches, enabling SVMs to scale to data-intensive applications. Thus, the remainder of the chapter continues to focus on the training of the support vector machine classifier.

7.3 Implementations

Support vector machines are only now making inroads into the data classification field. Platt has stated that there are two possible reasons for why researchers have been slow to apply SVMs to classification. One is the degree of sophistication needed to use these methods effectively with currently available software. This will change as more users adapt this method and use it. Although it is of some concern, this obstacle is one of familiarity with the method. The other reason is the ability of the SVM software to handle large problems in a reasonable period of time [4]. This is an area of current concern with support vector machines, especially how this method applies to data-intensive computing.

Although the classification function is the same for all versions of SVMs, the method of finding the parameters that make up the classification function is not. There are currently four major means of solving the optimization problem, which in turn yields the hyperplane normal vector and bias needed for the classification function. The first method appeared very early after Vapnik's introduction of the SVM method and is an adaptation of the adaline method used in neural networks. For example, it is implemented in GIST [5], a popular program among biologists. One chooses an initial configuration of values (usually $\alpha_i = 0$ for all i). One goes through the test vectors and looks for those misclassified using the current set of values. One then updates the parameters, α, in the direction to correct this error and then imposes the constraints. After many iterations, a set of variables that produces the minimal amount of errors is found. Although not particularly fast, this method is very simple and uses a minimum of memory. There are proofs that this procedure will converge quadratically [6, 7]. Unfortunately, this method relies on a fixed bias, but does not present a general solution.

The second method to appear was the application of quadratic programming techniques from optimization theory to the SVM problem. In particular, the interior point method of Karkumar, which solves the problem using conventional linear algebra and convex programming techniques. One use of the conjugate gradient technique in combination with several auxiliary Lagrange multipliers variables is called slacks. Initially, the system is allowed to step in the direction that most maximizes the dual Lagrangian and at the same time violates the Karush-Kuhn-Tucker (KKT) conditions by a small amount controlled by the slack variables (maximizes a larger dual Lagrangian involving these slacks). KKT violations are reduced with each step until they are close to zero. At this point, a solution has been found. The main drawback to this technique is that the Kernel Matrix is decomposed at each step in order to find a quasi inverse for the update step. This implies that this method requires on the order of N^3 operations and N^2 memory for N test vectors. Therefore, this method can be very expensive. One way of reducing the computational load is to approximate the Kernel Matrix using a lower rank) [8–10]. This reduces the number of operations to some fraction of the previous number. The new package PSVM uses this technique. Although the computational and memory cost can be reduced to some fraction of the former number, the underlying method is still proportional to the factors previously given. Therefore, for large data sets the amount of time to solution is too large for practical application and amount of memory needed is prohibitive. Moreover, experiments with this approach have shown a loss of accuracy, as the fraction of the kernel matrix retained is reduced below a certain threshold [8]. Another approach to reducing the cost of this technique is known as "chunking" and was developed very early in the history of SVMs by Osuna [11]. One deals with only a small subset of the training vector set at one time (such as one-tenth of the original set). After reaching a solution within the subset chosen, vectors that are not support vectors are replaced with new vectors and a new solution is generated. After each new solution, some vectors that were previously eliminated can be reintroduced. When the objective function is nearly constant for each new set, a solution is reached. The interior point method with chunking is implemented in one of the most popular programs known as SVMLight. One of the best reasons for using these methods is that they are based upon more traditional linear algebra operations. Existing linear algebra software such as LAPACK has been able to produce a very high number of floating point operations per second for these types of operations. Moreover, this method is fairly straightforward to adapt to high-performance distributed computing. Nevertheless, there are clearly problems if a large subset of vectors is needed to fully describe the hyperplane and bias. If this the case, then the active subset will grow to accommodate all of these vectors and the overall scaling degenerates to N^3.

A third approach is similar to the previous methods with the exception that the update is projected so that it always satisfies the KKT conditions. These use a conjugate gradient approach with Newton steps that are filtered in direction as well as length (projection). This type of optimization was originally developed by Dai and Fletcher [12]. A parallel version (pgpdt) and serial version (gpdt) have been released by the Serafini, Zanghirati, and Zanni [13, 14]. The memory and flops requirements are similar to the interior point methods. This method is implemented within the SVMLight framework of Joachims [15] and like the former methods uses chunking to reduce the problem size to a manageable level.

The fourth method is the sequential minimal optimization (SMO) method. Platt formulated this approach in 1998 [4, 16]. As previously mentioned, the most popular methods for solving dual Lagrangian equation at the time were conventional bound constrained quadratic programming solvers, which scale roughly as the cube of the number of input vectors (one must solve a linear equation at each iteration). Platt's implementation immediately became popular because it scales linearly. The idea comes from the related area of neural networks. In this area, perceptron or adaline methods had become the most popular means of solving the training problem (like the first method previously mentioned). These maximize a functional by updating one weight at a time. However, the constraint introduced by the derivative with respect to the bias precludes this approach when the bias is nonzero because any weight is linearly dependent on at least one other. This next simplest approach is updating two weights at once by changing one and allowing the change in one other to be dependent on this change in such a way to satisfy this constraint. Indeed, this is possible. In other words, we can maximize the objective function as much as possible using the two Lagrange multiplier weights subject to the conditions $0 \le \alpha_i \le C$ and $\sum_i \alpha_i y_i = 0$. Let us call these two multipliers α_1 and α_2. The constraint from the previous equations is written in the following form.

$$y_1\alpha_1 + y_2\alpha_2 = \gamma'$$

Clearly, this can be rewritten as $\gamma = \alpha_2 + s\alpha_1$ where $s = y_1 y_2$ and γ is a constant. The dual Lagrangian can then be expressed in terms of the variables α_1 and α_2.

$$\max L = -\frac{1}{2}\left(K_{22}\alpha_2^2 + K_{11}(\gamma - \alpha_2)^2 - 2K_{12}\alpha_2(s\gamma - s\alpha_2)\right)$$
$$+ \alpha_2 + s\alpha_2 - y_2(\gamma - \alpha_2)\lambda_1 - y_2\alpha_2\lambda_2 + \cdots$$

where $\lambda_1 = \sum_{k \ne 1} y_k\alpha_k K_{k1}$ and $\lambda_2 = \sum_{k \ne 2} y_k\alpha_k K_{k2}$ are constant with respect to changes in α_1 and α_2. After some algebra, the value of the update to α_2 is the following.

$$\alpha_{2,new} = (G_2 - sG_1)/(K_{11} + K_{22} - 2K_{12})$$

G_1 is the gradient of the dual Lagrangian with respect to α_1 and α_2 similarly for G_2. The value of $\alpha_{2,new}$ must be clipped so the constraint conditions are met. The lowest possible value for α_2 we will denote as L and highest possible is H. These are shown as the following.

$$L = \max\left(0, \gamma - \frac{1-s}{2}C\right)$$

$$H = \min\left(C, \gamma + \frac{1+s}{2}C\right)$$

Note that if the difference in α_2 and $\alpha_{2,new}$ is small (e.g., 10^{-12}) this means there is very little change in the multipliers or the objective function and we have an unsuccessful step. The only nontrivial procedure left is a way to pick which two weights or Lagrange multipliers to update. Platt gave one procedure where one goes through each of the weights sequentially and chooses the other weight to be the one with the maximal difference in the gradient of the pair. If one cannot take a successful step with these criteria, one chooses a random place in the list of weights and tries each sequentially. Finally, if no successful steps are made for any weight the solution has converged. After the first iteration, only those in the set $\{i : 0 \le \alpha_i < C\}$ are considered unless no changes are seen for all members of this set. Then, all are examined. Keerthi has shown that there is a much more efficient way of picking these weights [17]. First, we must define the status variable.

$$\Omega_i = \begin{cases} = 1, \alpha_i = C \\ = 0, 0 < \alpha_i < C \\ = -1, \alpha_i = 0 \end{cases}$$

We first find one weight, α_1, such that $y_1 G_1$ is maximal and $y_1 \Omega_1 \neq 1$. The second one, α_2, is chosen to be one such that $y_2 G_2$ is minimal and $y_2 \Omega_2 \neq -1$. If one cannot find two weights satisfying these conditions or no successful updates have occurred based upon these conditions, it can be shown that one is at the optimal solution and the training problem is solved.

The problem to discuss next is the case: $\eta = K_{11} + K_{22} - 2K_{12} < 0$. This can happen for two reasons. One is the case where the input examples contain redundant or nearly redundant vectors. In this case, the results should be zero; however, round off error can produce a very small negative result. The other reason is a choice of kernel function, which does not satisfy the proper conditions for being a norm. Platt advocated enforcing the extreme values in this case (setting α_2 equal to L or H), but a more recent approach is to change the definition of η to the value $\eta = \max(K_{11} + K_{22} - 2K_{12}, \tau)$ where τ is a very small but positive number, such as 10^{-12} [18]. This is equivalent to regularizing the kernel matrix. In some sense, we are using a dual soft-margin approach where the value of τ is chosen as the cost of L_2, which is the norm slack variable independent of the other soft-margin slack variable.

The initial conditions are $\alpha_i = 0$, $\Omega_i = -1$ and $G_i = 1$ for all vectors. Thus, the order of the input vectors determines which ones are picked for optimization first for an update. After each step, the gradient must be updated.

$$G_i = G_i - y_i(\Delta \alpha_2 K_{2i} y_2 + \Delta \alpha_1 K_{1i} y_1)$$

The process of updating pairs of weights is repeated until no new successful steps can be taken. One can find other criteria for terminating the calculation such as the value of the feasibility gap. Although using these conditions can greatly reduce the computation time without a sacrifice in accuracy, they are outside the scope of this chapter and the interested reader is referred to an excellent explanation of these criteria in a recent book [1].

After convergence, the hyperplane bias is found by an averaging over all α such that $0 \leq \alpha_i \leq C$.

$$b = \left(-\sum_{\Omega=0} G_i y_i\right) / N_{\Omega=0}$$

This outlines the procedure of solving the training problem for most of the SMO implementations available today such as LIBSVM (be aware that many toolboxes use the LIBSVM source code) [19]. For data-intensive computing, clearly the SMO method is most appropriate because it scales linearly and requires an amount of memory proportional to the number of vectors. Also, in LIBSVM there is the option to do "chunking" to reduce the active set size to fit in memory. In addition, it has been shown that one can cache kernel matrix rows. Thus, one can in principle reduce the training problems to one that is linear to the number of test vectors for computational flops and memory.

7.4 Computational Issues

The key issues for the any method in relation to data-intensive computing are the ability of the algorithm to handle large-scale problems with the hardware available now and in the future. The apparent trend for hardware is that the number of cores is doubling every eighteen months while the clock speed is only marginally improved in the same period of time. Thus, this requires the capability to use multiple cores to speed up the amount of flops and a large amount of memory to feed data to these cores. The author has recently shown that this is efficient using the SMP architecture provided by a single node of a high-end processor. The first issue is, of course, either precomputing the kernel matrix if needed or setting up the necessary data structure to cache kernel matrix rows. The precomputation of the kernel matrix is more scalable than cache technique because it is embarrassingly parallel. However, in cases where not enough is available to store that kernel matrix, one must resort to caching. Caching requires some synchronization between the different threads on each core. In turn, this can generate serial computation, which will negatively impact weak scaling. Most of the SMO time is spent in determining the maximal and minimal gradients within the condition previously set. This is a data-parallel operation with a final reduction step (finding the global max and min from the local values found by each core). This is, of course, quite scalable. The actual update of the weights is purely serial and could be a potential problem for weak scaling, however, because it is constant in the number of arithmetic operations strong scaling is unaltered. Thus, the SMO technique remains the method of choice for large-scale problems on SMP architectures. Even with the recent popularity of General Purpose Graphics Processors (GP-GPUs), which represent the extreme form of an SMP approach, this method is adaptable to the hardware at hand.

Another type of architecture of interest today is the supercomputer or distributed computers using networks to form a single system image. Each of the separate nodes or computational units of these computers is an SMP type machine exactly the same as the preceding. The difference is that many of these are connected with a network that can pass data between the nodes. These types of computers are in general attractive because many thousands of processors are available versus the dozen seen on a single node on an SMP machine or hundreds of a GP-GPU. There is also an abundance of memory with many terabytes available for use. However, the communication needed for synchronization negatively affects the performance of all four of these algorithms. At this time, it takes several microseconds to pass data from one computer to the next. In contrast, the SMP machines take about three orders of magnitude less time to do the same operation. Thus, all synchronizations previously mentioned will be a thousand times more expensive in the future. Parallel versions of the last three methods have been developed [20–22], but an efficient method that is extended to many processors over a local network is an area of current and future research.

7.4.1 Tests of the Sequential Minimal Optimization

A sixteen-node dual quad core computer was utilized for these calculations. Each node contains 8 AMD Barcelona processors (2.1 GHz) and 16 GB of memory. The amount of memory sets an upper limit of around 45,000 training vectors if the kernel matrix is precomputed. An important feature of this configuration is that each socket of four processors is connected to the other socket by a hypertransport link. This results in slower access times for a processor fetching data from memory of another socket compared to its own memory. As this chapter later shows, this situation requires that some data be replicated in order to get the best performance. The compiler used for these results was the gcc C++ compiler, g++ 4.2, available with most Linux distributions (exact settings available upon request from the authors). The Native POSIX Threads Library version 2.5 is available with the glibc provided the threads functionality. Red Hat Enterprise Linux 5 was the operating system on all nodes. There are three codes being compared for the data sets. The first two codes are object-oriented and do not copy the training vectors and scaling factors for the kernel matrix building step. One of these two uses a sparse vector form and the other a dense form (these codes are known as Sparse6 and Dense6 respectively). A third code uses a contiguous dense data format for storing the training vectors and does replicate this data during the kernel building phase. This code uses a dense vector format and is known as SVM7.

Two data sets are chosen to test the performance and accuracy of the code and three different implementations of the SMO SVM algorithm. The nature of the data sets determines which of these implementations performs the best. The Adult data set [4, 23] was used for testing with sparse data. The Adult data set attempts to predict if a household's income exceeds $50,000 (U.S. dollars) based upon census data. This data set is sparse and binary in nature (all features are either 0 or 1). This set is further decomposed into many subsets with varying number of training vectors. The a3a, a5a, a8a, and a9a subsets are used. These subsets contain 3,185, 6,414, 22,696, and 32,561 training vectors respectively. These contain 123 features with the maximum number of nonzero element for any vector being 14. For this case, a radial basis kernel function is used with a variance of 10 (coefficient of the exponential is 0.05) and the SVM cost parameter set equal to 2.5. The kernel matrix is scaled so that the diagonal values are 1. Although other parameters might be more optimal, these produced the best accuracy and ROC scores out of the few we tested. Moreover, the kernel parameters are the same as those chosen by Platt, which allows a direct comparison of the present results with the previously published ones (Platt uses a cost parameter of 1 [16]). The Adult data set is available from the LIBSVM Web site for download [19]. The original Web site for the Adult data set is the UCI machine learning repository [23]. This data set is also available from Platt [16] and available in another format on his Web page. As an initial test, we compared our results with those given in Platt's paper [16] with almost identical agreement. Regardless of the value of the cost parameter, the predictions are not completely accurate. For the adult data set with a cost of 2.5, a typical ROC score is around .90 whereas the accuracy is around 84 to 86 percent. The second data set chosen was a bioinformatics data set from a previous paper on the application of support vector machines to protein classification; SVM Homology Tool (SHOT) [25]. This data set is to test the performance of these codes for dense training vectors. All of the 2,176 features are nonzero. The large set is divided into two training sets of 10,000 (SHOT 10k) and 20,000 (SHOT 20k) training vectors respectively. Each has 2,177 features. We refer to these as the SHOT data sets. A previous work suggested that a polynomial kernel function yields good results [16]. Thus, a polynomial kernel function is used, $(x \cdot y + 10)^2$ where $x \cdot y$ is the usual dot product of vectors x and y. The kernel matrix is not scaled in this case. Instead, the features are all scaled to lie between 0 and 1. This is done to easily compare with LIBSVM [9], which does not allow the kernel matrix to be scaled. As with the previous set, the cost was set equal to 2.5. Again, these choices show to produce good results. The accuracy is shown to be around 90 percent (a ROC score of 0.91). As the reader sees later in this chapter, the time for creation of the kernel matrix is an order of magnitude larger than the time for solving the optimization problem. This is most likely the result of the quadratic scaling of this step versus the linear scaling of the SMO procedure.

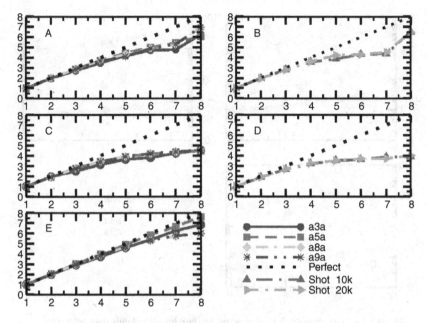

Figure 7.2. The speed up for the kernel matrix construction for each of the cases:
A) SVM7 for the Adult set, B) SVM7 for the SHOT data, C) Dense 6 for the Adult
Set, D) Dense6 for the SHOT data, E) Sparse6 on the Adult Data.

Two tasks are the most important for determining the speed of the present
code. First, the creation of the kernel matrix whereas the second is the solving
of the optimization problem by SMO. The results for the time to create the
kernel matrix for the Adult data set and the speedup for the process's versus
the number of cores is shown in Figures 7.2–7.4. As previously stated, this
calculation is embarrassingly parallel in terms of computation. In Figure 7.2,
note that the speed up is very good for all three codes up to four processors.
There the dense code, Dense6, begins to have problems scaling. However,
for the sparse code, Sparse6, and the data replicated code, SVM7, acceptable
speedup is seen up to eight cores, which is maximum number of this machine.
Also, note for this step that the dense codes are slower than the sparse code
by a factor two to four, as shown for the Adult data set. For the SHOT data
set, the sparse code is an order of magnitude slower (results not shown). For
the Adult data set, this result is readily explained. Because the Adult data set
is sparse, the dense codes are performing many wasted operations. In fact, the
sparse codes are performing only about ten percent of the flops per kernel row.
Moreover, the sparse code, Sparse6, scales much better than the dense version
of the same code, Dense6. Because the data is sparse, this also makes sense

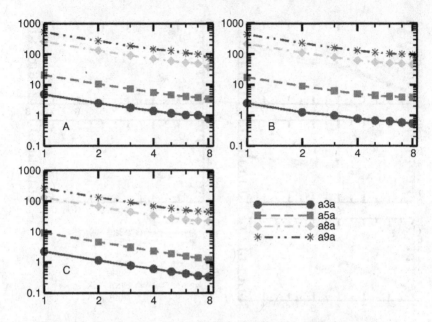

Figure 7.3. The time on a log-log scale for building the Adult data set kernel matrix versus number of cores for A) SVM7, B) Dense6, and C) Sparse6.

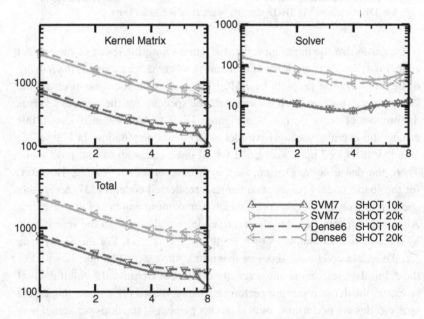

Figure 7.4. The time on a log-log scale for constructing the kernel matrix, solving the SMO problem, and total time with the Bioinformatics data sets.

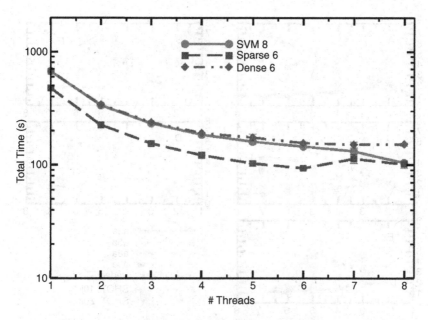

Figure 7.5. The time on a log-log scale for building the kernel matrix for the a9a Adult data set versus number of cores for SVM7, Dense6, and Sparse6.

for the following reasons. The sparse vectors are of different lengths and the time to compute the kernel matrix element for each pair will vary greatly. Thus, each thread is writing the results of the computation and loading a new vector at different times with respect to other threads. This eliminates any memory access conflicts. In contrast, the dense code has vectors of fixed length, which implies that all threads will complete the kernel matrix computation and try to load new data at nearly the same time. One will note from the previously mentioned figures that threads on the same socket are not as affected by this as one might imagine. If more than one socket is needed (more than four threads), the hypertransport link is not so robust and a definite drop off is noticed. The data replicated code, SVM7, was developed for this very reason. SVM7 scales well because it eliminates these conflicts by allowing each thread to have its own copy of the needed data. Although it is clear from Figure 7.2 that the hypertransport link problem still influences performance, this is less of a problem for SVM7 (the problem of communicating kernel matrix elements from each thread to a single memory location remains).

The performance of all three programs is contrasted for the largest sparse data set, a9a, in Figure 7.5. As the number of threads increases, the duplication of data allows SVM7 to perform nearly as well as Sparse6. Obviously, this

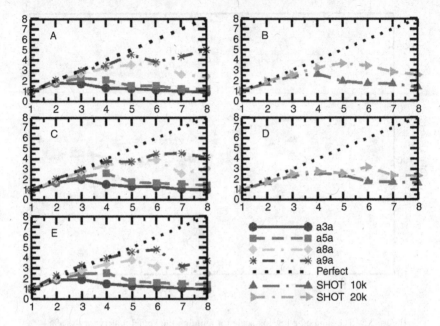

Figure 7.6. The speedup for solving the SMO problem for each of the cases: A) SVM7 on the the Adult data set, B) SVM7 on the SHOT data set, C) Dense6 on the Adult data set, D) Dense6 on the SHOT data set, E) Sparse6 on the Adult Data set.

duplication is enabling better performance. In contrast to the results for the Adult data set, the dense codes are up to an order of magnitude faster for the dense SHOT data set. Also, the excellent scaling of the Sparse6 code is not seen here, because each thread is in fact accessing data from memory at the same time as all other threads. Only the SVM7 code performs reasonably well here.

The second task is solving the optimization problem by the SMO procedure. As previously mentioned, there is a crucial synchronization point followed by a small part of serial code. The speedups and average timings are shown in Figures 7.5–7.7. Note that this part of the algorithm is exactly the same for all three problems. It is clear to see that though scaling is possible, this problem prevents the almost linear scaling seen with the kernel matrix construction. For small data, sets this leads to a complete lack of scaling when the number of threads is greater than two. However, as the number of training vectors grows the scaling of the code improves because the time of computation dominates over the synchronization time. Note that in this part of the program, there is not replication of data, which does lead to some degradation of performance

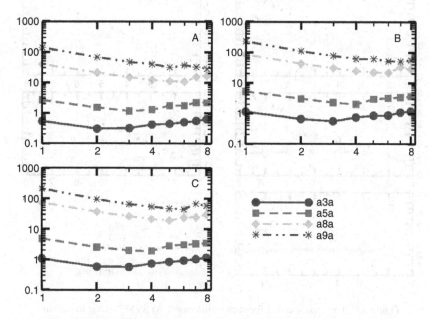

Figure 7.7. The time on a log-log scale for solving the SMO problem with the Adult data set kernel matrix versus number of cores for A) SVM7, B) Dense6, and C) Sparse6.

when attempting to use threads on different sockets. We finally show the total speed up for the adult and bioinformatics sets in Figures 7.4, 7.8, and 7.9. These show the relative importance of having each part of the program scale well. As mentioned before, the time for this step rapidly decreases compared to the kernel matrix construction time. Thus, for large data sets, one should concentrate on the kernel matrix construction for the very best performance (even a code that is twice as fast can produce very little change in the total time to solution).

The present code is compared to serial performance of LIBSVM and the parallel performance of the PSVM implementations in Tables 7.1–7.4. The serial and best parallel runtime is shown for the present code. Note that comparing these results is hard. Each of these codes has different convergence criteria and the exact details of the implementation differ from one code to the next. However, this comparison is useful for exploring the issues in each implementation.

PSVM uses an interior point method to solve the quadratic optimization. As previously explained, the kernel matrix is replaced by a lower rank representation [8]. The assumed rank of this matrix can greatly affect the accuracy [8].

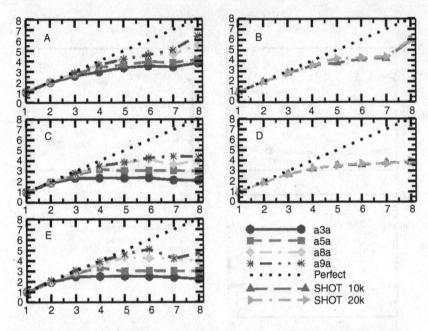

Figure 7.8. The total speedup for each of the cases: A) SVM7 on the the Adult data set, B) SVM7 on the SHOT data set, C) Dense6 on the Adult data set, D) Dense6 on the SHOT data set, E) Sparse6 on the Adult Data set.

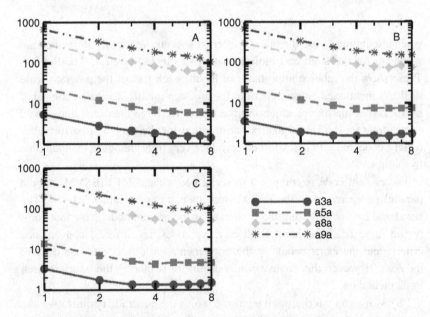

Figure 7.9. The total time on a log-log scale with the Adult data set versus number of cores for: A) SVM7, B) Dense6, and C) Sparse6.

Table 7.1. *Results for Adult A3a set*

Program	Time (sec)	# Support Vectors	Bias	Accuracy
LIBSVM-No shrink	1.89	1,270	0.05	84.34
LIBSVM-Shrink	1.30	1,273	0.05	84.34
SVM7 serial	5.5	1,270	0.05	84.34
6 threads	1.42			
Dense6 serial	2.42	1,270	0.05	84.34
6 threads	1.52			
Sparse6 serial	2.22	1,270	0.05	84.34
5 threads	1.33			
PSVM 1 core	4216.305	1,283	0.05	84.18
16 cores	3099.93			

Table 7.2. *Results for Adult A9A set*

Program	Time (sec)	# Support Vectors	Bias	Accuracy
LIBSVM (no shrink)	2128.98	11,533	−0.3	85.00
LIBSVM (shrink)	226.99	11,638	−0.3	85.00
SVM7 serial	642.2	11,533	−0.3	85.00
8 threads	104.22			
Dense6 serial	497.82	11,533	−0.3	85.00
8 threads	152.14			
Sparse6 serial	368.546	11,533	−0.3	85.00
8 threads	101.37			

Table 7.3. *Bioinformatics 10K set*

Program	Time (sec)	# Support Vectors	Bias	Accuracy
LIBSVM-No shrink	29571	3,189	8.22	84.65
LIBSVM-Shrink	2991	3,230	8.22	84.65
SVM7 serial	716.73	3,189	8.22	84.65
8 threads	120.48			
Dense6 serial	790.99	3,189	8.22	84.65
8 threads	209.45			

Table 7.4. *Bioinformatics 20K set*

Program	Time (sec)	# Support Vectors	Bias	Accuracy
LIBSVM-No shrink	179,931.4	6,550	9.624	84.203
LIBSVM-Shrink	68,811	6,716	9.624	84.203
SVM7 serial	2,885.45	6,550	9.624	84.203
8 threads	490.33			
Dense6 serial	3,179.60	6,550	9.624	84.203
8 threads	996.6			

We assume a rank ratio of 0.7 for these tests. The PSVM runtimes are dominated by a serial Cholesky factorization, which prevents any substantial speedup with the parameters and data set chosen. Lower rank ratio would reduce the time required for the Cholesky Factorization and thus improve the speedup. However, in cases where the actual rank of matrix is greater than that assumed the accuracy is degraded. Thus, this code forces a trade-off in accuracy for speed. The runtimes for the a9a and SHOT data with PSVM were truncated at one day are not shown. This code can be very useful in cases where the rank of the kernel matrix is much less than the total number of vectors. This is not the case for the present data sets.

The other code, LIBSVM, uses both caching and shrinking to speed up the computation and reduce the amount of memory needed. From the results shown in the table, this greatly speeds up the computation compared to using all training vectors at once. This has not been implemented in the present code, though this enhancement is added in the near future. The second way LIBSVM tries to speed up the computation is to replace the kernel matrix construction step with a cache of kernel matrix rows (when a step requires a kernel matrix row not in cache, the vector that was used the longest ago in the past is replaced with one that is computed). Provided enough memory is allocated for caching, it is not necessary to recompute rows with this method. For small sparse data sets, this can result in a dramatic speedup in the code because only a few kernel matrix rows may be needed. In contrast, for data sets that are large, the cost of computing a kernel matrix row can be very expensive and the amount of memory available is limited. Not only would one need to recompute the same kernel matrix rows more than once but for each row computation all of the training vectors must be accessed. The advantage to using a cache is that ideally any size training set can be treated, provided one can fit two rows of the kernel matrix in memory at one time. As shown in Tables 7.1, 7.2, 7.3, and 7.4, a precomputed kernel is faster for larger data sets, but the size of this matrix is limited by the amount of available memory (for 32 GB of memory, we are limited to a training set of approximately 50,000 vectors). LIBSVM also assumes a sparse data format, which can be very slow when this assumption is not true such as the SHOT data set. In all cases, the present codes perform well with respect to this and other implementations. The accuracy of the present codes is basically identical to LIBSVM.

Although these are clear trade-offs, the present approach compares well across the spectrum of data set sizes and types of data. It is expected that in the future, the number of cores available for a single computer will increase at roughly the same rate as Moore's Law. The amount of memory available per computer is also expected to increase in coming years. The present code is well poised to take advantage of these increases to tackle larger data sets and to train much faster for the data sets of the same size as the current data sets.

7.5 Conclusion

It is clear that SVMs can be utilized to provide an accurate and scalable means of binary classification and the sequential minimal optimization method is currently the best candidate for this task because it allows linear scaling in both flops and memory. The key questions for the future is adapting current implementations to ever larger data sets and the methodologies to utilize current and future data- intensive computing platforms. A critical step along this path is to take advantage of multiple cores within a compute node by developing efficient strategies for threading SVM training. This is motivated by the continued success of SVMs as a reliable classification methodology and the steady increases of data volumes that are being used to drive SVM training across a wide spectrum of applications. In many cases, such as with streaming sensor input, training vectors are dense and of high dimensionality. For applications where this high dimensionality is needed because of the complexity of the underlying phenomena, a large number of training vectors must be used to adequately sample the solution space. Computational limitations that force users to sample the data sets to create smaller training data may remove critical detail in the training space and undermine the quality of the resulting classifier. For this reason, we are highly motivated to enable training on very large data sets. To this end, a multithreaded version of the sequential minimal optimization has been developed and shown to perform well for large data sets. However, for small data sets, the computational scaling is adversely affected by the crucial serial section of the SMO algorithm. It can be questioned if this is really an issue since for small data sets, because one can solve the problem using the completely serial algorithm in short time if this is the case. The need for a parallel approach is not warranted for such small sets. On the other hand, for large data sets the improved scaling of using POSIX threads is clearly beneficial because a serial approach is limited to the number of flops that a single core can produce. We demonstrate clearly that we can take advantage of the modern multicore architectures.

References

1. Christianini, N. and Shawe-Taylor, J. *An Introduction to Support Vector Machines and other Kernel Based Learning Methods*. Cambridge, UK: Cambridge University Press, 2000.
2. Boser, B. E., Guyon, I. M., and V. N. Vapnik. "A Training Algorithm for Optimal Margin Classifiers." In *Proceedings of the 5th Annual ACM Workshop on Computational Learning Theory*, edited by D. Haussler, 144–52. New York: ACM Press, 1992.
3. Jin, J. "Impossibility of Successful Classification When Useful Features are Rare and Weak." *Proceedings of the National Academy of Sciences of the United States of America* 106, no. 22 (2009): 8859–64.
4. Platt, J. "Using Analytic QP and Sparseness to Speed Training of Support Vector Machines." *Proc. Advances in Neural Information Processing Systems* 11, 557–63. Cambridge, MA: MIT Press, 1999.
5. Brown, M. P. S., Grundy, W. N., Lin, D., Cristianini, N., Sugnet, Furey Jr., C., T. S., Ares, M., and Haussler, D. Knowledge-Based Analysis of Microarray Gene Expression Data Using Support Vector Machines. *Proceedings of the National Academy of Science* 97, no. 1 (2000): 262–67.
6. Frieß, T. T., Cristianini, N., and Campbell, C. *The Kernel Adatron: a Fast and Simple Learning Procedure for Support Vector Machines. Proceedings of the Fifteenth International Conference on Machine Learning*. Madison, Wisconsin: Morgan Kaufmann, 1998.
7. Opper, M. "Learning Times of Neural Networks: Exact Solution for a Perceptron Algorithm." *Physical Review A* 38 (1988): 3824–26.
8. Chang, E., Zhu, K., Wang, H., Bai, H., Li, J., Qiu, Z., and Cui, H. 2008. "Parallelizing support vector machines on distributed computers." In *Advances in Neural Information Processing Systems 20*, J. Platt, D. Koller, Y. Singer, and S. Roweis Eds., MIT Press, Cambridge, MA, 257–64.
9. *PSVM, accessed* August 2010, http://code.google.com/p/psvm.
10. Fine, S., Scheinberg, K., Cristianini, N., Shawe-Taylor, J., and Williamson, B. "Efficient SVM Training Using Low-Rank Kernel Representations." *Journal of Machine Learning Research* 2 (2001): 243–64.
11. Osuna, R., Freund, R., and Girosi, F. "Training Support Vector Machines: an Application to Face Detection." In *Proceedings of the Conference on Computer Vision and Pattern Recognition, 130*, 1997.
12. Dai, Y. H., and Fletcher, R. *New Algorithms for Singly Linearly Constrained Quadratic Programs Subject to Lower and Upper Bounds*. Research Report NA/216, Department of Mathematics, University of Dundee, 2003.

13. Zanghirati, G., and Zanni, L. "A Parallel Solver for Large Quadratic Programs in Training Support *Vector Machines.*" *Parallel Computing* 29 (2003): 535–51.
14. Serafini, T. Zanghirati, G., and Zanni, L. "Gradient Projection Methods for Large Quadratic Programs and Applications in Training Support Vector Machines." *Optim. Meth. Soft.* 20 (2005): 353–78.
15. Joachims, T. "Making Large-Scale SVMLearning Practical." In *Advances in Kernel Methods – Support Vector Learning*, edited by B. Schölkopf, C. Burges, and A. Smola. Boston: MIT-Press, 1999.
16. Platt, John C. "Fast Training of Support Vector Machines Using Sequential Minimal Optimization." In *Advances in Kernel Methods – Support Vector Learning*, edited by B. Schölkopf, C. Burges, and A. Smola. Boston: MIT-Press, 1998.
17. Keerthi, S. S., Shevade, S. K., Bhattacharyya, C., and Murthy, K. R. K. "Improvements to Platt's SMOAlgorithm for SVMClassifier Design." *Neural Computation* 13, no. 3 (2001): 637.
18. Fan, R. E., Chen, P. H., and Lin, C. J. "Working set selection using second order information for training SVM." *Journal of Machine Learning Research* 6, (2005): 1889–1918.
19. Chih-Chung Chang and Chih-Jen Lin. "LIBSVM: A Library for Support Vector Machines," *accessed* August 2010, http://www.csie.ntu.edu.tw/~cjlin/libsvm.
20. Cao, L. J., Ong, C. J., Zhang, J. Q., Periyathamby, U., Fu, X. J., and Lee, H. P. "Parallel Sequential Minimal Optimization for the Training of Support Vector Machines," *IEEE Transactions on Neural Networks* 17, no. 4 (2006): 1039–49.
21. MILDE, accessed August 2010, http://www.nec-labs.com/research/machine/ml_website/software.php?project=milde.
22. Woodsend, K., and Gondzio, J. "Hybrid MPI/OpenMPI Parallel Support Vector Maschine Training." *Journal of Machine Learning Research* 10 (2009): 1937.
23. UCI Machine Learning Repository, University of California, School of Information and Computer Science, accessed May 2009, http://www.ics.uci.edu/~mlearn/MLRepository.html.
24. SVMLink from John Platt's web page, accessed August 2010, http://research.microsoft.com/enus/projects/svm/default.aspx.
25. Webb-Robertson, B-J. Oehmen, C., and Shah, A. "A Feature Vector Integration Approach for a Generalized Support Vector Machine Pairwise Homology Algorithm." *Computational Biology and Chemistry* 32, no. 6 (2008): 458–61.

8

Beyond MapReduce: New Requirements for Scalable Data Processing

Bill Howe and Magdalena Balazinska

8.1 Introduction and Background

The MapReduce programming model has had a transformative impact on data-intensive computing, enabling a single programmer to harness hundreds or thousands of computers for a single task and get up and running in a matter of hours. Processing with thousands of computers require a different set of design considerations dominate: I/O scalability, fault tolerance, and flexibility rather than absolute performance. MapReduce, and the open-source implementation Hadoop, are optimized for these considerations and have become very successful as a result.

It is difficult to quantify the popularity of the MapReduce framework directly, but one indication of the uptake is the frequency of the search term. Figure 8.1 illustrates the search popularity for terms "mapreduce" and "hadoop" over the period 2006 to 2012.[1] We see a spike in popularity for the term "mapreduce" in late 2007, but more or less constant popularity since. For the term "hadoop," however, we see a steady increase to about twelve times that of "mapreduce."

These data suggest that MapReduce and Hadoop are generating interest, as seen from the number of downloads, successful startups [12, 19, 47], projects [41, 53, 57], and interest from the research community [15, 18, 62, 63, 72, 78]. These data suggest a significant increase in interest in both MapReduce and Hadoop.

The MapReduce framework provides a simple programming model for expressing loosely coupled parallel programs by providing two serial functions, *Map* and *Reduce*. The Map function processes a block of input producing a sequence of (key, value) pairs, while the Reduce function processes a set of values associated with a single key. The framework itself is responsible for "shuffling" the output of the Map tasks to the appropriate Reduce task using

---

[1] Source: Google Trends.

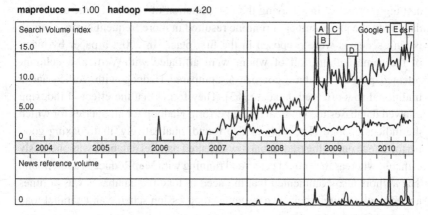

Figure 8.1. Search popularity for the terms "mapreduce" and "hadoop" from 2006 to 2012. (*Source:* Google Trends.)

a distributed sort. The model is sufficiently expressive to capture a variety of algorithms and high-level programming models while allowing programmers to largely ignore the challenges of distributed computing and focus instead on the semantics of their task. Examples include machine learning [53], relational query processing [45, 58, 63, 72], web data processing [21], and spatio-temporal indexing [9]. Hadoop and the MapReduce model have been shown to scale to hundreds or thousands of nodes as early as 2009 [63]. MapReduce clusters can be constructed inexpensively from commodity computers connected in a shared-nothing configuration (that is, neither memory nor storage are shared across nodes).

Although the discussion of MapReduce frequently turns to performance and scalability, it is important to realize that the original motivation was to simplify parallel processing on large-scale clusters, calling to mind the title of the original 2004 MapReduce paper by Dean et al. [21].

The popularity of MapReduce indicates that it filled a real gap in the IT landscape, but it is reasonable to ask why this gap existed. In particular, parallel databases (such as Teradata [71]) purport to offer scalable data manipulation capabilities, but MapReduce and its implementation in Hadoop, offers essentially none of the hallmark features of databases: schemas, indexing, a query language, a formal data model, or transactions. Are these features unnecessary for those applications well-served by Hadoop and MapReduce?

This question was explored by database leaders Mike Ston[e]braker, David DeWitt, and several colleagues in a 2008 blog post titled, "MapReduce: A Major Step Backwards" [27]. The authors derided the lack of support for schemas, arguing (correctly) that leaving the interpretation of type and structure of the data up to the programmer at runtime resulted in more frequent errors – which is why schemas were proposed in the first place. In 2009, a paper by many of the same authors (all of whom were affiliated with Vertica, a column-oriented parallel database company), compared Hadoop with Vertica and a traditional row-oriented database [63]. They found that the effect of indexing allowed databases to significantly outperform Hadoop for all queries for which the indices applied. The authors also found, qualitatively, that coaxing good performance out of the traditional row-oriented parallel database was onerously difficult, whereas they could get up and running with MapReduce in a few hours. The authors also commented that the need to load the databases was at times a roadblock (though their own systems compression scheme and parallel load features ultimately won out).

Given this evidence, one might conclude that the point in the design space claimed by parallel databases was simply different than that claimed by MapReduce, and that they target different applications entirely. In fact, these same authors have clarified their position in a Communications of the ACM article in 2010 [69], concluding that parallel databases and MapReduce are complementary, primarily because parallel databases are not designed for the extract-transform-load tasks at which MapReduce excels.

But this resolution of the question does not explain the trend seen in the ecosystem of technologies that extend MapReduce with new features. Many, if not all, of these features are those found in mature database products. Yahoo's Pig system can superimpose schema information on datasets in HDFS, the file system used by Hadoop. The Apache Hbase project provides indexing. The HIVE system from Facebook, now an Apache project, can compile SQL statements into a sequence of MapReduce jobs. HadoopDB, a research project at Yale, integrates a database system on each node with Hadoop to control the parallel query execution. Microsoft Dryad, DryadLINQ, and more recently SCOPE – which are not MapReduce-based systems but provide a similar parallel dataflow programming framework – use algebraic optimization of relational algebra expressions, just like databases (as do Pig and HIVE to some extent). So the trend observed is that MapReduce "rebooted" the database architecture, throwing out all features except parallel processing. But over time, classical database features are creeping back in. One might imagine that MapReduce would not have been quite so successful if a good open-source parallel database existed as an alternative.

Acknowledging that the pendulum is swinging back toward a database-style feature set, what new features and new requirements are emerging that will take MapReduce and other parallel dataflow systems beyond the capabilities of databases? This chapter explores three such features and reports on some progress to date implementing them. Specifically, it considers how Hadoop can be modified to support efficient recursive algorithms and to tolerate skew (or "straggler" tasks) in the context of scientific computing. The chapter ends with a discussion of future trends toward more interactive, cross-scale analysis as opposed to the "brute force" batch-oriented approach of MapReduce.

8.2 HaLoop: Iterative Processing on Large Clusters

MapReduce [22] has become popular for programming commodity computer clusters to perform large-scale data processing in a single pass, but many data analysis techniques require *iterative* computations, including PageRank [60], HITS (Hypertext-Induced Topic Search) [48], recursive relational queries [6], clustering, neural-network analysis, social network analysis, and network traffic analysis. These techniques have a common trait: Data are processed iteratively until the computation satisfies a termination condition. The MapReduce framework does not directly support these iterative data analysis applications. Instead, programmers typically implement iterative programs by manually issuing multiple MapReduce jobs and orchestrating their execution using a driver program [53].

There are two key problems with manually orchestrating an iterative program in MapReduce. The first is that even though much of the data may be unchanged from iteration to iteration, the data must be reloaded and reprocessed at each iteration, wasting I/O, network bandwidth, and CPU resources. The second problem is that the termination condition may involve detecting when a *fixpoint* has been reached; that is, when the application's output does not change for two consecutive iterations. This condition may itself require an *extra* MapReduce job on each iteration, again incurring overhead in terms of scheduling extra tasks, reading extra data from disk, and moving data across the network. To illustrate these problems, consider the following two examples.

Example 8.1 PageRank: PageRank is a link analysis algorithm that assigns weights (ranks) to each vertex in a graph by iteratively computing the weight of each vertex based on the weight of its inbound neighbors. In the relational algebra, the PageRank algorithm can be expressed as a join followed by an update with two aggregations. These steps must be repeated by a driver program until a termination condition is satisfied (such as the rank of each page converges or a specified number of iterations has been performed).

url	rank
www.a.com	1.0
www.b.com	1.0
www.c.com	1.0
www.d.com	1.0
www.e.com	1.0

url_source	url_dest
www.a.com	www.b.com
www.a.com	www.c.com
www.c.com	www.a.com
www.e.com	www.d.com
www.d.com	www.b.com
www.c.com	www.e.com
www.e.com	www.c.com
www.a.com	www.d.com

(a) Initial Rank Table R_0 (b) Linkage Table L

$$MR_1 \begin{cases} T_1 = R_i \bowtie_{\|url\|=\|url\_source\|} L \\ T_2 = \gamma_{\|url\|,\|rank\|,\frac{\|rank\|}{\text{COUNT}(\|url\_dest\|)} \to \|new\_rank\|}(T_1) \\ T_3 = T_2 \bowtie_{\|url\|=\|url\_source\|} L \end{cases}$$

$$MR_2 \begin{cases} R_{i+1} = \gamma_{\|url\_dest\| \to \|url\|, \text{SUM}(\|new\_rank\|) \to \|rank\|}(T_3) \end{cases}$$

url	rank
www.a.com	2.13
www.b.com	3.89
www.c.com	2.60
www.d.com	2.60
www.e.com	2.13

(c) Loop Body   (d) Rank Table R_3

Figure 8.2. An illustration of PageRank expressed in relational algebra. The input is an initial set of urls with default rank (a) and a set of links between urls (b). On each iteration, the rank table from the previous iteration is joined with the link table, and the contributions from each incoming link are aggregated to compute a new rank. The process finishes after a fixed number of iterations, or until the ranks do not change significantly.

Figure 8.2 shows a concrete example. R_0 (Figure 8.2a) is the initial rank table, and L (Figure 8.2b) is the linkage table. Two MapReduce jobs (MR_1 and MR_2 in Figure 8.2c) are required to implement the loop body of PageRank. The first MapReduce job joins the rank and linkage tables. Mappers emit records from the two relations with the join column as the key and the remaining columns as the value. Reducers compute the join for each unique source URL as well as the rank contribution for each outbound edge (new_rank). The second MapReduce job computes the aggregate rank of each unique destination URL: the map function is the identity function and the reducers sum the rank contributions of each incoming edge. In each iteration, R_i is updated to R_{i+1}. For example, one could obtain R_3 (Figure 8.2d) by iteratively computing R_1, R_2, R_3.

In the PageRank algorithm, the linkage table L is invariant across iterations. Because the MapReduce framework is unaware of this property, however, L is processed and shuffled at each iteration. Worse, the invariant linkage data may frequently be larger than the resulting rank table. Finally, determining whether the ranks have converged requires an extra MapReduce job on each iteration.

Example 8.2 Descendant Query: Given the social network relation in Figure 8.3a, who is within two friend-hops from Eric? To answer this query, we can first find Eric's direct friends, and then all the friends of these friends. A related

name1	name2
Tom	Bob
Tom	Alice
Elisa	Tom
Elisa	Harry
Sherry	Todd
Eric	Elisa
Todd	John
Robin	Edward

$$MR_1 \left\{ \; T_1 = \Delta S_i \bowtie_{\Delta S_i.\text{name2}=F.\text{name1}} F \quad T_2 = \pi_{\Delta S_i.\text{name1},F.\text{name2}}(T_1) \right.$$

$$MR_2 \left\{ \; T_3 = \bigcup_{0 \le j \le (i-1)} \Delta S_j \quad \Delta S_{i+1} = \delta(T_2 - T_3) \right.$$

(a) Friend Table F (b) Loop Body

Eric(ΔS_0)
|
Elisa(ΔS_1)

Tom(ΔS_2)   Harry(ΔS_2)

name1	name2
Eric	Elisa
Eric	Tom
Eric	Harry

(c) Result Generating Trace   (d) Result Table ΔS

Figure 8.3. A query to compute the descdendants in a social network. (a) The input is a binary friend relation. (b) The loop body computes the next generation of friends, removes duplicates, and appends the new records to the result. (c) A graphical illustration of the computation. (d) The final result of the computation in this example.

query is to find all people who can be reached from Eric following the friend relation F. These queries can be implemented by a driver program that executes two MapReduce jobs (MR_1 and MR_2 in Figure 8.3b), either for two iterations or until a fixpoint has been reached, respectively. The first MapReduce job finds a new generation of friends by joining the friend table F with the friends discovered in the previous iteration, ΔS_i. The second MapReduce job removes duplicate tuples from ΔS_i that also appear in ΔS_j for $j < i$. The final result is the union of results from each iteration.

Let ΔS_i be the result of the join after iteration i, computed by joining ΔS_{i-1} with F and removing duplicates. $\Delta S_0 = \{$Eric, Eric$\}$ is the trivial friend relationship that initiates the computation. Figure 8.3c shows how results evolve from ΔS_0 to ΔS_2. Finally, $\Delta S = \bigcup_{0 < i \le 2} \Delta S_i$ is returned as the final result, as in Figure 8.3d.

As in the PageRank example, a significant fraction of the data (the friend table F) remains constant throughout the execution of the query, yet still gets processed and shuffled at each iteration.

Many other data analysis applications have characteristics similar to the preceding two examples: A significant fraction of the processed data remains invariant across iterations, and the analysis should typically continue until a fixpoint is reached. Examples include most iterative model-fitting algorithms (such as k-means clustering and neural network analysis), most web/graph ranking algorithms (such as HITS [48]), and recursive graph or network queries.

This section presents a new system called *HaLoop* that is designed to efficiently handle the preceding types of applications. HaLoop extends MapReduce and is based on two simple intuitions. First, a MapReduce cluster can cache the invariant data in the first iteration and then reuse them in later iterations. Second, a MapReduce cluster can cache reducer outputs, which makes checking for a fixpoint more efficient, without an extra MapReduce job.

HaLoop includes the following contributions:

- **New programming model and architecture for iterative programs:** HaLoop handles loop control that would otherwise have to be manually programmed. It offers a programming interface to express iterative data-analysis applications.
- **Caching for loop-invariant data:** HaLoop caches and indexes data that are invariant across iterations in cluster nodes during the first iteration of an application. Caching the invariant data reduces the I/O cost for loading and shuffling them in subsequent iterations.
- **Caching to support fixpoint evaluation:** HaLoop caches and indexes a reducer's local output. This avoids the need for a dedicated MapReduce step for fixpoint or convergence checking.
- **Experimental study:** We evaluated our system on iterative programs that process both synthetic and real-world datasets. HaLoop outperforms Hadoop in all metrics; on average, HaLoop reduces query runtimes by 1.85, and shuffles only 4 percent of the data between mappers and reducers.

8.2.1 HaLoop Overview

Figure 8.4 illustrates the architecture of HaLoop, a modified version of the open source MapReduce implementation Hadoop [37].

HaLoop inherits the basic distributed computing model and architecture of Hadoop. HaLoop relies on a distributed file system (HDFS [39]) that stores each job's input and output data. The system is divided into two parts: one master node and many slave nodes. A client submits jobs to the master node. For each submitted job, the master node schedules a number of parallel tasks to run on slave nodes. Every slave node has a task tracker daemon process to communicate with the master node and manage each task's execution. Each task is either a map task (which usually performs transformations on an input data partition, and calls a user-defined map function with one (key, value) pair each time) or a reduce task (which usually copies the corresponding partition

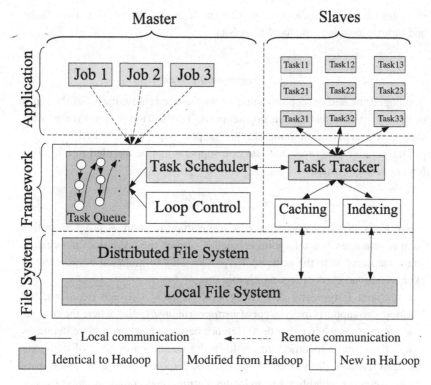

Figure 8.4. The HaLoop framework, a variant of Hadoop MapReduce framework.

of mapper output, groups the input keys, and invokes a user-defined reduce function with one key and its associated values each time). For example, in Figure 8.4, there are three jobs running in the system: Job 1, Job 2, and Job 3. Each job has three tasks running concurrently on slave nodes.

In order to accommodate the requirements of iterative data analysis applications, several changes are made to the basic Hadoop MapReduce framework. First, HaLoop exposes a new application programming interface to users that simplifies the expression of iterative MapReduce programs. Second, HaLoop's master node contains a new loop control module that repeatedly starts new MapReduce steps that compose the loop body, until a user-specified stopping condition is met. Third, HaLoop caches and indexes application data on slave nodes. As shown in Figure 8.4, HaLoop relies on the same file system and has the same task queue structure as Hadoop, but the task scheduler and task tracker modules are modified, and the loop control, caching, and indexing modules are new. The task tracker not only manages task execution, but also manages caches and indices on the slave node, and redirects each task's cache and index accesses to the local file system.

8.2.2 Programming Model

The PageRank and descendant query examples are representative of the types of iterative programs that HaLoop supports. This section presents the general form of the recursive programs that are supported and a detailed API.

The iterative programs that HaLoop supports can be distilled into the following core construct:

$$R_{i+1} = R_0 \cup (R_i \bowtie L)$$

where R_0 is an initial result and L is an invariant relation. A program in this form terminates when a fixpoint is reached – when the result does not change from one iteration to the next, i.e. $R_{i+1} = R_i$. This formulation is sufficient to express a broad class of recursive programs.

A fixpoint is typically defined by exact equality between iterations, but HaLoop also supports the concept of an *approximate fixpoint*, where the computation terminates when either the difference between two consecutive iterations is less than a user-specified threshold or the maximum number of iterations has been reached. Both kinds of approximate fixpoints are useful for expressing convergence conditions in machine learning and complex analytics. For example, for PageRank, it is common to either use a user-specified convergence threshold ε [60] or a fixed number of iterations as the loop termination condition.

Although the recursive formulation describes the class of iterative programs intend to support, this work does not develop a high-level declarative language for expressing recursive queries. Rather, the focus is on providing an efficient foundation API for iterative MapReduce programs; a variety of high-level languages (such as Datalog) are likely to be implementable on this foundation.

To write a HaLoop program, a programmer specifies the loop body (as one or more mapreduce pairs) and optionally specifies a termination condition and loop-invariant data. Now consider HaLoop's API. Map and Reduce are similar to standard MapReduce and are required; the rest of the API is new and is optional.

To specify the loop body, the programmer constructs a multistep MapReduce job, using the following functions:

- Map transforms an input ⟨key, value⟩ tuple into intermediate ⟨in_key, in_value⟩ tuples.

- Reduce processes intermediate tuples sharing the same in_key, to produce ⟨out_key, out_value⟩ tuples. The interface contains a new parameter for cached invariant values associated with the in_key.
- AddMap and AddReduce express a loop body that consists of more than one MapReduce step. AddMap (AddReduce) associates a Map (Reduce) function with an integer indicating the order of the step.

HaLoop defaults to testing for equality from one iteration to the next to determine when to terminate the computation. To specify an approximate fixpoint termination condition, the programmer uses the following functions.

- SetFixedPointThreshold sets a bound on the distance between one iteration and the next. If the threshold is exceeded, then the approximate fixpoint has not yet been reached, and the computation continues.
- The ResultDistance function calculates the distance between two out_value sets sharing the same out_key. One out_value set v_i is from the reducer output of the current iteration and the other out_value set V_{i-1} is from the previous iteration's reducer output. The distance between the reducer outputs of the current iteration i and the last iteration $i - 1$ is the sum of ResultDistance on every key. (It is straightforward to support additional aggregations besides sum.)
- SetMaxNumOfIterations provides further control of the loop termination condition. HaLoop terminates a job if the maximum number of iterations has been executed, regardless of the distance between the current and previous iteration's outputs. SetMaxNumOfIterations can also be used to implement a simple for−loop.

To specify and control inputs, the programmer uses:

- SetIterationInput associates an input source with a specific iteration because the input files to different iterations may be different. For example, in Example 8.1, at each iteration $i + 1$, the input is $R_i \cup L$.
- AddStepInput associates an additional input source with an intermediate mapreduce pair in the loop body. The output of preceding mapreduce pair is always in the input of the next mapreduce pair.
- AddInvariantTable specifies an input table (an HDFS file) that is loop-invariant. During job execution, HaLoop will cache this table on cluster nodes.

Figure 8.5 shows the difference between HaLoop and Hadoop, from the application's perspective: in HaLoop, a user program specifies loop settings and

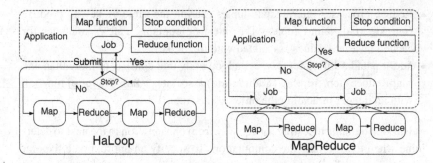

Figure 8.5. Boundary between an iterative application and the framework (HaLoop versus Hadoop). HaLoop knows and controls the loop, while Hadoop only knows jobs with one mapreduce pair.

the framework controls the loop execution, but in Hadoop, it is the application's responsibility to control the loops.

8.2.3 Caching and Indexing

Thanks to the inter-iteration locality offered by the task scheduler, access to a particular loop-invariant data partition is usually only needed by one physical node. To reduce I/O cost, HaLoop caches those data partitions on the physical node's local disk for subsequent reuse. To further accelerate processing, it indexes the cached data. If a cache becomes unavailable, it is automatically reloaded, either from map task physical nodes or from HDFS. HaLoop maintains three types of caches: reducer input cache, reducer output cache, and mapper input cache. Each of them fits a number of application scenarios. Application programmers can choose to enable or disable a cache type using the HaLoop API.

8.2.4 Reducer Input Cache

If an intermediate table is specified to be loop-invariant (via the HaLoop API AddInvariantTable) and the reducer input cache is enabled, HaLoop will cache reducer inputs across all reducers and create a local index for the cached data. Note that reducer inputs are cached before each reduce function invocation, so that tuples in the reducer input cache are sorted and grouped by reducer input key.

Let us consider the social network example (Example 8.3) to see how the reducer input cache works. Three physical nodes n_1, n_2, and n_3 are involved in the job, and the number of reducers is set to 2. In the join step of the first iteration, there are three mappers: one processes F-split0, one processes

name1	name2
Tom	Bob
Tom	Alice
Elisa	Tom
Elisa	Harry

(a) F-split0

name1	name2
Sherry	Todd
Eric	Elisa
Todd	John
Robin	Edward

(b) F-split1

name1	name2
Eric	Eric

(c) ΔS_0-split0

Figure 8.6. Mapper input splits in example 1.3.

F-split1, and one processes ΔS_0-split0. The three splits are shown in Figure 8.6. The two reducer input partitions are shown in Figure 8.7. The reducer on n_1 corresponds to hash value 0, whereas the reducer on n_2 corresponds to hash value 1. Then, because table F (with table ID "#1") is set to be invariant by the programmer using the AddInvariantTable function, every reducer will cache the tuples with table ID "#1" in its local file system.

In later iterations, when a reducer passes a shuffled key with associated values to the user-defined Reduce function, it also searches for the key in the local reducer input cache to find associated values and passes them together to the Reduce function (note that HaLoop's modified Reduce interface accepts this parameter). Also, if the reducer input cache is enabled, mapper outputs in the first iteration are cached in the corresponding mapper's local disk, for future reducer cache reloading.

In the physical layout of the cache, keys and values are separated into two files, and each key has an associated pointer to its corresponding values. Sometimes the selectivity in the cached loop-invariant data is low. Thus, after reducer input data are cached to local disk, HaLoop creates an index over the keys and stores it in the local file system too. Because the reducer input cache is sorted and then accessed by reducer input key in the same sorted order, the disk seek operations are only conducted in a forward manner, and in the worst case, in each iteration, the input cache is sequentially scanned from the local disk only once.

The reducer input cache is suitable for PageRank, HITS, various recursive relational queries, and any other algorithm with repeated joins against large invariant data. The reducer input cache requires that the partition function f

name1	name2	table ID
Elisa	Tom	#1
Elisa	Harry	#1
Robin	Edward	#1
Tom	Bob	#1
Tom	Alice	#1

(a) partition 0

name1	name2	table ID
Eric	Elisa	#1
Eric	Eric	#2
Sherry	Todd	#1
Todd	John	#1

(b) partition 1

Figure 8.7. Reducer input partitions in example 1.3.

for every mapper output tuple t satisfies that: (1) f must be deterministic, (2) f must remain the same across iterations, and (3) f must not take any inputs other than the tuple t. In HaLoop, the number of reduce tasks is unchanged across iterations, therefore the default hash partitioning satisfies these conditions.

8.2.5 Reducer Output Cache

The reducer output cache stores and indexes the most recent local output on each reducer node. This cache is used to reduce the cost of evaluating fixpoint termination conditions. That is, if the application must test the convergence condition by comparing the current iteration output with the previous iteration output, the reducer output cache enables the framework to perform the comparison in a distributed fashion.

The reducer output cache is used in applications where fixpoint evaluation should be conducted after each iteration. For example, in PageRank, a user may set a convergence condition specifying that the total rank difference from one iteration to the next is below a given threshold. With the reducer output cache, the fixpoint can be evaluated in a distributed manner without requiring a separate MapReduce step. After all Reduce function invocations are done, each reducer evaluates the fixpoint condition within the reduce process and reports local evaluation results to the master node, which computes the final answer.

The reducer output cache requires that in the last map-reduce pair of the loop body, the mapper output partition function f and the reduce function satisfy the following conditions: if $(k_{o1}, v_{o1}) \in$ reduce(k_i, V_i), $(k_{o2}, v_{o2}) \in$ reduce(k_j, V_j), and $k_{o1} = k_{o2}$, then $f(k_i) = f(k_j)$. That is, if two Reduce function calls produce the same output key from two different reducer input keys, both reducer input keys must be in the same partition so that they are sent to the same reduce task. Further, f should also meet the requirements of the reducer input cache. Satisfying these requirements guarantees that reducer output tuples in different iterations but with the same output key are produced on the same physical node, which ensures the usefulness of reducer output cache and the correctness of the local fixpoint evaluation. Our PageRank, descendant query, and k-means clustering implementations on HaLoop all satisfy these conditions.

8.2.6 Mapper Input Cache

Hadoop [37] attempts to co-locate map tasks with their input data. On a real-world Hadoop cluster [13], the rate of data-local mappers is around 70 percent to 95 percent, depending on the runtime environment. HaLoop's mapper input

cache aims to avoid non-local data reads in mappers during non-initial iterations. In the first iteration, if a mapper performs a non-local read on an input
split, the split will be cached in the local disk of the mapper's physical node.
Then, with loop-aware task scheduling, in later iterations, all mappers read
data only from local disks, either from HDFS or from the local file system.
The mapper input cache can be used by model-fitting applications such as
k-means clustering, neural network analysis, and any other iterative algorithm
consuming mapper inputs that do not change across iterations.

8.2.7 Cache Reloading

There are a few cases where the cache must be reconstructed: (1) the hosting
node fails, or (2) the hosting node has a full load and a map or reduce task
must be scheduled on a different substitution node. A reducer reconstructs the
reducer input cache by copying the desired partition from all first-iteration
mapper outputs. To reload the mapper input cache or the reducer output cache,
the mapper/reducer only needs to read the corresponding chunks from the
distributed file system, where replicas of the cached data are stored. Cache
reloading is completely transparent to user programs.

8.2.8 Experimental Evaluation

Previous sections compared the performance of iterative data analysis applications on HaLoop and Hadoop. Because the use of the reducer input cache, the
reducer output cache, and the mapper input cache are all independent options,
each were evaluated separately.

8.2.9 Evaluation of Reducer Input Cache

This suite of experiments used virtual machine clusters of 50 and 90 slave nodes
in Amazon's Elastic Compute Cloud (EC2). There is always one master node.
The applications were PageRank and descendant query. Both are implemented
in both HaLoop (using the new programming model) and Hadoop (using the
traditional driver approach).

The experiment involves both semi-synthetic and real-world datasets:
Livejournal[2] (18GB, social network data), Triples[3] (120GB, semantic web
data), and Freebase[4] (12GB, concept linkage graph). The Reducer Input

---

[2] http://snap.stanford.edu/data/index.html.
[3] http://challenge.semanticweb.org/.
[4] http://www.freebase.com/.

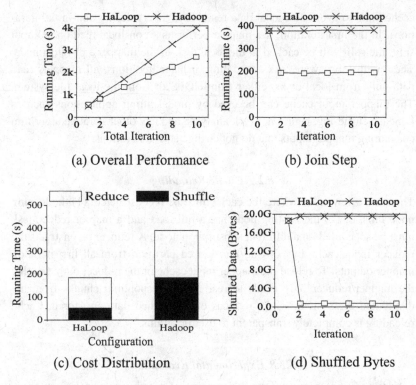

Figure 8.8. PageRank performance: HaLoop versus Hadoop (Livejournal Dataset, 50 nodes).

Cache experiments were performed on Amazon AWS using the default small instances.[5]

The PageRank query was executed on the Livejournal and Freebase datasets and the descendant query on the Livejournal and Triples datasets. Figures 8.8–8.11 show the results for Hadoop and HaLoop. The number of reduce tasks is set to the number of slave nodes. The performance with fail-overs has not been quantified; all experimental results are obtained without any node failures.

Overall, as the figures show, for a ten-iteration job, HaLoop lowers the runtime by 1.85 on average when the reducer input cache is used. As discussed later, the reducer output cache creates an additional gap between Hadoop and HaLoop but the impact is less significant on overall runtime. The following presents these results in more detail.

---

[5] http://aws.amazon.com/ec2/instance-types/.

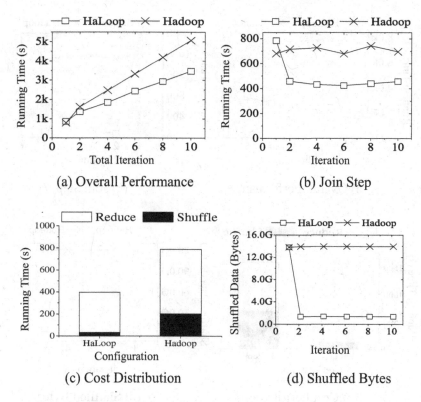

Figure 8.9. PageRank Performance: HaLoop versus Hadoop (Freebase Dataset, 90 nodes).

Overall runtime: In this experiment, SetMaxNumOfIterations, rather than fixedPointThreshold and ResultDistance, was used to specify the loop termination condition. The results are plotted in Figure 8.8a, Figure 8.9a, Figure 8.10a, and Figure 8.11a.

In the PageRank algorithm, there are two steps in every iteration: join and aggregation. The running time in Figure 8.8a and Figure 8.9a is the sum of join time and aggregation time over all iterations. In the descendant query algorithm, there are also two steps per iteration: join and duplicate elimination. The running time in Figure 8.10a and Figure 8.11a is the sum of join time and "duplicate elimination" time overall iterations.

HaLoop always performs better than Hadoop. The descendant query on the Triples dataset has the best improvement, PageRank on Livejournal and Freebase have intermediate gains, but the descendant query on the Livejournal dataset has the least improvement. Livejournal is a social network dataset with

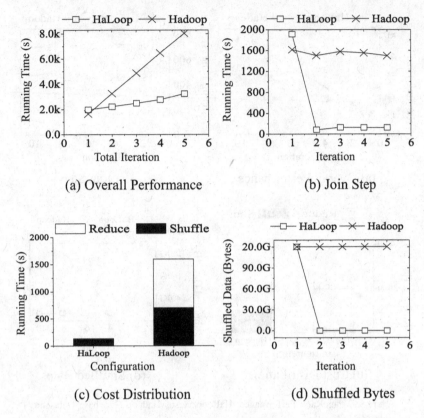

Figure 8.10. Descendant query performance: HaLoop versus Hadoop (Triples Dataset, 90 nodes).

high fan-out and reachability. As a result, the descendant query in later iterations (>3) produces so many duplicates that duplicate elimination dominates the cost, and HaLoop's caching mechanism does not significantly reduce overall runtime. In contrast, the Triples dataset is less connected, thus the join step is the dominant cost and the cache is crucial.

Join step runtime: HaLoop's task scheduling and reducer input cache potentially reduce join step time, but do not reduce the cost of the "duplicate elimination" step for the descendant query, nor the final aggregation step in PageRank. Thus, to partially explain why overall job running time is shorter with HaLooop, consider the performance of the join step across iterations. Figure 8.8b, Figure 8.9b, Figure 8.10b, and Figure 8.11b plot join time in each iteration. HaLoop significantly outperforms Hadoop.

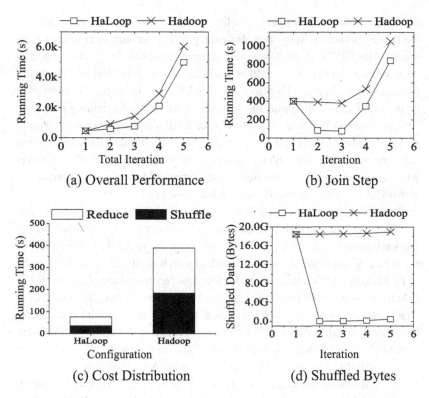

Figure 8.11. Descendant query performance: HaLoop versus Hadoop (Livejournal Dataset, 50 nodes).

In the first iteration, HaLoop is slower than Hadoop, as shown in (a) and (b) of all four figures. The reason is that HaLoop performs additional work in the first iteration: HaLoop caches the sorted and grouped data on each reducer's local disks, creates an index for the cached data, and stores the index to disk. That is, in the first iteration, HaLoop does the exact same thing as Hadoop, but also writes caches to local disk.

Cost distribution for the join step: To better understand HaLoop's improvements to each phase, consider the cost distribution of the join step across Map and Reduce phases. Figure 8.8c, Figure 8.9c, Figure 8.10c, and Figure 8.11c show the cost distribution of the join step in a certain iteration (here it is iteration 3). The measurement is time spent on each phase. In both HaLoop and Hadoop, reducers start to copy data immediately after the first mapper completes. "Shuffle time" is normally the time between reducers starting to copy map output data and reducers starting to sort copied data; shuffling is concurrent with the rest of the unfinished mappers. The first completed mapper's running time in the two algorithms is very short, for example, 1–5 seconds to read data from one 64 MB HDFS block. If the first mapper's running time were plotted as "map phase," the duration would be too brief to be visible compared to shuffle phase and reduce phase. Therefore, the "shuffle time" in the plots is allowed to be the usual shuffle time plus the first completed mapper's running time. The "reduce time" in the plots is the total time a reducer spends after the shuffle phase, including sorting and grouping as well as accumulated Reduce function call time. Note that in the plots, "shuffle time" plus "reduce time" constitutes what is reffered to as the "join step." Considering all four plots, the conclusion is that HaLoop outperforms Hadoop in both phases.

The "reduce" bar is not visible in Figure 8.10c, although it is present. The "reduce time" is not 0, but rather very short compared to "shuffle" bar. It takes advantage of the index HaLoop creates for the cache data. Then the join between ΔS_i and F will use an index seek to search qualified tuples in the cache of F. Also, in each iteration, there are few new records produced, so the join's selectivity on F is very low. Thus, the cost becomes negligible. By contrast, for PageRank, the index does not help much, because the selectivity is high. For the descendants query on Livejournal (Figure 8.11), in iteration > 3, the index does not help either, because the selectivity becomes high.

I/O in shuffle phase of join step: To tell how much shuffling I/O is saved, the amount of shuffled data in to the join step of each iteration was compared. Because HaLoop caches loop-invariant data, the overhead of shuffling these invariant data are completely avoided. These savings contribute an important part of the overall performance improvement. Figure 8.8d, Figure 8.9d, Figure 8.10d, and Figure 8.11d plot the sizes of shuffled data. On average, HaLoop's join step shuffles 4 percent as much data as Hadoop's does.

8.2.10 Evaluation of Reducer Output Cache

This experiment shares the same hardware and dataset as the reducer input cache experiments. To see how effective HaLoop's reducer output cache is, the cost of fix-point evaluation was compared across iterations. Because the descendant query has a trivial fixpoint evaluation step that only requires testing to see if a file is empty, evaluate PageRank on the Livejournal and Freebase datasets. In the Hadoop implementation, the fixpoint evaluation is implemented by an extra MapReduce job. On average, compared with Hadoop, HaLoop reduces the cost of this step to 40 percent, by taking advantage of the reducer output cache and a built-in distributed fixpoint evaluation. Figure 8.12a and b shows the time spent on fixpoint evaluation in each iteration.

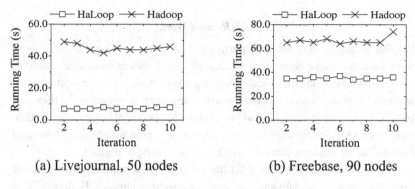

(a) Livejournal, 50 nodes   (b) Freebase, 90 nodes

Figure 8.12. Fixpoint evaluation overhead in pagerank: HaLoop versus Hadoop.

8.2.11 Evaluation of Mapper Input Cache

Because the mapper input cache aims to reduce data transportation between slave nodes but we do not know the disk I/O implementations of EC2 virtual machines, this suite of experiments uses an 8-node physical machine cluster. PageRank and descendant query cannot utilize the mapper input cache because their inputs change from iteration to iteration. Thus, the application used in the evaluation is the k-means clustering algorithm. We used two real-world Astronomy datasets (multi-dimensional tuples): cosmo-dark (46 GB) and cosmo-gas (54 GB). All nodes in these experiments contain a 2.60 GHz dual quad-core Intel Xeon CPU with 16 GB of RAM. We vary the number of total iterations, and plot the algorithm running time in Figure 8.13. The mapper locality rate is around 95 percent since there are not concurrent jobs in our lab HaLoop cluster. By avoiding nonlocal data loading, HaLoop performs marginally better than Hadoop.

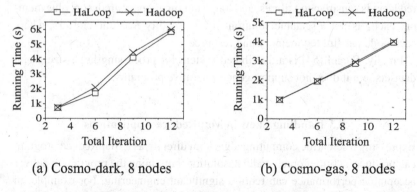

(a) Cosmo-dark, 8 nodes   (b) Cosmo-gas, 8 nodes

Figure 8.13. Performance of k- means: HaLoop versus Hadoop.

8.2.12 Related Work

Parallel database systems [28] partition data storage and parallelize query workloads to achieve better performance. However, they are sensitive to failures and have not been shown to scale to thousands of nodes. Various optimization techniques for evaluating recursive queries have been proposed in the literature [6, 81]. The existing work has not been shown to operate at large scale. Further, most of these techniques are orthogonal to our research; we provide a low-level foundation for implementing data-intensive iterative programs.

More recently, MapReduce [22] has emerged as a popular alternative for massivescale parallel data analysis in shared-nothing clusters. Hadoop [37] is an open-source implementation of MapReduce. MapReduce has been followed by a series of related systems, including Dryad [46], Hive [41], Pig [57], and HadoopDB [2]. Like Hadoop, none of these systems provides explicit support and optimizations for iterative or recursive types of analysis.

Mahout [53] is a project whose goal is to build a set of scalable machine learning libraries on top of Hadoop. Because most machine learning algorithms are model fitting applications, nearly all of them involve iterative programs. Mahout uses an outside driver program to control the loops, and new Map-Reduce jobs are launched in each iteration. The drawback of this approach was previously discussed. Like Mahout, we are trying to help iterative data analysis algorithms work on scalable architectures, but we are different in that we are modifying the fundamental system: we inject the iterative capability into a MapReduce engine.

Twister [30] is a stream-based MapReduce framework that supports iterative programs, in which mappers and reducers are long running with distributed memory caches. They are established to avoid repeated mapper data loading from disks. However, Twister's streaming architecture between mappers and reducers is sensitive to failures, and long-running mappers/reducers plus memory cache is not a scalable solution for commodity machine clusters, where each node has limited memory and resources.

Finally, Pregel [54] is a distributed system for processing large-size graph datasets, but it does not support general iterative programs.

8.3 Handling Skew in MapReduce Applications

Expressing a scientific computing algorithm directly as a MapReduce program can produce a "brute force" scalable solution, but tuning the program to deliver acceptable performance can require significant engineering. For example, in prior work, we found that a naïve implementation of a data clustering algorithm on a real astronomy simulation dataset took twenty hours to complete on an 8-node Dryad [45] cluster. In contrast, an optimized version took only seventy minutes, but took multiple weeks to develop and debug by a team of domain and computer scientists [51].

A crucial problem in optimizing MapReduce programs is *skew* – imbalance in runtimes of different tasks that washes out parallel performance. There are a variety of sources of skew: imbalance in data assigned to each task, problems at the hardware layer that cause one node to run slower than others, algorithmic sensitivity to the input data distribution. Data load can often be balanced automatically, and the response to hardware problems is typically just to restart the task elsewhere. It is the third type of skew – algorithmic sensitivity to inputs – that we consider in this work.

Specifically, we explore a class of algorithms called *spatial feature extraction* algorithms that are common in scientific computing and particularly suscep- tible to skew effects. We describe a new generalization of MapReduce called SkewReduce that can automatically mitigate skew effects in many such cases.

We observe that these applications share a common structure that can be par- allelized using the following strategy: (1) Partition the multidimensional space and assign each node a contiguous region, (2) run a serial form of the analysis locally on each region, extracting locally found features and labeling the input data with these features if necessary, (3) efficiently merge the local results by considering only those features that cross region boundaries, relabeling the input data as necessary. Although this formulation is simple and sound, a naïve implementation on existing parallel data processing engines is dominated by skew effects and other performance problems.

The standard approach to handling skew in parallel systems is to assign an equal number of data values to each partition via hash partitioning or clever range partitioning. These strategies effectively handle *data skew*, which occurs when some nodes are assigned more data than others. *Computation skew*, more generally, results when some nodes take longer to process their input than other nodes and can occur even in the absence of data skew – the runtime of many scientific tasks depends on the data values themselves rather than simply the data size [43].

Existing parallel-processing engines offer little support for tolerating general computation skew, so scientific programmers are typically forced to develop ad hoc solutions. At realistic scales, these ad hoc solutions not only require inti- mate familiarity with the source data, but also expertise in distributed program- ming, scheduling, out-of-core processing, performance monitoring and tuning, fault-tolerance techniques, and distributed debugging. SkewReduce efficiently reduces computational skew and helps scientific programmers express their solutions in popular parallel processing engines such as MapReduce.

In addition to skew, two other sources of performance problems are the merge and data labeling steps. Because of large data volumes, it may not be efficient or even possible to execute the merge phase on a single node. Instead, feature reconciliation must be performed incrementally in a hierarchical fashion. Similarly, intermediate results must be *set aside* to disk during the merge phase, then relabeled in parallel after the merge phase is complete to obtain the final result. Although both these strategies can be implemented in existing systems, doing so is nontrivial. Additionally, the same type of translation is repeated independently for each new feature extracting application.

To use SkewReduce, the programmer defines three (non-parallel) data processing functions and two cost functions to guide optimization. Given these functions, the framework provides a parallel evaluation plan that is demonstrably efficient and – crucially – skew-tolerant. The plan is then executed in a Hadoop cluster. We show that this framework delivers significant improvement over the status quo. The improvement is attributable primarily to the reduction of skew effects, as well as the elimination of performance issues in the merge and labeling steps. Further, we argue that the cognitive load for users to provide the suite of control functions is significantly less than that required to develop an ad hoc parallel program. In particular, the user remains focused on their application domain: they specify their analysis algorithm and reason about its complexity, but do not concern themselves with distributed computing complications.

This work delivers the following contributions: a SkewReduce system for efficiently processing spatial feature extraction scientific user-defined functions. SkewReduce comprises (1) a simple API for users to express multi-dimensional feature extraction analysis tasks and (2) a static optimization engine designed to produce a *skew-resistant plan* for evaluating these tasks. SkewReduce is implemented using Hadoop [37]. (3) Experimental results demonstrating the efficacy of the framework on real data from two different science domains. The results show that SkewReduce can improve query runtime by a factor of up to eight compared with an unoptimized implementation.

8.3.1 Motivation

We begin by describing three motivating applications from different scientific domains. We then discuss the commonalities between these applications and the challenges that arise when trying to implement them on a MapReduce-type platform.

Cosmological simulations are used to study the structural evolution of the universe on distance scales ranging from a few million light-years to several billion light-years. In these simulations, the universe is modeled as a set of particles. These particles represent gas, dark matter, and stars, and interact with each other through gravity and fluid dynamics. Every few simulation timesteps, the simulator outputs a *snapshot* of the universe as a list of particles, each tagged with its identifier, location, velocity, and other properties. The data output by a simulation can thus be stored in a relation with the following schema:

$$\text{Particles}(id,\ time, x, y, z, v_x, v_y, v_z, \cdots)$$

State of the art simulations (such as Springel *et al.* 2005 [66]) use over 10 billion particles producing a data set size of over 200 GB per snapshot and are expected to significantly grow in size in the future.

Astronomers commonly used various sophisticated clustering algorithms [33, 49, 75] to recognize the formation of interesting structures such as galaxies. The clustering algorithm is typically executed on one snapshot at a time [51]. Given the size of individual snapshots, however, astronomers would like to run their clustering algorithms on a parallel data processing platform in a shared-nothing cluster.

A flow cytometer measures scattered and fluoresced light from a stream of particles, using data analysis to recognize specific microorganisms. Originally devised for medical applications, it has been adapted for use in environmental microbiology to determine the concentrations of microbial populations. Similar microorganisms exhibit similar intensities of scattered light, as in Figure 8.14.

In an ongoing project in the Armbrust Lab at the University of Washington [5], flow cytometers are being continuously deployed on ocean-going vessels to understand the ocean health. All data is reported to a central database for ad hoc analysis and takes the form of points in a six-dimensional space, where each point represents a particle or organism in the water and the dimensions are the measured properties.

As in the astrophysics application, scientists need to cluster the resulting 6-D data. As their instruments increase in sophistication, so does the data volume, calling for efficient analysis techniques that can run in a shared-nothing cluster.

As a final example, consider the problem of analyzing collections of 2-D images. In many scientific disciplines, scientists process such images to extract objects (or features) of interest: galaxies from telescope images, hurricanes

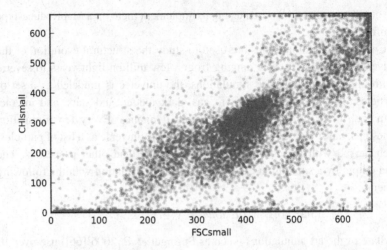

Figure 8.14. A scatter plot of flow cytometry measurements. Each point represents an organism and clusters represent populations. The axes correspond to different wavelengths of light.

from satellite pictures, and so on. As these images grow in size and number, parallel processing becomes necessary.

Each of these scientific applications follow a similar pattern: data items (events, particles, pixels) are embedded in a metric space, and the task is to identify and extract emergent features from the low-level data (populations and galaxies). These algorithms then typically return (a) a set of features (significantly smaller than the input data), (b) a modified input dataset with each element tagged with the corresponding feature (potentially as large as the input), or (c) both. For example, the output of the astronomy clustering task is a list of clusters with the total number of particles in each and a list of the original particles annotated with their cluster identifier.

Parallel implementation challenges: A straightforward way to parallelize such feature extraction applications in a compute-cluster with N nodes is the following: (1) split the input into N equal-sized hypercubes, (2) extract features in each partition and annotate the input with these initial features, (3) reconcile features that span partition boundary, relabeling the input as appropriate. With existing parallel processing systems, there are several challenges with expressing this seemingly simple algorithm in a manner that achieves high performance.

First, the data distribution in many scientific applications is highly skewed. Even worse, the processing time of many feature-extraction algorithms depends not only on the number of data points but also on their distribution in space.

For example, in a simple clustering algorithm used in astrophysics called "friends-of-friends" [20], clusters correspond to connected components of the graph induced by the "friend" relationship – two particles are friends if they are within a given distance threshold. To identify a cluster, the algorithm starts with a single point, then searches a spatial index to find its immediate friends. For each such friend, the algorithm repeats the search recursively. In a sparse region with N particles, the algorithm completes in $O(N \log N)$ time (such as, all particles are far apart). In a dense region, however, a single particle can be a friend of all the other particles and vice versa. Thus, the algorithm takes $O(N^2)$ time. In the two simulation snapshots that we received from astronomers [51], we found that the number of friends associated with a given particle varied between 2 and 387, 136. As a result, without additional optimizations, a dense region takes much longer to process than a sparse one even when both contain the same number of total particles [51]. The consequence is a type of computational skew, where some data partitions require dramatically more time than others to process. Computational skew is the reason that the naïve parallel implementation of the astronomy clustering application mentioned previously required over twenty hours, while an optimized one took only seventy minutes on the same dataset [51]. Our key motivation is that *existing platforms do nothing to reduce computational skew*. In our case, developing a skew-resistant algorithm (by optimizing index traversal to avoid quadratic behavior in the dense region) required significant effort from multiple experts over several weeks [51].

Second, the feature reconciliation phase (which we refer to as the "merge" phase) can be both CPU and memory intensive. For example, to reconcile clusters at the boundary of two data partitions requires processing all particles within a small distance of that boundary. If the space is initially carved into N partitions, it may not be efficient or even possible for a single node to reconcile the data across all these partition boundaries in one step. Instead, reconciliation should be performed in a hierarchical fashion, reconciling increasingly large regions of the space, while keeping the amount of data to process at each step approximately constant (that is, the memory requirement cannot increase as we move up the hierarchy). At the same time, while the local data processing and later merge steps proceed, the input data must be labeled and relabeled as necessary, for example, to track feature membership. Although it is possible to implement both functions using existing systems, expressing them using current APIs is non-trivial.

Problem statement summary: The goal of SkewReduce is to enable scientists to *easily express and efficiently execute* feature-extraction applications at very large scale without consideration of resource constraints and data or computation skew issues.

Table 8.1. *Summary of notation*

T	A record in the original input data file assigned to a region (such as, a particle in an astronomy simulation).
S	A record set aside during the process phase or merge phase (such as, a particle far away from a partition boundary tagged with a local cluster id).
F	An object representing a set of features extracted during the process phase for a given region. May not be relational. Includes enough information to allow reconciliation of features extracted in different partitions (such as, the clusters identified so far and the particles near a partition boundary).
Z	A record in the final result set (such as, a particle tagged with a global cluster id).

8.3.2 SkewReduce

SkewReduce has two components. The first component is an API for expressing spatial feature-extraction algorithms such as the preceding. The functions in our API are translated into a dataflow that can run in a MapReduce-type platform [21, 37, 45]. The second component of SkewReduce is a static optimizer that partitions the data to ensure skew-resistant processing if possible. The data partitioning is guided by a user-defined cost function that estimates processing times.

8.3.2.1 Basic SkewReduce API

Informed by the success of MapReduce [21], the basic SkewReduce API is designed to be a minimal control interface allowing users to express feature extraction algorithms in terms of serial programs over familiar data structures. The *basic SkewReduce API* is the minimal interface that must be implemented to use our framework. The basic API is:

$$\texttt{process} \quad :: \quad \langle \text{Seq. of } T \rangle \rightarrow \langle F, \text{Seq. of } S \rangle$$
$$\texttt{merge} \quad :: \quad \langle F, F \rangle \rightarrow \langle F, \text{Seq. of } S \rangle$$
$$\texttt{finalize} \quad :: \quad \langle F, S \rangle \rightarrow \langle \text{Seq. of } Z \rangle$$

The notation used in these types is defined in Table 8.1. At a high-level, *T* refers to the input data. *F* is the set of features and *S* is an output data field that must be tagged with the features *F* to form *Z*. The previous three functions lead to a very natural expression of feature extracting algorithms: First, partition the data (not shown). Second, apply process to each partition to get an initial set of local features and an initial field. Third, merge, or reconcile, the output of each local partition to identify a global set of features. Finally, adjust the output of the original process functions given the final, global structures output by merge. For example, in the case of the astronomy simulation clustering task, process identifies local clusters in a partition of the 3-D space. merge hierarchically reconciles local clusters into global clusters. Finally, the finalize function relabels particles initially tagged by process with a local cluster ID using the appropriate global cluster ID.

The functions of the SkewReduce API loosely correspond to the API for distributed computation of algebraic user-defined aggregates found in OLAP systems and distributed dataflow frameworks. For example, Yu *et al.* [80] Propose a parallel aggregation framework consisting of functions initialreduce, combine, and finalreduce. The function initialreduce generates intermediate partial aggregates, combine merges partial aggregates, and the final aggregate value can be further transformed by finalreduce.

The distinguishing characteristic of our API is that our analog of the initial-reduce and finalreduce functions return two types of data: a representation of the extracted features and a representation of the "tagged" field. A given algorithm may or may not use both of these data structures, but we have found that many do.

We now present the three functions in SkewReduce's API in more detail.

8.3.2.2 Process: Local Computation with Set-Aside

The process function locally processes a sequence of input tuples producing F, a representation of the extracted features, and Seq. of S, a sequence of tuples that are set aside from the hierarchical reconciliation. In our astronomy simulation use-case, process performs the initial clustering of particles within each partition. Although we can forward all the clustering results to the merge function, only particles near the boundary of the fragment are necessary to merge clusters that span two partitions. Thus, process can optionally *set aside* those particles and results that are not required by the following merges. This optimization is not only helpful to reduce the memory pressure of merge but also improves overall performance by reducing the amount of data transferred over the network. In this application, our experiments showed that almost 99 percent of all particles can thus be set aside after the Process phase.

8.3.2.3 Merge: Hierarchical Merge with Set-Aside

The merge function is a binary operator that combines two intermediate results corresponding to two regions of space. It takes as input the features from each region and returns a new merged feature set. The two feature set arguments are assumed to fit together in the memory of one node. This constraint is a key

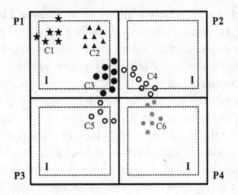

Figure 8.15. Illustration of the merge step of the clustering algorithm in the SkewReduce framework. Data is partitioned into four chunks. Points with the same shape are in the same global cluster. Point with different colors but with identical shapes are in different local clusters (for example the circles in the middle of the figure). Each P*i* labels the cell boundary and each *I* labels the interior region. Only points outside of *I* are needed in the subsequent merge phase. After the hierarchical merge phase, three cluster mappings are generated: (C4,C3), (C5,C3), and (C6,C3). Such mappings are used to relabel local cluster ids during the finalize phase.

defining characteristic of our target applications. This assumption is shared by most user-defined aggregate frameworks [59, 67, 80]. However, SkewReduce provides more flexibility than systems designed with trivial aggregation functions such as sum, count, and average in mind. Specifically, we acknowledge that the union of all feature sets may not fit in memory, so we allow the merge function to set aside results at each step. In this way, we ensure that the size of any value of type *F* does not grow larger than memory. We acknowledge that some applications may not exhibit this property, but we have not encountered them in practice. We assume that both functions process and merge set aside data of the same form. This assumption may not hold in general, but so far we have found that applications either set aside data in the process phase or in the merge phase, but not both.

In our running example, the merge function combines features from adjacent regions of space, returning a new feature object comprising the bounding box for the newly merged region of space, the cluster id mappings indicating which local clusters are being merged, and the particles near the boundary of the new region. Figure 8.15 illustrates the merge step for four partitions P1 through P4. The outer boxes, P*i*, represent the cell boundaries. The inner boxes, *I*, are a fixed distance ϵ away from the corresponding edge of the region. The local clustering step, process, identified a total of six clusters labeled C1 through C6.

Each cluster comprises points illustrated with a different shade of gray and shape. However, there are only three clusters in this dataset. These clusters are identified during the hierarchical merge step. Clusters C3, C4, C5, and C6 are merged because the points near the cell boundaries are within distance ϵ of each other. In Figure 8.15, C2 does not merge with any other cluster because all points in C2 are sufficiently far from P1's boundary. We can thus safely discard C2 before merging: These points are not needed during the merge phase. In general, we can discard all the points in the larger I regions before merging, reducing the size of the input to the merging algorithm. This reduction is necessary to enable nodes to process hierarchically larger regions of space without exhausting memory.

8.3.2.4 Finalize: Join Features with Set-Aside Data

The finalize function can be used to implement a join between the final collection of features and the input representation as output by the process and merge functions. This function is useful for tagging the original data elements with their assigned feature. The finalize function accepts the final feature set from the merge phase and a *single tuple* set aside during processing. The Skew-Reduce framework manages evaluation of this function over the entire distributed dataset.

Our emphasis on distinguishing "features" and "set aside" data may at first appear to be over-specialized to our particular examples, but we find the idiom to be quite general. To understand why, consider the analogous distinction between vector and raster representations of features. For example, Geographic Information Systems (GIS) may represent a geographic region as an image with each pixel assigned a value of "road," "waterway," and "building," (the raster representation). Alternatively, these objects may be represented individually by line segments, polygons, or some other complex object (the vector representation). Neither representation is ideal for all algorithms, so both are frequently computed and maintained. In our running example, the tagged particles are analogous to the raster representation – each point in the original dataset is labeled with the feature to which it contributes.

The user specifies these three functions, and SkewReduce automatically partitions the input data into hypercubes and schedules the execution of the process, merge, and finalize operators in a Hadoop cluster. The partition plan is derived by SkewReduce's optimizer, as discussed in what follows.

In many application domains the process function satisfies the *motonicity* property. The process function is monotonic if, for datasets R, S where $R \subseteq S$, the execution time $\text{time}[\text{process}(R)] \leq \text{time}[\text{process}(S)]$. Intuitively, as data size increases, so must the local processing cost.

The SkewReduce's optimizer is designed primarily for applications where this property holds. However, it can still handle applications that violate this property, a case that will be considered when the optimizer is discussed.

For the applications we encounter in practice, we find that process is far more expensive than merge, which causes aggressive partitioning to be generally beneficial. In these cases, the limiting factor in partitioning is the scheduling overhead. In contrast, if merge is expensive or comparable relative to process, partitioning simply ensures that no node is allocated more data than will fit in its memory.

Optional Pre-Processing: The process function operates on a set of records Seq. of T. In some applications, especially those operating on arrays, individual records are not cells but rather small neighborhoods of cells, sometimes called *stencils*. This distinction is not an issue for process, which receives as input a contiguous block of cells and can thus extract stencil neighborhoods unilaterally. However, because the optimizer operates on a sample of the input data, SkewReduce must apply a preprocessing step that extracts application-defined *computational units* before sampling them. For this reason, although not part of the basic API, we allow a user to provide a custom function to transform a sequence of "raw" records into a sequence of computational units, Seq. of T.

8.3.2.5 Cost Functions

We have presented the basic SkewReduce API, but we have not explained how skew is handled. Both the process and merge phases of the API are crucially dependent on the initial partitioning of data into regions. Feature extraction applications often exhibit both data skew and computational skew, and both are determined by how the data are partitioned. Datasets prone to significant data and computational skew (usually as a result of extreme variations in data density) can be processed efficiently if an appropriate partition-and-merge plan can be found. As we will show, plan quality can be improved dramatically if the user can estimate the runtime costs of their process and merge functions.

We allow the user to express these costs by providing two additional cost functions C_p and C_m, corresponding to process and merge, respectively. These cost functions operate serially on samples of the original dataset returning a real number; that is:

$$C_p \quad :: \quad (S, \alpha, B) \to \mathbb{R}$$
$$C_m \quad :: \quad (S, \alpha, B) \times (S, \alpha, B) \to \mathbb{R}$$

where S is a sample of the input, α is the sampling rate, and B is a bounding hypercube.

The cost functions accept both a representation of the data (the sample S) and a representation of the region (the bounding hypercube B, represented as a sequence of ranges, one for each dimension). The cost of the feature extraction algorithms we target is frequently driven by the distribution of the points in the surrounding space. One approach to estimate cost inexpensively is therefore to build a histogram using the bounding hypercube and the sample data and compute an aggregate function on that histogram. The sampling rate α allows the cost function to properly scale up the estimate to the overall dataset. When discussing cost functions in the remainder of this paper, we omit the bounding hypercube and sampling rate parameters when they are clear from the context.

Given a representative sample, the cost functions C_p and C_m must be representative of actual runtimes of the process and merge functions. More precisely, the functions must satisfy the following properties.

- **Fidelity:** For samples R, S, if $C_P(R) < C_P(S)$, then time[process(R)] < time[process(S)] (intuition: the true cost and the estimated cost impose the same total order on datasets). Similarly, for samples R, S, T, U, if $C_m (R, S)$ < $C_m(T, U)$, then time[merge(R, S)] < time[merge(T, U)].
- **Boundedness:** For some constants ρ_p and ρ_m and samples R and S, time[process(R)] $= \rho_p C_p(R)$ and time[merge(R, S)] $= \rho_m C_m (R, S)$.

For the boundedness condition, we can estimate the constant factors ρ_p and ρ_m in at least two ways. The first method is to run the process and merge algorithms over a data sample and compute the constants. This type of approach is related to curve fitting for UDF cost estimation [8]. The second method is to derive new constants for a new cost function from past executions of the same analysis.

Many MapReduce-style analytic systems are running on top of chunk-based distributed file systems such as GFS, HDFS, and S3 and use the chunk as a unit of task distribution and computation. SkewReduce takes a similar approach and requires that the process and merge functions have the ability to process at least one chunk-size of input data without running out of memory. Alternatively, we could optionally allow users to specify memory usage estimation functions that take a form analogous to the cost functions above. In both cases, the optimizer ensures a partition plan with sufficient granularity that no operator runs out of memory.

8.3.3 SkewReduce's Optimizer

There are two potential optimization goals for a SkewReduce application: minimize execution time or minimize resource usage. SkewReduce's current optimizer adopts a traditional approach and *minimizes the query execution time subject to a constraint on the number of available machines in a cluster.* This constraint can be dictated by the size of a locally available cluster or by monetary reasons when using a pay-as-you-go platform such as Amazon EC2 [3]. SkewReduce's optimizer could be used to try alternative cluster sizes if a user tries to find some desired price-performance trade-off, but we leave it for future work to automate such exploration.

SkewReduce's optimizer is designed to operate on a small sample of the entire data set, so that the optimizer can execute on a user's desktop before the user acquires or even just reserves any resources on a large cluster. In this paper, we do not address the problem of how the user generates such a sample. Such samples are already commonly used for debugging in these environments.

At a high level, SkewReduce's optimizer thus works as follows: given a sample S of the input data, process and merge functions and their corresponding cost functions C_p and C_m, a compute cluster-size constraint of M nodes, and a scheduling algorithm, the optimizer attempts to find the *partitioning plan* that minimizes the total query execution time. The user-supplied cost functions and the scheduling algorithm guide the optimizer's search for the best plan. SkewReduce works best with a task scheduler that minimizes makespan subject to task dependencies. However, it uses the scheduler as a black box and can therefore work with various schedulers.

Because the scheduler is modeled as a black box and the cost functions may not be completely accurate, SkewReduce does not guarantee to generate an optimal plan. However, our previous experiments show that it finds very efficient plans in practice (Figure 8.16).

We begin by defining the SkewReduce partition plan, execution plan, and the optimization problem more precisely.

Partition plan: A SkewReduce partition plan is a full binary tree where all intermediate nodes represent merge operators and all leaf nodes represent process operators. Each node in the tree is associated with a bounding hypercube defining the region of space containing all data in the partition. The hypercubes at a given height in the tree partition the space; there are no gaps or overlaps.

Valid partition plan: A partition plan is valid if no node in the plan is expected to receive more data than will fit in memory. The memory size is applied after scaling the sample data back to the original input data size, assuming the sample, S, is representative. For example, if a one percent data sample leads to a partition with 2,000 particles, and we know that a single node cannot process more than 100,000 particles, the plan will not be valid because $2{,}000 * 100 > 100{,}000$.

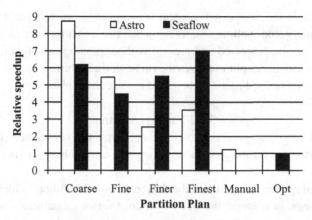

Completion time (hours for Astro, minutes for Seaflow)						
Dataset	Coarse	Fine	Finer	Finest	Manual	Opt
Astro	14.1	8.8	4.1	5.7	2.0	1.6
Seaflow	87.2	63.1	77.7	98.7	-	14.1

Figure 8.16. Relative speed of different partitioning strategies compared with the optimized plan (Opt). The table shows the actual completion time for each strategy (units are hours for Astro and minutes for Seaflow). Manual plan is shown only for the Astro dataset. Overall, SkewReduce's optimization significantly improves the completion time.

Execution plan: A SkewReduce execution plan comprises a partition plan and its corresponding schedule using a job scheduling algorithm schedule. A valid execution plan is a valid partition plan and its schedule.

Optimization problem: Given a sample S of the input data, process and merge functions with their corresponding cost functions and constants (ρ_p, ρ_m), a compute cluster of M nodes, a scheduling algorithm, and constant operator scheduling delay (Δ), return the valid execution plan that is estimated to minimize query runtime.

8.3.3.1 Optimizing the Partition Plan

The search space of the optimizer is the set of all possible partitions of the hy-percube defined by the input data. The optimizer enumerates potentially interesting partition plans in this search space using a greedy strategy. This greedy strategy is motivated by the fact that all process cost functions are assumed to be monotonic.

Starting from a single partition that corresponds to the entire hypercube bounding the input data I, and thus also the data sample, S, the optimizer greedily splits the most expensive leaf partition in the current partition plan. The optimizer stops splitting partitions when two conditions are met: (a) All partitions can be processed and merged without running out of memory; (b) No further leaf-node split improves the runtime; that is further splitting a node increases the expected runtime compared to the current plan.

8.3.3.2 Partition Splitting

When splitting a hypercube in two, the optimizer has two choices to make: which axis to use for the split and at what point along this axis to perform the split.

An ideal split should partition the data into two subpartitions with identical real runtimes. In contrast, the worst split creates two subpartitions with very different real runtimes, with the runtime for the slower subpartition similar to the presplit runtime.

For a low-dimensional data, typically 3 to 4, the optimizer exhaustively tries to split the data along each of the available axes because the optimization process is low-overhead (as we show later in Figure 8.19). For a high dimensional data, the user can supply a heuristic to filter out bad split axes to improve optimization time. We define the best split to be the one that minimizes the maximum cost C_p of any of the subpartitions created without violating the merge memory requirement.

To select the point along an axis where to split the data, different algorithms are possible. We present and compare three strategies. All three methods require that the examined sample data be sorted along the splitting axis with tie-breaking using values in other dimensions. Thus, we sort the sample data before run the strategy.

Discrete: The Discrete approach considers splitting the data at each one of n uniformly-spaced points along the splitting-axis. n is given as a parameter. For each point, the discrete strategy computes the cost of splitting the data at that point. The discrete approach is thus the most general strategy because it can work even when the cost function is not monotonic. It simply tries all possible splitting points assuming a given minimum granularity. On the other hand, this strategy may not return the best estimated splitting point, especially if n is small.

Binary search: This approach requires that cost functions be monotonic and performs a binary search for the best split point. The algorithm terminates after examining all $\log |S|$ candidate split points. Binary search always returns the optimal split as estimated by the cost function.

Incremental update: The incremental update approach requires that the cost function be monotonic and incrementally updatable. That is, whenever the cost

Table 8.2. *Datasets used in the evaluation*

Dataset	Size	# Items	Description
Astro	18 GB	900 M	Cosmology simulation
Seaflow	1.9 GB	59 M	Flow Cytometry

function is updated with a sample through an API call, the new cost is returned. Given these restrictions, the incremental update approach achieves the best optimization performance. The approach searches for the best split point in two phases. The algorithm starts with two empty subpartitions. It continuously adds samples to these subpartitions starting at both ends of partitioning axis. Each new data point is added to the partition currently estimated to have the lower runtime. The algorithm terminates when all samples have been assigned to a subpartition and the splitting point is the midpoint between the last sample inserted into each partition.

If multiple points fall on the partition boundary, the algorithm enters a second phase, where it computes the fraction of such points that were assigned to each partition. At runtime, when the entire dataset is partitioned, points on the same partition boundary are randomly distributed to subpartitions according to these precomputed proportions.

8.3.3.3 Estimating the Cost of a Schedule

The newly split partitions are only added if the candidate plan yields a better total runtime than the current plan. We estimate the runtime by calling a black box scheduling function schedule. To match the units of the operator costs to those of the scheduling overheads, we scale the process and merge costs using the precomputed ρ_p, ρ_m constants, thus converting these costs into time units.

Converting a schedule to a cost estimate is straight forward; we invoke the scheduling algorithm with the costs of all operators and M slots as input then take the total runtime. While we leave the scheduling algorithm as a black box, we found that Longest Processing Time (LPT) scheduling algorithm [35] works well in practice and satisfies all necessary features such as job dependency and multiple slots. Thus, we use LPT algorithm in the prototype.

8.3.4 Evaluation

In this section, we evaluate the performance of SkewReduce on the friends-of-friends clustering task over datasets from two different domains: astronomy and oceanography. Table 8.2 summarizes the properties of the two datasets.

We implemented friends-of-friends in a straightforward fashion without any optimizations, and using a standard KD-tree for storing local data and looking up friends.

Summary: We answer the following questions: (1) Does SkewReduce improve task completion times compared to uniform data partitioning, and, if so, is the difference significant? (2) How important is the fidelity of the cost model for SkewReduce's optimization? (3) How does the sample size affect cost estimates and ultimately performance? (4) What is the overhead of scheduling and optimization in SkewReduce? Our results show that SkewReduce imposes a negligible overhead (Figure 8.19) and can decrease total runtime by a factor of 2 or more compared to uniform data partitioning (Figure 8.16). We also find that small sample sizes of just 1 percent suffice to guide optimization, but the quality of the resulting plan does depend on the characteristics of the sample (Figures 8.17 and 8.18). Finally, a cost function that better captures the analysis algorithms helps SkewReduce find better plans, but even an approximate cost function can improve runtime compared to not using SkewReduce at all.

Implementation: The SkewReduce prototype consists of two Java classes: the SkewReduce optimizer and the SkewReduce execution engine. The optimizer takes the cost model and sample data as input and produces an optimized partition plan and a corresponding schedule. The execution engine converts the plan into a graph of Hadoop jobs and submits them to Hadoop according to the schedule from the optimizer. SkewReduce deploys a full MapReduce job for the initial data partitioning task (if necessary) and for each finalize operator, but deploys a map-only job for each process or merge operator. This design gives us better control over the timing of the schedule because Hadoop only supports user specified priorities at the job level rather than at the task level.

SkewReduce minimizes the scheduling overhead by using asynchronous job completion notifications of the Hadoop client API. Optionally, the user can implement the finalize operator as a Pig script [58] instead of a MapReduce program.

Setup: We perform all experiments in an eight-node cluster running Hadoop 0.20.1 with a separate master node. Each node uses two 2 GHz quad-core CPUs, 16 GB of RAM, and two 750 GB SATA disk drives (RAID 0). All nodes are used as both compute and storage nodes. The HDFS block size is set to 128 MB and each node is configured to run at most four map tasks and four reduce tasks concurrently.

We compare SkewReduce to various uniform data partitioning algorithms. We use the LPT scheduling algorithm for the SkewReduce optimizer. Uniform alternatives cannot use this approach because they do not have any way to estimate how long different tasks will take to process the same amount of data.

Table 8.3. *Cost-to-time conversion constant for cost models (ρ_p, ρ_m, scale)*

	Data Size			Histogram 1D			Histogram 3D		
Astro	83	4.3	10^{-6}	1500	2.9	10^{-12}	3.0	40	10^{-7}
Seaflow	4.8	1.6	10^{-5}	9.3	130	10^{-12}	6.0	200	10^{-8}

Default optimization parameters: SkewReduce's optimizer assumes a MapReduce job scheduling overhead (Δ) of 10 seconds [63]. Unless indicated otherwise, experiments use a sample size of one percent. The default cost function builds a 3D equi-width histogram of the data. Each bucket covers a range equal to the friend distance threshold along each dimension. The cost is computed as the sum of squared frequencies for all buckets. Each frequency is scaled back by the sample size (such as, for a one percent sample, all bucket frequencies are multiplied by 100) before squaring. The intuition behind this cost model is this: To identify a cluster, the friends-of-friends algorithm starts with a point and recursively finds friends and friends-of-friends using the KD-tree until no new friends can be added. This process yields quadratic runtime in dense regions, because every point is a friend of every other point. We obtain the conversion constants ρ_p, ρ_m (shown in Table 8.3) by executing ten micro-benchmark runs of the analysis task over a one percent data sample.

8.3.4.1 Overall SkewReduce Performance

In this section, we present experimental results that answer the following question: Does SkewReduce improve task completion times in the presence of computational skew compared to uniform data partitioning? Is the improvement significant? To answer this question, we measure the total runtime of the plans generated by SkewReduce for both datasets. We compare them against the runtimes of a manually crafted plan called *Manual* and plans with various uniform partitioning granularities: *coarse, fine, finer*, and *finest*. All plans are generated from the same one percent data sample. *Coarse* mimics Hadoop, which assigns a Map task to each HDFS chunk. Similarly, *Coarse* partitions the data into fragments that each contains the same number of data points. It does so by repeatedly splitting the region to bisect the data, one axis at a time in a round robin fashion, just like a KD-tree using a Recursive Coordinate Bisection (RCB) scheme [7]. *Coarse* stops splitting when the size of each partition is less than 128 MB. Fine stops splitting only when each partition is 16 MB. *Finer* and *Finest* partition the fine partitions further until each partition holds 4 MB and

2 MB, respectively. Finally, we prepared the Manual plan by tweaking the fine plan based on the execution results: we merged partitions experiencing no skew and split slow partitions further. We prepared a manual plan only for the Astro dataset due to the tedious nature of this task. Figure 8.16 shows the relative completion times of all plans compared to the optimized plan, labeled as Opt. We also report the actual completion time of each plan in the accompanying table.

The results from both datasets illustrate that fine-grained uniform splitting only improves performance up to a certain point before runtimes increase again because of overheads associated with scheduling and executing so many partitions. The SkewReduce optimizer's plan, however, guided by user-defined cost functions, is more than twice as fast as the best uniform plan. For the Astro dataset, SkewReduce improves the completion time of the clustering task by a factor of more than 8 compared with *Coarse*, which is the strategy equivalent to the default approach in MapReduce-type systems. SkewReduce's performance is even a bit better than the Manual plan. For the Seaflow dataset, the *Opt* runtime is a factor of 3 better than *Fine* and a factor of 6 better than *Coarse*.

Overall, SkewReduce can thus significantly improve the runtime of this analysis task.

8.3.4.2 Sample Size

In this section, we examine the effects of the sample size on SkewReduce's performance and answer the following question: What sample sizes are required for SkewReduce to generate good plans?

SkewReduce's optimization is based solely on the sample, and an unrepresentative sample may affect the accuracy of the optimizer's cost estimates. To measure the effect on accuracy, we prepared three independent samples with varying sampling rates, then generated and executed an optimized plan using the best cost function, Histogram 3D.

Figures 8.17 and 8.18 show the results from the Astro and Seaflow datasets, respectively. In both figures, the optimizer's cost estimates improve as the sample size increases but the convergence is not smooth. Surprisingly, the estimated runtime of the Astro dataset does not fluctuate as much as that of the Seaflow dataset even at lower sampling rates. The reason is that the extreme density variations in the Astro dataset that drive the performance are still captured even in a small sample. In contrast, the Seaflow sample may or may not exhibit significant skew. We also find that a larger sample does not always guarantee a better plan. In Figure 8.18, the sampling rate of 10 percent does not yield a better plan than a five percent sampling rate. The conclusion is that the quality

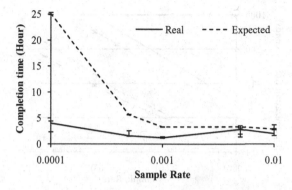

Figure 8.17. Completion time for the Astro dataset with varying sample rates. Error bars show the minimum and maximum values obtained for each sampling rate.

of optimization may vary subject to the representativeness of the sample. Interestingly, the runtime of this suboptimal plan is still a factor of 2 improvement compared to the plans based on uniform partitioning as shown in Figure 8.16.

8.3.4.3 SkewReduce Overhead

We study SkewReduce's overhead and answer the following question: How long does SkewReduce's optimization take compared with the time to process the query?

Figure 8.19 shows the runtime of the prototype optimizer using the Data Size and the Histogram 3D cost functions for each dataset. At a one percent sampling rate, the optimization takes 18 seconds using 594 K samples from the

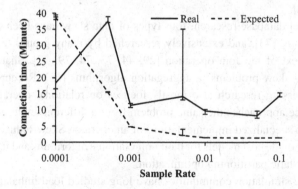

Figure 8.18. Completion time for the Seaflow dataset with varying sample rates. Error bars show the minimum and maximum values obtained for each sampling rate.

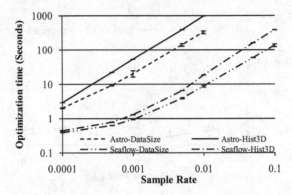

Figure 8.19. Optimization time with varying sample rates and cost functions.
With a 0.01 sample rate, there are 590 K samples for the Seaflow dataset and 9.1M
samples for Astro.

Seaflow dataset and 15 minutes using 9.1 M samples from the Astro dataset.
Considering that the prototype is not parallelized and does not manage memory
in any sophisticated way, the runtime is still a small fraction of the actual runtime
of the algorithm for each dataset. With an efficient parallel implementation, the
SkewReduce optimizer could potentially run with a more complex cost function
or use multiple samples to produce a better plan.

8.3.5 Related Work

Effective handling of skew is an important problem in any parallel system
because improper skew handling can counter all the benefits of parallel processing [26].

In parallel database research, four types of data skew have been identified
by Wolf *et al.* [73], and extensively researched by many groups, especially,
in the context of the Join operation [29, 44, 73, 74, 79, 77]. Shatdal *et al.*
investigated skew problems in aggregation algorithms [65]. Recent adaptive
query processing research also mostly focuses on relational operators [23].
SkewReduce approaches the same problem from a different angle. Instead of
focusing on specialized implementations of an operator, SkewReduce requests
that users provide cost models for their nonrelational algorithms and it performs
cost-based static partitioning optimization.

Scientific simulation communities have long studied load imbalance problems in parallel systems. Just as in parallel database systems, there exist many
mature infrastructures to run parallel simulations in a scalable manner [25,
55, 61]. The primary technique for attacking skew is adaptively repartitioning

(or regridding) the data by periodically monitoring the application runtime statistics or through explicit error measures of the parallel simulation [24]. The SkewReduce optimization resembles these programs, but uses sampling to optimize statically. Also, the partitioning is strictly guided by the user cost functions rather than errors in the simulation. Several cosmological simulations partition the workload based on gravitational potential and construct a tree to balance parallel spatial index lookup as well as computation [68]. Skew-Reduce shares the same spirit with those simulations but provides a generic, domain-independent framework to statically optimize the partition plan using user-defined cost functions and execute it in a shared-nothing cluster.

MapReduce and similar large scale data analysis platforms handle machine skew using speculative execution [21, 45, 37]. Speculative execution simply relaunches slow tasks on multiple different machines and takes the result of the first replica to complete. Speculative execution is effective in heterogeneous computing environments or when machines fail. However, it is not effective against data skew because rerunning the skewed data partition even on a faster machine can still yield a very high response time. Lin analyzed such impact of data skew of a MapReduce program [52]. Handling data skew in these systems is, in general, at a relatively early stage. Pig supports skewed join as proposed by DeWitt *et al.* [29] in its latest 0.5.0 release. To the best of our knowledge, this is the only effort to handle data skew problems in MapReduce-based systems. Qiu *et al.* implemented three applications for bioinformatics using cloud technologies and reported their experience and measurement results [64]. Although they also found skew problems in two applications, they discussed a potential solution rather than tackling the problem. SkewReduce is aiming to offer a more general skew-resistant solution to applications running on these types of platforms.

8.4 Looking Ahead: Complex Data, Massive Scale, and Interactive Speeds

As we have shown in the previous two sections, MapReduce in particular and parallel data processing systems in general can use significant enhancements to support the need of today's users. In this section, we argue that going forward even more fundamental changes are necessary.

In both science and industry, data is being acquired aggressively from any available source, stored indefinitely, used both in longitudinal historical studies and real-time decision support, fed through predictive statistical models, and visualized interactively. The implied requirements for a scalable analytics platform are significant: the infrastructure must handle *any data* (structured, unstructured, arrays, meshes, and images), at *any scale* (from 100s of MB to 100s of TB, at potentially interactive speeds), for *any workload* (filtering, sampling, streaming, interactive, and batch). Today's systems are not equipped to cover this design space: They focus on large-scale, batch processing [21, 37, 45], structured-data processing [36, 71], or small-scale interactive analytics and visualization (for example, MATLAB and R). There exist various efforts to better support existing requirements for data analytics [14, 70, 82], but none of these systems addresses the complete challenge of *any scale*, *any data*, and any *workload* analytics.

We consider requirements for a new cloud-based database system called NuageDB that is designed to support data analytics in a more comprehensive fashion than MapReduce and its contemporaries, aiming to help users spend less time "managing" data and more time extracting information from it.

Consider these examples: Oceanographers routinely compare observed data from instruments with simulation output [42]. The simulation output is large (potentially 100s of TB) and non-relational (mesh-structured [42]). The observed data is relatively small (perhaps 10s of GB) but can be extremely complex and therefore difficult to integrate. For example, consider the Acoustic Doppler Current Profiler (ADCP), which measures velocity in a vertical column of water by emitting sound waves and measuring the reflection time from particles in the water. To preprocess ADCP data, an analyst may extract a subset of the timeseries (say, one day's worth) and interactively clean and transform the data using MATLAB, Python, or R, generating visualizations at each step to assess the results. Once satisfied, the analyst's goal is to apply the same transformation to the full dataset, join the result with the simulation output, and continue alternating between interactive data exploration and batch data processing. The challenge is that each task requires a different tool, each with a different data model, programming model, performance characteristics, and tuning parameters. As a result, we routinely encounter scientists who spend more time context-switching between tools (reading documentation, installing software, learning languages, and debugging programs) than they spend analyzing data. This situation motivates a new, comprehensive analysis platform satisfying three requirements:

1. **Any scale:** A system that can scale to terabytes or petabytes, but also offer competitive interactive performance over small datasets. Science data comes in all sizes from a few megabytes to hundreds of terabytes (such as, [76]). Correspondingly, queries can run from milliseconds to hours. NuageDB's goal is to efficiently handle both ends of the scale spectrum within a single data analysis system.

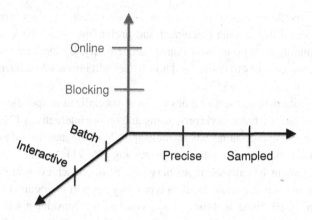

Figure 8.20. Basic query execution patterns in NuageDB. These patterns are orthogonal and can thus be combined. For example, a user can run a precise, online, and interactive query or a sampled blocking yet interactive query.

2. **Any data:** A system able to process any data type. Scientists manipulate diverse types of data from structured records to images and time-series data. To manage this diversity, we aim to to tolerate unstructured data but exploit structure when it exists and extract it whenever possible. In particular, NuageDB does not mandate an up-front schema like conventinoal relational database engines [63], but can exploit schema information when it exists (unlike MapReduce-like systems [21, 37, 45]). Similar to some recent parallel data processing systems [1, 10, 41], NuageDB avoids the cost of repeatedly parsing untyped data for each query. However, NuageDB also captures, infers, and exploits other types of structure, incrementally evolving raw data into relations equipped with typed attributes, integrity constraints, and descriptive metadata.

3. **Any workload:** A system that can optimize for both interactive and batch queries, returning either approximate or exact results. We observe that science analytics involves a combination of interactive, exploratory queries and long-running batch queries (Fig. 8.20). Resource management in such context is challenging. Today, companies often create multiple physical clusters to accommodate different types of workloads [72]. Additionally, the latency to cloud systems is still too high to efficiently run interactive visualization applications, forcing users to manually download subsets of the data to their desktops.

To optimize these diverse workloads, the key idea is that the scope of NuageDB query optimization is an entire session rather than a single query: a user who downloads a small subset, processes it repeatedly, then runs a large job motivates different data placement and prefetching strategies than a user who is scanning a single massive dataset sequentially. By reasoning about the workload, we also seek to understand how a user will interact with query results and optimize accordingly [17].

Current data management engines are over-specialized to specific contexts. Some focus only on batch-style processing and ignore interactivity [21, 37, 45]. Others cannot scale to hundreds or thousands of computers in a data center, as needed for multi-tenant petascale processing [36, 71]. Recent cloud-based data management systems sacrifice query capabilities to achieve scalability [4]. Some systems may constrain the data types they support to documents [16].

To help satisfy these ambitious requirements, we consider novel features to exploit both shared cloud resources for massive scalability as well as local resources for low-latency work:

- A structural inference engine that can incrementally and semiautomatically extract features from datasets useful for optimization and physical organization (such as, schema, partitioning information, statistical samples, outliers, or constraints).
- A workload pattern language to help the system infer and exploit colocation and optimization opportunities before the jobs themselves are available.
- A storage manager that automatically creates different sizes of virtual clusters within a single massive-scale physical one and collocates data likely to be queried together.
- A caching and pre-fetching subsystem that can speculatively "guess" what the user will ask for and eagerly push results toward the client to reduce latency. Tree of operators with support for both.
- An efficient pre-emption mechanism to maximize utilization and afford fault-tolerance.

In the rest of this section, we elaborate on these features.

8.4.1 Structural Inference

One strength of the MapReduce model is its ability to deal with "ad hoc data" – data that must be processed without access to a schema. The price to pay is that every Map function must parse, transform, interpret, or otherwise prepare the data for processing on the fly.

NuageDB attempts to offer the best of both worlds by taking a "schema later" approach: data initially requires no schema but types, constraints, and properties can be extracted incrementally through the ordinary use of the system (HadoopDB [1] and LearnPADS [31, 32]). To achieve this flexibility, we adopt a data model that can operate on ad hoc files but facilitates "incremental structuralization" to well-defined relations. The fundamental unit of processing is the *dataset*, representing an (initially) uninterpreted sequence of bytes, possibly spanning multiple files.

Incremental structure: A dataset can be recognized as a *table*, which is a partitioned sequence of records where each record shares a common schema. Attribtues constituting the table can be extracted incrementally by using one or more user-defined *parse functions*. Each extracted attribute logically becomes a new attribute of the table and is accessible by queries that reference the original table. Parse functions can be applied as part of query processing via a special operator, allowing new attributes to be computed on the fly from raw data as needed.

Incremental constraints: In addition to types, NuageDB also incrementally extracts other useful data properties including integrity constraints, (specifically keys, or functional dependencies, and inclusion dependencies), sort orders, and statistics. We encode these constraints as properties with special semantics and make them accessible during query processing. The approach is for NuageDB to mine the data and automatically infer that some properties may hold. Each inferremake them property is presented to the user who can either confirm or invalidate it. Properties can thus be in one of four states: (1) inferred, (2) confirmed, (3) violated, or (4) invalidated. A violated property is one that was asserted but was discovered to not hold. In addition to types, relational databases teach us that integrity constraints are an important source of optimization opportunities and application correctness guarantees. Specifically, keys, functional dependencies, inclusion dependencies, sort orders, and statistics all inform optimization strategies. We encode these constraints as properties blessed with special semantics by the system and accessible during query processing. Overall, data thus evolves incrementally from an opaque BLOB to a typed relation equipped with integrity constraints and other properties.

Extensible optimization rules: The set of properties that can be inferred by NuageDB and used for optimization is extensible by the user. The user provides custom rewrite rules that may rely on certain properties holding (such as, sort order, value constraints, or functional dependencies), as well as functions to verify or enforce these properties. We will describe the details in the full paper.

8.4.2 A Workload Pattern Language

We observe that even before the first query is written, a user can often sketch the access pattern of their workload and that this information can be used to optimize query processing. For example, an observational oceanographer processing ADCP data might describe their task in English: "First, I will download last month's ADCP data, then create a progressive series of visualizations." Even though we know nothing about the actual queries that will be executed, we can speculate about the workload overall: We know the user will be accessing a particular dataset (ADCP data), extracting a subset, and then running a series of interactive queries. We can encode this high-level workload as the string $dRT \cdots T$, where d indicates the input dataset, R indicates a *reduction* of the dataset, and $T \cdots T$ indicates a series of *transformations* on the reduced data.

We generalize this example to derive a pattern language for workloads. A *basic workload pattern* is a word in the alphabet $D \cup \{R, S, T\}$, where D is a set of symbols representing dataset names, and R, S, and T are *query class operators* indicating a *reduction*, *sample*, and *transformation*. A reduction indicates a highly selective filter and the result is assumed to be small enough for efficient local processing. When NuageDB encounters the reduction operator, it may decide to build an index. The sample operator indicates that the user need not have exact answers but can tolerate a statistical sample. A sample is assumed to be significantly smaller than the original dataset. NuageDB can respond to the sample operator by preparing or colocating the appropriate samples. The transformation operator indicates an arbitrary query that produces a result of similar size to the input.

A basic workload pattern can only express compositions of queries. To express a series of independent queries on the same dataset, we introduce three more symbols to the alphabet: $\{\hat{R}, \hat{S}, \hat{T}\}$. Consider the difference between dRT and $d\hat{R}T$. The former indicates a transformation of a reduced dataset (so T is inexpensive), while the latter indicates a reduction query, followed by a transformation of the original dataset d (so T is expensive). Nested expressions are also allowed in order to express operations on multiple datasets. For example, $(de)R$ indicates that datasets d and e are both reduced together in one operation, perhaps a join. The expression $(dReR)T$ indicates a reduction of d, a reduction of e, followed by a transformation of both datasets together.

Semantics: The semantics of a workload pattern is defined in terms of a stack representing the user's workspace. Processing the string from left to right, a dataset symbol indicates a push of that dataset onto the stack. A query class operator indicates to replace the top of the stack with the result of the query. A hat operator (such as, R) reads the top of the stack, but does not consume it or replace it. Parentheses indicate creation of a new substack that can be manipulated by query class operators just like an individual dataset.

Laws: Internally, NuageDB applies a set of rewrite rules to simplify the expression and afford reasoning. The rule $SR \rightarrow S$ captures the intuition that

Table 8.4. *Examples of workload patterns*

Pattern	Intuition
$dR\hat{T}^+$	Reduce a dataset and query it interactively.
$dS\hat{T}^+dT$	Debug a query on a sample, then apply it to the whole dataset.
$(dR)^+$	Iteratively inspect subsets of a large dataset.
$d\hat{S}^+$	Iteratively extract samples of a large dataset (such as, Monte Carlo experiments).
$(dRe)T$	Filter a dataset, join with another dataset.
$(defgh)T^+$	Analyze a collection of related datasets.

a reduction of a sample requires no additional work from NuageDB than a sample alone – there is no value in indexing a random sample. Other laws include $RR \rightarrow R$ (a composition of reductions collapse into a single reduction for planning purposes), $SS \rightarrow S$ (a composition of sample operations collapse to a single sample operation), $OR \leftrightarrow O$ (an online query can be filtered on the fly), and $OS \leftrightarrow SO$ (sampling an online query may be cheaper than creating a sample first then streaming the results, unless the samples have already been constructed), $xSySzS \rightarrow (xyz)S$ (sampling the three datasets parallel), $dTdT \rightarrow dTT$ (two independent queries can share a scan).

Examples: Table 8.4 shows several example workload patterns and the intuition for the underlying scenarios.

Sources and use cases: To facilitate workload pattern specifications, we envision a workflow-style GUI including a drop-down menu of common patterns. NuageDB can also automatically infer workflow patterns from query logs, or predict them by monitoring a user's actions on the fly [52]. Also, the user need not be the only source of these expressions. Workflow patterns can be used to describe and classify applications, they can be inferred post hoc from logs, or they can be predicted by monitoring and classifying a user's actions on the fly [52]. There are many uses to workflow patterns: NuageDB uses workflow patterns primarily for query optimization, but there are other applications. We can classify workloads by estimating the number of large-scale operations (such as, the expression $dRTTT$ has only one large-scale operation, which may be amenable to indexing, whereas $dTdTdT$ involves three independent queries over the same large dataset). We can combine multiple users' workload expressions to analyze opportunities for data colocation.

Previous work on workload specification relies on users providing explicit query templates [56]; in contrast, we only ask users to specify the high-level properties of their queries.

8.4.3 Virtual Clusters

NuageDB is intended to be deployed in a large, shared-nothing cluster in a cloud. At cloud scale, the parallel database strategy of sharding each dataset across all nodes [36, 71] is not usable as it would create overly small data partitions. On the other hand, the HDFS [37] or GFS [34] strategy of randomly allocating data to nodes in the cluster does not promote collocation of datasets that need to be queried together. In contrast, our strategy is to improve data locality by creating virtual microclusters for collocating related datasets, where collocation and partitioning decisions are informed by the actual and expected query workloads.

NuageDB partitions tables into blocks, which are distributed across machines. In contrast to other systems, NuageDB collocates all blocks for a dataset on the same rack whenever possible, then replicates the dataset to two other racks, one in the same and one in another data center.

As queries are executed on the datasets, NuageDB monitors query performance. When queries are CPU bound, NuageDB responds by repartitioning into smaller blocks and spreading them across a larger number of nodes. When contention arises on popular datasets, these datasets get replicated onto additional racks.

To increase data locality, NuageDB attempts to collocate datasets likely to be accessed together by clustering on workload patterns, metadata, or the query log. For example, when an astronomer uploads a new snapshot from a cosmological simulation, she can express a workload pattern indicating that this dataset will often be queried together with earlier snapshots. The system then collocates the new data on the same rack as some of the other identified datasets. If the user does not identify any other datasets, the data placement is determined by mining the query log: NuageDB periodically mines the query log and clusters users into groups based on the data they access. NuageDB then preferably collocates datasets of users in the same group.

This data placement strategy must respect capacity constraints and be sensitive to possibly complex collaborations among users. For example, another astronomer in a different country may compare his analysis result with the new snapshot for validation. Should his data be collocated with the snapshot or with his other datasets? To address this challenge, NuageDB dynamically relocates the data based on "what if" analysis results [11]: if past queries would have run faster given a different data location and replication strategy, NuageDB applies that strategy. This approach assumes that past query patterns are an indicator of future ones. More advanced strategies for inferring future queries are also possible. For example, if a dataset receives periodic appends, future queries will likely focus on the new rather than old data [40]. NuageDB also leverages workload pattern descriptions to optimize data placement across a whole query session.

8.4.4 Caching

As previously discussed, NuageDB supports interactive queries in part by reserving resources for such queries on all nodes, which enables the system to prefetch, cache in memory (at least in part), and efficiently process interactively queried data. Latency to the cloud is still unacceptably high for some applications (for example, interactive visualization). To reduce latency, NuageDB pushes data toward the user when interactive performance is requested. To do so, users register their local machines with the NuageDB cloud and run a local instance of a NuageDB node as a virtual machine.

To analyze data in an interactive session, the user can either (1) label their queries as "interactive" or (2) produce a workload specification for the entire query session. In the former case, NuageDB uses the local cache as in traditional systems, using the growing query log to optimize caching decisions [50]. In the latter case, however, NuageDB can perform more advanced optimizations because it has information about the entire query session to come. Current NuageDB optimizations include the following: (1) pre-fetch and push to local cache data that is going to be queried interactively, (2) run batch queries in the cloud but push results toward the client if the user plans interactive drill-down analysis, and (3) relocate data within the cloud itself (such as, if a user wants to interactively analyze a small amount of data, gather it into a single machine to reduce the overhead of distributed processing.

8.4.5 Preemptive Scheduling

Supporting queries with low-latency requirements together with large-scale ad hoc queries is challenging [72]: batch queries can consume all the resources causing time-sensitive queries to experience unacceptably high latency. One approach is to separate workloads across different physical clusters [72], but this requires significant dataset replication to ensure availability. Alternatively, a sophisticated scheduler can help ensure that different workload types get predefined fraction of resources or that some queries get priority over others [38].

NuageDB uses a variant of Hadoop's capacity scheduler [38] but with important differences. First, to support interactive queries whose data can be located on any machine, NuageDB reserves a fraction of resources *on each machine* for short or interactive queries. Our key innovation then lies in aggressively using these "reserved" cycles for batch queries and efficiently preempting parts of a batch computation when cycles are reclaimed. NuageDB's approach works as follows: when a batch query is scheduled, a fraction of each operator's partitions are allocated resources as in Hadoop or a typical parallel DBMS. The remaining partitions are scheduled using "borrowed" resources. To efficiently support preemptions, partitions running on borrowed resources use *shared storage* to checkpoint their output and internal state. As a result, these partitions run slower than the others but can easily be restarted from the latest checkpoint on another machine. NuageDB takes this performance penalty into account and schedules proportionally less work to these tasks.

Acknowledgments

The content of this book chapter is based in part on work done in collaboration with Yingyi Bu, Michael D. Ernst, YongChul Kwon, and Jerome Rolia. The research presented here was also supported in part by NSF CluE grant IIS-0844572, NSF grant IIS-0844580, NSF CAREER Award IIS-0845397, NSF grant CNS-0855252, NSF CRI grant CNS-0454425, Woods Hole Oceanographic Institute Grant OCE-0418967, an HP Labs Innovation Research Award, gifts from Amazon, Yahoo! and Microsoft Research, Balazinska's Microsoft Research New Faculty Fellowship, the University of Washington eScience Institute, and the Yahoo! Key Scientific Challenges program.

References

1. Abouzeid A., Bajda-Pawlikowski K., Abadi D., Silberschatz A., and Rasin A. "An Architectural Hybrid of MapReduce and DBMS Technologies for Analytical Workloads." In *Proc. of the 35th VLDB Conf.*, 2009.
2. Abouzeid A., Bajda-Pawlikowski K., Abadi D. J., Rasin A., and Silberschatz A. "HadoopDB: An Architectural Hybrid of MapReduce and DBMS Technologies for Analytical Workloads." *VLDB* 2, no. 1 (2009): 922–33.
3. Amazon Elastic Compute Cloud (Amazon EC2). http://aws.amazon. com/ec2/. Accessed May 2012.
4. Amazon SimpleDB. http://www.amazon.com/simpledb/. Accessed May 2012.
5. Oceanic remote chemical analyzer (ORCA). http://armbrustlab. ocean.washington .edu/.
6. Bancilhon F., and Ramakrishnan R. "An Amateur's Introduction to Recursive Query Processing Strategies." In *SIGMOD Conference*, pages 16–52, 1986.
7. Berger M. J., and Bokhari S. H. "A Partitioning Strategy for Nonuniform Problems on Multiprocessors." *Computers, IEEE Transactions on*, C-36(5), 1987.
8. Boulos J., and Ono K. "Cost Estimation of User-Defined Methods in Object-Relational Database Systems." *SIGMOD Record*, 28, no. 3 (1999).

9. Cary A., Sun Z., Hristidis V., and Rishe N. "Experiences on processing spatial data with mapreduce." In *Proceedings of the 21st International Conference on Scientific and Statistical Database Management*, SSDBM 2009, pages 302–19, Berlin, Heidelberg: Springer-Verlag, 2009.

10. Chaiken R., Jenkins B., Larson P.-Å., Ramsey B., Shakib D., Weaver S., and Zhou J. SCOPE: "Easy and Efficient Parallel Processing of Massive Data Sets. In *Proc. of the 34th VLDB Conf.*, pages 1265–76, 2008.

11. Chaudhuri S., and R. Narasayya V. "Self-Tuning Database Systems: A Decade of Progress." In *Proc. of the 33rd VLDB Conf.*, pages 3–14, 2007.

12. Cloudera. http://www.cloudera.com/.

13. Nsf cluster exploratory program. http://www.nsf.gov/pubs/2008/nsf08560/nsf08560.htm. Accessed July 7, 2010.

14. Cohen J., Dolan B., Dunlap M., Hellerstein J. M., and Welton C. "MAD skills: New Analysis Practices for Big Data." *Proc. of the VLDB Endowment*, 2, no. 2 (2009): 1481–92.

15. Condie T., Conway N., Alvaro P., Hellerstein J. M., Elmeleegy K., and Sears R. "MapReduce Online." In *Symposium on Networked Systems Design and Implementation*, pages 21–21, 2010.

16. CouchDB. http://couchdb.apache.org/. Accessed May 2012.

17. Dageville B., Das D., Dias K., Yagoub K., Mohamed Z., and Mohamed Z. "Automatic SQL Tuning in Oracle 10g." In *Proc. of the 30th VLDB Conf.*, pages 1098–1109, 2004.

18. Das S., Sismanis Y., Beyer K. S. Gemulla R., Haas P. J., and McPherson J. "Ricardo: Integrating R and Hadoop." In *Proc. of the ACM SIGMOD International Conference on Management of Data*, pages 987–98, 2010.

19. Datameer. http://www.datameer.com./. Accessed May 2012.

20. Davis M., Efstathiou G., Frenk C. S., and White S. D. M. "The Evolution of Large-Scale Structure in a Universe Dominated by Cold Dark Matter." *Astroph. J.* 292 (May 1985): 371–94.

21. Dean J. and Ghemawat S.. MapReduce: "Simplified Data Processing on Large Clusters." In *Proc. of the 6th OSDI Symp.*, 2004.

22. Dean J. and Ghemawat S. "MapReduce: Simplified Data Processing on Large Clusters." In *OSDI*, pages 137–50, 2004.

23. Deshpande A., Ives Z., and Raman V. Adaptive Query Processing. *Foundations and Trends in Databases* 1, no. 1 (2007): 139.

24. Devine K., Boman E., and Karypis G. *Parallel Processing for Scientific Computing*, chapter 6. Society for Industrial and Applied Mathematics, 2006.

25. Devine K., Boman E., Heapby R., Hendrickson B., and Vaughan C. Zoltan Data Management Service for Parallel Dynamic Applications. *Computing in Science and Eng.* 4, no. 2 (2002): 90–96.

26. DeWitt D., and Jim G. Parallel Database Systems: The Future of High Performance Database Systems. *CACM*, 35, no. 6 (1992): 85–98.

27. Dewitt D., and Stonebraker M. MapReduce: A major step backwards. http://databasecolumn.vertica.com/database-innovation/mapreduce-a-major-step-backwards/.

28. DeWitt D. J., and Gray J. Parallel Database Systems: The Future of High Performance Database Systems. Commun. *ACM* 35, no. 6 (1992): 85–98.

29. DeWitt D. J., Naughton J. F., Schneider D. A., and Seshadri S. "Practical Skew Handling in Parallel Joins." In *Proc. of the 18th VLDB Conf.*, 1992.

30. Ekanayake J., and Pallickara S. "MapReduce for Data Intensive Scientific Analysis." In *IEEE eScience*, pages 277–84, 2008.

31. Fisher K., Walker D., and Zhu K. Q. "Learnpads: Automatic Tool Generation from Ad Hoc Data." In *SIGMOD Conference*, pages 1299–1302, 2008.

32. Fisher K., Walker D., Zhu K. Q., and White P. "From Dirt to Shovels: Fully Automatic Tool Generation from Ad Hoc Data." In *POPL*, pages 421–34, 2008.

33. Gelb J. M., and Bertschinger E. Cold Dark Matter. 1: The Formation of Dark Halos. Astroph. *J.* 436 (December 1994): 467–90.

34. Ghemawat S., Gobioff H., and Leung S.-T. "The Google File System." In *Proc. of the 19th SOSP Symp.*, pages 29–43, 2003.

35. Graham R. L. Bounds on Multiprocessing Timing Anomalies. *SIAM Journal on Applied Mathematics*, 17, no. 2 (1969): 416–29.

36. Greenplum database. http://www.greenplum.com/. Accessed May 2012.

37. Hadoop. Accessed July 7, 2010. http://hadoop.apache.org/.

38. Hadoop – capacity scheduler guide. http://hadoop.apache.org/mapreduce/docs/current/capacity_scheduler.html.

39. Hdfs. Accessed July 7, 2010. http://hadoop.apache.org/common/docs/current/hdfs_design.html.

40. Bingsheng H., Yang M., Guo Z., Chen R., Su B., Lin W., and Zhou L. "Comet: Batched Stream Processing for Data Intensive Distributed Computing." In *Proc. of the 1st ACM symposium on Cloud computing*, pages 63–74, 2010.

41. Hive. http://hadoop.apache.org/hive/.

42. Howe B., and Maier D. "Algebraic Manipulation of Scientific Datasets." In *VLDB '04: Proceedings of the 30th International Conference on Very Large Data Bases*, Toronto, Ontario, CA, 2004.

43. Howe B., Maier D., and Bright L. "Smoothing the Roi Curve for Scientific Data Management Applications." In *Proc. of the Third CIDR Conf.*, 2007.

44. Hua K. A., and Lee C. "Handling Data Skew in Multiprocessor Database Computers Using Partition Tuning. In *Proc. of the 17th VLDB Conf.*, 1991.

45. Isard M., Budiu M., Yu Y., Birrell A., and Fetterly D. "Dryad: Distributed Data-parallel Programs from Sequential Building Blocks." In *Proc. of the EuroSys Conf.*, pages 59–72, 2007.

46. Isard M., Budiu M., Yu Y., Birrell A., and Fetterly D. "Dryad: Distributed Data-Parallel Programs From Sequential Building Blocks." In *EuroSys*, pages 59–72, 2007.

47. Karmasphere. http://www.karmasphere.com/. Accessed May 2012.

48. Kleinberg J. M. Authoritative Sources in a Hyperlinked Environment. *J. ACM*, 46 no. 5 (1999): 604–32.

49. Knollmann S. R., and Knebe A. "AHF: Amiga's Halo Finder." *Astroph*. J. Suppl. 182 (June 2009): 608–24.

50. Kossmann D., Franklin M. J., Drasch G., and Ag W. Cache Investment: Integrating Query Optimization and Distributed Data Placement. *ACM TODS* 25, no. 4 (2000): 517–58.

51. Kwon et al. Scalable Clustering Algorithm for N-Body Simulations in a Shared-Nothing cluster. Technical Report UW-CSE-09-06-01, Dept. of Comp. Sci., Univ. of Washington, 2009.

52. Lin J. "The Curse of Zipf and Limits to Parallelization: A Look at the Stragglers Problem in MapReduce." In *7th Workshop on Large-Scale Distributed Systems for Information Retrieval*, 2009.

53. Mahout. http://lucene.apache.org/mahout/. Accessed July 7, 2010.

54. Malewicz G., Austern M. H., Bik A. J. C., Dehnert J. C., Horn I., Leiser N., and Czajkowski G. "Pregel: A System for Large-Scale Graph Processing." In *SIGMOD Conference*, pages 135–46, 2010.

55. Oliker L., and Biswas R. Plum: Parallel Load Balancing for Adaptive Unstructured Meshes. *J. Parallel Distrib. Comput.* 52, no. 2 (1998): 150–77.

56. Olston C., Bortnikov E., Elmeleegy K., Junqueira F., and Reed B. "Interactive Analysis of Web-Scale Data." In *Fourth CIDR Conf. – Perspectives*, 2009.

57. Olston C., Reed B., Srivastava U., Kumar R., and Tomkins A. "Pig Latin: A Not-So-Foreign Language for Data Processing." In *SIGMOD Conference*, pages 1099–10, 2008.

58. Olston C., Reed B., Srivastava U., Kumar R., and Tomkins A.. "Pig Latin: A Not-So-Foreign Language for Data Processing." In *Proc. of the SIGMOD Conf.*, pages 1099–10, 2008.

59. Oracle. http://www.oracle.com/database/.

60. Page L., Brin S., Motwani R., and Winograd T. The PageR-ank Citation Ranking: Bringing Order to the Web. Technical Report 1999-66, Stanford InfoLab, 1999.

61. Parashar M., Liu H., Li Z., Matossian V., Schmidt C., Zhang G., and Hariri S. AutoMate: Enabling Autonomic Applications on the Grid. *Cluster Computing* 9, no. 2 (2006): 48–57.

62. Pavlo A., Paulson E., Rasin A., Abadi D. J., DeWitt D. J., Madden S., and Stonebraker M. "A Comparison of Approaches to Large-Scale Data Analysis." In *SIGMOD Conference*, pages 165–78, 2009.

63. Pavlo A., Paulson E., Rasin A., Abadi D. J., DeWitt D. J., Madden S., and Stonebraker M. "A Comparison of Approaches to Large-Scale Data Analysis." In *Proc. of the SIGMOD Conf.*, pages 165–78, 2009.

64. Qiu X., Ekanayake J., Beason S., Gunarathne T., Fox G., Barga R., and Gannon D. "Cloud Technologies for Bioinformatics Applications." In *MTAGS '09: Proceedings of the 2nd Workshop on Many-Task Computing on Grids and Supercomputers*, pages 1–10, 2009.

65. Shatdal A. and Naughton J. "Adaptive Parallel Aggregation Algorithms." In *Proc. of the SIGMOD Conf.*, 1995.

66. Springel V., White S. D. M., Jenkins A., Frenk C. S., Yoshida N., Gao L., Navarro J., Thacker R., Croton D., Helly J., Peacock J. A., Cole S., Thomas P., Couchman H., Evrard A., Colberg J., and Pearce F. "Simulations of the Formation, Evolution and Clustering of Galaxies and Quasars." *NATURE* 435 (June 2005): 629–36.

67. Sql server. http://www.microsoft.com/sqlserver/. Accessed May 2012.

68. Stadel J. G.. *Cosmological N-body Simulations and Their Analysis.* PhD thesis, University of Washington, 2001.

69. Stonebraker M., Abadi D. J., DeWitt D. J., Madden S., Paulson E., Pavlo A., and Rasin A. Mapreduce and Parallel Dbmss: Friends or Foes? *CACM*, 53, no. 1 (January 2010).

70. Stonebraker M., Becla J., DeWitt D., Lim K.-T., Maier D., Ratzesberger O., and Zdonik S. "Requirements for Science Data Bases and SciDB." In *Fourth CIDR Conf. – Perspectives*, 2009.

71. Teradata. http://www.teradata.com/.
72. Thusoo A., Shao Z., Anthony S., Borthakur D., Jain N., Sarma J. S., Murthy R., and Liu H. "Data Warehousing and Analytics Infrastructure at Facebook." In *Proc. of the ACM SIGMOD International Conference on Management of Data*, pages 1013–20, 2010.
73. Walton C. B., Dale A. G., and Jenevein R. M. "A Taxonomy and Performance Model of Data Skew Effects in Parallel Joins." In *Proc. of the 17th VLDB Conf.*, 1991.
74. Snodgrass R. T., Li W., and Gao D. "Skew Handling Techniques in Sort-Merge Join." In *Proc. of the SIGMOD Conf.*, 2002.
75. Weinberg D. H., Hernquist L., and Katz N. "Photoionization, Numerical Resolution, and Galaxy Formation." *Astroph. J.* 477 (March 1997): 8–+.
76. Xldb workshop. http://www-conf.slac.stanford.edu/xldb/. Accessed May 2012.
77. Xu Y., and Kostamaa P. "Efficient Outer Join Data Skew Handling in Parallel DBMS." In *VLDB*, 2009.
78. Xu Y., Kostamaa P., and Gao L. "Integrating Hadoop and Parallel DBMs." In *Proc. of the ACM SIGMOD International Conference on Management of Data*, pages 969–74, 2010.
79. Xu Y., Kostamaa P., Zhou X., and Chen L. "Handling Data Skew in Parallel Joins in Shared-Nothing Systems." In *Proc. of the SIGMOD Conf.*, pages 1043–52, 2008.
80. Yu Y., Gunda P. K., and Isard M. "Distributed Aggregation for Data-Parallel Computing: Interfaces and Implementations." In *Proc. of the 22nd SOSP Symp.*, 2009.
81. Zhang W., Wang K., and Chau S.-C. "Data Partition and Parallel Evaluation of Datalog Programs." IEEE Trans. Knowl. *Data Eng.*, 7, no. 1 (1995): 163–76.
82. Zhang Y., Herodotou H., and Yang J. RIOT: I/O-Efficient Numerical Computing Without SQL. In *Proc. of the Fourth CIDR Conf.*, 2009.

9

Let the Data Do the Talking: Hypothesis Discovery from Large-Scale Data Sets in Real Time

Christopher Oehmen, Scott Dowson, Wes Hatley,
Justin Almquist, Bobbie-Jo Webb-Robertson,
Jason McDermott, Ian Gorton, and Lee Ann McCue

9.1 Discovering Biological Mechanisms through Exploration

The availability of massive amounts of data in biological sciences is forcing us to rethink the role of hypothesis-driven investigation in modern research. Soon thousands, if not millions, of whole-genome DNA and protein sequence data sets will be available thanks to continued improvements in high-throughput sequencing and analysis technologies. At the same time, high-throughput experimental platforms for gene expression, protein and protein fragment measurements, and others are driving experimental data sets to extreme scales. As a result, biological sciences are undergoing a paradigm shift from hypothesis-driven to data-driven scientific exploration. In hypothesis-driven research, one begins with observations, formulates a hypothesis, then tests that hypothesis in controlled experiments. In a data-rich environment, however, one often begins with only a cursory hypothesis (such as some class of molecular components is related to a cellular process) that may require evaluating hundreds or thousands of specific hypotheses rapidly. This large number of experiments is generally intractable to perform in physical experiments. However, often data can be brought to bear to rapidly evaluate and refine these candidate hypotheses into a small number of testable ones. Also, often the amount of data required to discover and refine a hypothesis in this way overwhelms conventional analysis software and hardware. Ideally advanced hardware can help the situation, but conventional batch-mode access models for high-performance computing are not amenable to real-time analysis in larger workflows. We present a model for real-time data-intensive hypothesis *discovery* process that unites parallel software applications, high-performance hardware, and visual representation of the output. This process uses MeDICi, a middleware integration framework, to coordinate analytical task scheduling and data moving – making the power of parallel computing more accessible to bench biologists who need it. This chapter illustrates examples of this discovery model using real-world biological data sets from which testable hypotheses were derived.

The first step toward discovering a hypothesis from large-scale data is to understand the fundamental measurements that can be made on a system. For the case of biology, we focus on understanding living systems by identifying chemical fragments present in cells. At the molecular level, the collection of a cell's genes (such as its *genome*) is often referred to as a "blueprint," but it is more like a super-catalog – containing information about all the *possible* parts that might be synthesized by the cell. At any given moment, two cells with identical genomes can have very different appearance and behavior. This is because not all the genes are used by a cell all the time. In response to a constantly changing environment genes are "turned on" or "turned off," producing a constantly changing list of active parts. Genes that are "turned on" serve as circulating templates for larger working molecules or *proteins*. The proteins that are present in a cell at a given time give a more comprehensive picture of what processes the cell is capable of engaging in at that time. These proteins and genes constantly interact with each other, with the cell's surroundings, and with the internal environment of the cell to regulate the cell's state, and adapt that state to maximize survival.

Conventional molecular biology has focused on understanding genes and proteins and how they operate in living systems. As aspects of the genetic code have been elucidated, researchers have widened the scope of their investigation to incorporate interactions between multiple genes, protein systems, and finally to the full complement of genes and proteins in cells or groups of cells. In tandem with and in many ways driving this broadening of scope high-throughput sequencing technologies have driven an exponential increase in the rate that new gene sequences can be discovered and published. One example of this trend is illustrated by the Joint Genome Institute's (JGI) Integrated Microbial Genomes project [1], which curates a collection of public sequenced genomes. The 2.4 release of the IMG database grew by more than 10 percent since the 2.3 release only three months prior – a trend that is indicative of the ever-growing volume of sequenced genomes. This flood of sequence data provides rich opportunities for uncovering relationships between organisms.

At the same time, high-throughput experimental platforms such as gene-chips and mass-spectrometry-based technologies have enabled breakthrough improvements in the rate at which genes and gene products can be detected in cells. In principal, this should enable researchers to gain insight into the underlying processes at work in these systems. Better understanding these relationships enables, for instance, identification of highly conserved proteins that are suggestive of ubiquitous and essential functions. Likewise, these patterns can help identify unique proteins that may indicate functions specific to a particular organism. Yet the complexity of the mapping between genes, proteins, metabolic pathways, and cell behaviors is staggering. It is not always possible to observe these complex interaction systems and devise a hypothesis *a priori*. Often the best we can do is conjecture that some processes are related, or even more generally assert that a particular environmental treatment will cause differences that can be measured.

To unwind the complexity in these systems is a key computational task, which is also often a bottleneck for genome studies, as is analyzing the coding capacity of a genome in relation to other species' genomes. The two key tasks associated with multiple whole-genome sequence comparison are: 1) comparing all predicted protein sequences of a genome relative to those of other genomes and 2) representing the results of this sequence analysis in a way that facilitates the identification of features of interest (such as highly conserved versus unique proteins).

9.1.1 Whole-Genome Comparison

Performing multiple whole-genome comparisons requires mapping homologous relationships of the proteins in each genome. *Homologs* are defined as proteins or genes sharing a common evolutionary ancestor. *Orthologs* are homologous proteins in different organisms, such as proteins separated by a speciation event, and are likely to be functionally equivalent (for a recent review, see [2]). *Paralogs* are homologous proteins that arose from a gene duplication event and perform very similar functions often with subtle and important differences. Identifying homologs, orthologs, and paralogs provides a map for comparing organisms' functional capabilities, and hence is a key task used to: transfer functional annotations from proteins of known function to proteins of newly sequenced organisms [3], map functional relationships based on co-conservation [4, 5], assess evolutionary relationships between species [6], and identify putative drug targets [7].

9.1.2 Common Practices in HPC Computational Biology

The majority of biologists who want to evaluate a large-scale multiple-genome hypothesis are faced with an unpleasant choice. Either they must prefilter the data, favoring that which is likely to produce an answer of interest, or they must accept heroic computational run times as a rate-limiting step in their research. In the first case, the biologist is often prevented from finding the unexpected (and, therefore, most valuable) results because data has been limited to accommodate tools of choice. In the second case, run-time parameters, data sets, and hypotheses must be so carefully chosen as to be correct on the first pass, because rerunning or exploratory analysis are virtually impossible to complete within a reasonable time. We view data-intensive computing as a central player in eliminating this unpleasant choice, instead offering the compute power of high-performance computing (HPC) platforms in a real-time exploratory model where iteration, refinement, and repetition can be completed in a short time. This chapter presents a collection of commonly performed analysis tasks, driven at a multiple whole-genome scale using tools implemented on HPC platforms and a demonstration of how analysis pipelines can be created from a laptop that allow interaction between the user, the visual representation of analysis output, and the underlying HPC systems. In effect, this creates an exploratory environment that facilitates hypothesis generation.

9.2 Data-Intensive Tools and Methods

Many different areas of bioinformatics and biology utilize common analysis tasks. Perhaps the most fundamental tasks for sequence analysis focus on finding similarities between genes (and the corresponding proteins) that comprise a species' genome. Some of the basic computational tasks that enable this analysis are sequence alignment, homology detection, and ortholog identification. In the following sections, we describe optimized implementations of computational tools, designed for these tasks, as well as a visual engine and middleware components to make the power of these optimized implementations accessible to research biologists.

9.2.1 High-Performance Sequence Analysis: ScalaBLAST

The BLAST [8] algorithm compares a query gene(s) or protein(s) sequence with the sequences in a database by identifying an optimal local alignment between sequences, if such an alignment exists. For each database sequence match to a query, BLAST returns a similarity score and statistical confidence, which form the basis of many other forms of analysis. ScalaBLAST [9] is a high-performance implementation of BLAST, which operates by distributing the work of the sequence analysis tasks across many processors, sharing a single image of the target database in globally accessible memory to prevent the need for many copies of large database files or I/O bottlenecks associated with multiple processors reading them across a parallel file system. ScalaBLAST has been shown to scale to thousands of processors, and has been specially modified for this application to accommodate ortholog identification by reorganizing the calculations into species-specific comparisons.

9.2.2 Sensitive Remote Homolog Detection: SHOT

SHOT [10] is an algorithm for detecting related proteins that have poor sequence similarity. This is done by transforming protein sequences into sets of features and identifying homologous pairs using a trained support vector machine (SVM) classifier. Though there are many SVM-based homology tools, SHOT is one of the few that reports similarity scores between pairs of proteins (as opposed to classifying protein sequences into pre-determined families). It is also faster and has much higher sensitivity than alternatives that depend on iterative BLAST-based methods [10].

The SHOT classifier is generated by a data-intensive training process that uses a basis set of proteins whose pairwise homology is known *a priori*. Using this classifier, a SHOT homology score for a new query protein is calculated as a linear combination of inner products between support vectors reported by the training process, and a vectorized form of new records. Because training the classifier is done rarely (for example, only after updates to the basis set), training is done offline of the query sequence analysis process, in effect hiding from users the computational cost of training the classifier. The analysis phase of SHOT can then be implemented using an embarrassingly parallel scheduling approach to simultaneously score many independent homology calculations.

9.2.3 Identifying Orthologs: InParanoid

Several methods have been developed to predict orthologs and paralogs [11–18]. These methods typically rely on sequence homology, clustering, evolutionary distance, family tree analysis, or a combination of these techniques. Among the bioinformatics tools available for ortholog and paralog detection, InParanoid [13] provides a good balance of specificity and sensitivity [19, 20]. InParanoid is a Perl script that uses the output of BLAST to detect homology between pairs of proteins to build maps of orthologs between pairs of genomes. Comparing two small genomes (typical microbes, for example) using InParanoid is relatively straightforward and readily accomplished within a few hours on a single-processor computer. However, this compute time dramatically increases when performing this analysis for a larger number of genome pairs, and/or analyzing larger genomes (mammalian genomes, for example). Specifically, for orthologs among a group of more than two genomes, the InParanoid process must be repeated for all pairs of genomes in the group, leading to a large investment in compute time for BLAST calculations, followed by post-processing of pairwise ortholog records to identify orthologous groups, referred to as "ortholog graphs."

Source code for InParanoid 1.35 was obtained from http://inparanoid.sbc. su.se/ and was rewritten in C++ (hereafter referred to as InParanoidC++). Translation of InParanoid from Perl to C++ included key changes that do not affect the numerical output of the code, but which significantly enhance performance. New data structures were created to associate information directly with each protein being tracked. These new structures replaced the need for several hash tables used in the original Perl script for tracking information, including hit scores and ortholog graph membership. There were also several auxiliary bookkeeping matrices that were eliminated to improve performance and scalability.

Features were also added to InParanoidC++. The original Perl code contained global variables that could be changed in order to customize the behavior of the script. These were replaced by command line options. A feature was also added to provide flexibility in the sequence overlap requirement. For a pair of sequences, this feature specifies the required length of the sequence alignment (from BLAST) as the percentage of the full length of each sequence. The user can specify this overlap cutoff as well as whether only one or both proteins of an orthologous pair of proteins must satisfy it. By default, 50 percent of the sequence length of one protein (of an orthologous pair) must align. We also add the ability to output the results in XML and to include additional information that is useful for constructing visualizations with the output. Features in InParanoidC++ not included are the bootstrapping routine and the ability to use outgroups, but these can be easily included in the future. Comparison of several sample sets verified that InParanoid and InParanoidC++ produced identical results.

InParanoid optionally launches serial BLAST jobs to create the pairwise alignments needed for ortholog prediction. This feature was removed from InParanoidC++ because BLAST tends to be the rate limiting step in the ortholog prediction process. Instead, we precompute BLAST scores using ScalaBLAST on a multiprocessor architecture, then feed that output to InParanoidC++ for rapid ortholog prediction. The change in run-time resulting from the combination of ScalaBLAST and InParanoidC++ make it feasible to include ortholog identification in real-time iterative analytical pipelines.

9.2.4 Interactive Visual Representation and Browsing: Starlight

Starlight [21], available from Future Point Systems, Inc., is an information visualization application capable of organizing and integrating a variety of

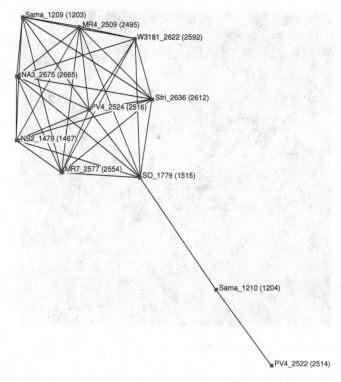

Figure 9.1. A complex ortholog graph.

structured and unstructured information types to generate interactive graphical representations of relationships among the data. Starlight allows for layering and filtering of many types of data. Here we use Starlight to create visual representations of sequence similarity scores and ortholog identifications from multiple genome data sets.

Two Starlight visualization types are generated in this chapter: ortholog graphs and remote homology graphs. Ortholog graphs (Figure 9.1) illustrate proteins that are highly similar, and therefore likely to perform the same basic function, across multiple species. In ortholog graphs, each node is a protein and each edge is an orthologous link determined by ScalaBLAST and InParanoidC++. Nodes can be color-coded to indicate the species of origin for each protein. If a given protein is unique to a single species it will not be connected to any other proteins. If a given protein is encoded by exactly two species, one would see a pair of nodes connected by an edge. If a protein has orthologs in several species, one would find a fully connected graph with the number of nodes indicating how many species share this function. However, because genes in a genome can be deleted or duplicated, leading

Figure 9.2. Remote homology graph.

to loss of function or evolution of similar functions, the relationship between
homologous proteins in an arbitrary collection of species can be very complex.
Although fully connected graphs are easy to describe and find automatically,
the human eye is the only tool that can intuitively recognize some of the more
complex relationships from a visual representation of the ortholog graphs, as
shown in Figure 9.1. By coloring the edges in this figure by the strength of the
similarity between nodes, the "head" of the cluster contains both strong and
weak orthologs, evidenced by its combination of lower scores (lighter color
edges) and higher scores (darker color edges).

Remote homolog graphs (Figure 9.2) can be thought of as a projection from
a central protein of known function onto proteins of unknown function. For
these graphs, a collection of "basis proteins," about which much is known
structurally or functionally, are used to classify proteins of interest into groups
or families. As with the ortholog graphs, nodes are proteins. However, a protein
in the center of a graph is one of the basis proteins, and protein homologs from
the genomes under study are located around the periphery of the basis protein.
In this case, edges indicate a remote homology relationship as determined by
SHOT, and the edges can be color-coded by species. These graphs look almost
like pie charts because there are no links between the peripheral proteins.

The distribution of edge colors gives an indication of the expansion or contraction of a protein family or structural fold in a particular species relative to the other species under study.

Starlight can also be used to integrate ancillary, unstructured data that may be available for genomes or proteins. For example, protein functional category information is available in the protein tables for prokaryotic genomes at.[1] Functional annotations can also be obtained from Pfam [22],[2] or by *ad hoc* comparison of proteins to the Pfam hidden Markov models using the HMMER software.[3] Incorporating additional records such as these to the existing data set of orthologous relationships is as simple as appending fields that contain these additional functional categorizations. Once added, users can query, search, and filter their data based on these data fields. These additional data are often heterogeneous: for some proteins, no functional categorization is available, whereas others may have single or multiple hierarchical functional categorizations. Starlight accommodates all of these variants without special handling.

9.2.5 *Middleware for Data-Intensive Computing: MeDICi*

The MeDICi Integration Framework (MIF) [23] is a component-based integration platform for creating complex scientific and analytical applications from the composition of independently developed software modules. The MIF employs abstractions and underlying supporting mechanisms to facilitate the handling of very large data sets and high-volume data streams in a distributed application. It also supports the integration of modules written in any language and running on any execution platform into a single distributed application. We present an example multiple whole-genome analysis processing pipeline using the analysis tools previously described running on HPC platforms where appropriate, integrated using MIF. This enables use of HPC systems, visual applications, and sophisticated analytical tools from a laptop in real time for biological hypothesis discovery.

9.3 Real-Time Data-Intensive Hypothesis Discovery

The following sections present a pair of case studies that utilize the various analytic components previously described. These case studies serve to illustrate how data-intensive computing is utilized for genome-scale hypothesis discovery studies in biology.

---

[1] http://www.ncbi.nlm.nih.gov/genomes/lproks.cgi.
[2] http://pfam.janelia.org/.
[3] http://hmmer.janelia.org/.

The data on which we demonstrate hypothesis discovery are collections of openly available bacterial genomes. Species of the genus *Shewanella* are gamma-proteobacteria that have remarkable anaerobic respiratory versatility, displaying the ability to transfer electrons to various heavy metals, including environmental contaminants such as iron, uranium, and chromium [24]. As a result, there is great interest in exploring their potential as constitutive agents for environmental remediation activities, such as cleaning up contaminated ground surrounding retired nuclear and chemical production facilities. In general, this metabolic versatility is a feature of *Shewanella* as a genus, however individual species have diverse respiratory capabilities and display considerable diversity with respect to physiologic characteristics such as nutrient requirements. This is reflective of the wide variety of habitats in which these organisms are found. Simultaneously examining the genome data available for several of the *Shewanella* species provides a means to identify the genes and proteins responsible for the unique characteristics of each species and could lead to testable hypotheses about species physiology and bioremediation potential.

There are several confounding aspects to understanding how *Shewanella* species are related. Many species encode multiple homologous proteins, making a one-to-one mapping of their functions nontrivial. Homologous proteins within a species (such as paralogs) perform similar but distinct functions, and are therefore informative when studying type versatility, but are not straightforward to map across genomes.

Given this complexity, it is important to look globally at the full protein complement of these species and to examine the data in a comparative manner. Furthermore, proteins can be described using a variety of overlapping ontologies – in terms of their biological pathways in which they participate, by the specific biochemical reactions they catalyze, by their cellular location, or by the physical attributes of their structure. Each of these ontologies gives some information about what the protein does. Text information across all these ontologies must be integrated with numerical data describing the relationship between the proteins when evaluating biological hypotheses. Users need to interactively project, filter, and group proteins by any one of these or other derived categorical descriptors.

Once presented with this interactive data set, one can develop a cursory hypothesis using a high-level visual representation of patterns within the data. This hypothesis can be refined by iteratively selecting and analyzing subsets of the data, looking for patterns that converge on a testable hypothesis. In this way, one can allow the data to reveal its underlying structure and patterns.

Table 9.1. Shewanella *species in genome set 1 (GS1)*

Species	Num Proteins	Abbreviation
S. putrefaciens CN-32	4006	CN32
Shewanella sp. ANA-3	4389	ANA3
S. oneidensis MR-1	4396	SONE
S. denitrificans OS217	3778	Sden
S. loihica PV-4	3868	PV4
S. amazonensis SB2b	3654	Sama
S. putrefaciens W3–18-1	4078	W3181
Shewanella sp. MR-7	4040	MR7
Shewanella sp. MR-4	3940	MR4
S. frigidimarina NCIMB 400	4063	Sfri

9.3.1 *Exploratory Look into* Shewanella *Functions*

This discussion explores orthologous relationships between ten *Shewanella* species by using ScalaBLAST and InParanoidC++ to infer all the orthologous protein pairs and visualization of the resulting ortholog graphs using Starlight. In the study, we imported functional information about the proteins from Pfam [22], a public database that organized proteins into families based on shared homology. Adding this additional functional information to the Starlight visualization allowed us to query and filter the output based on text found in the Pfam descriptions of each protein.

The genome data set used in the first case study (GS1) was a collection of ten predicted proteomes (the predicted set of all proteins encoded in a genome) of the genus *Shewanella*, which were obtained from the Joint Genome Institute download site.[4] The formal species names, protein counts, and abbreviated names for the GS1 data set are listed in Table 9.1.

Ortholog relationships between the species in GS1 were calculated using ScalaBLAST and InParanoidC++. The resulting ortholog graphs from the ten species were visualized using Starlight. Pfam descriptions for each protein were added to the Starlight records for all ten species in GS1 where such data was available for a protein.

Prediction of orthologs among all ten *Shewanella* species in GS1 required fory-five pairwise proteome comparisons. We examined the run times for completing this task using conventional BLAST with the InParanoid Perl script compared to using ScalaBLAST with InParanoidC++. Table 9.2 presents these run

---

[4] http://genome.jgi-psf.org/mic_home.html.

Table 9.2. *Ortholog prediction run times*

Analysis	Num Processors	Time (min)
InParanoid	1	45.05
InParanoidC++	1	0.54
BLAST + InParanoid	10	146.7
ScalaBLAST + InParanoidC++	10	105.4
ScalaBLAST + InParanoidC++	512	5.4

times for ortholog identification alone (InParanoid vs. InParanoidC++) and for the total times (BLAST + InParanoid versus ScalaBLAST + InParanoidC++).

To test only the InParanoid versus InParanoidC++ run times, precomputed BLAST output for all forty-five pairwise comparisons was used. For this benchmark, the option to InParanoid indicating that it should not launch serial BLAST was selected allowing the run time to arise from ortholog prediction times alone. The ortholog prediction performed by InParanoid was significantly faster using the C++ version versus the Perl version, as shown in Table 9.2. InParanoidC++ ran, on the average, in 2.5 percent of the time it took for the conventional InParanoid to run, giving an average eighty-fivefold speedup for whole genome ortholog prediction using the GS1 data set.

To measure the impact of combining ScalaBLAST and InParanoidC++, this calculation was repeated, but InParanoid called BLAST for each genome pair. For this test, ten processors were used on which InParanoid was manually launched on independent subsets of the genome pairs. Wall-clock times were recorded and compared with the run time of ScalaBLAST running on ten processors followed by InParanoidC++ for all genome pairs. Table 9.2 presents these run times. The difference in run time for these two tests was almost entirely because of the improvement in the ortholog prediction phase, as the BLAST times were nearly equal. However, because ScalaBLAST was inherently scalable to many processors regardless of the number of genomes under study, total run time was greatly reduced using larger systems with the ScalaBLAST + InParanoidC++ combination. For example, combining ScalaBLAST and InParanoidC++ using 512 processors completed the entire sequence analysis and ortholog identification phase in 5.4 minutes, making it reasonable to incorporate this analysis into a real-time hypothesis discovery pipeline.

We visualized the output of ortholog prediction between these ten *Shewanella* species as a collection of graphs using Starlight, where the graph nodes represented proteins and the edges represented predicted orthologous relationships. This approach allowed visual inspection and browsing of the

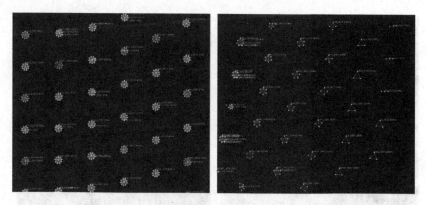

Figure 9.3. Sample of ortholog graphs for the GS1 data set.

entire ortholog record, with immediate identification of simple multiple-species ortholog groups – proteins for which an ortholog relationship was identified between any specific number of species. This relationship was represented in the ortholog graph record as fully connected graphs (such as cliques) with one protein from each species: for the set of ten species, fully connected graphs had ten nodes and forty-five edges. For any *subset* of the ten species, fully connected graphs with fewer than ten nodes were also readily identified. Figure 9.3 illustrates fully connected ortholog graphs.

A hallmark phenotypic characteristic of the *Shewanella* genus was the ability to use a wide array of terminal electron acceptors during anaerobic respiration [25]. Among the ten species in GS1, all except for Sden had the ability to use nitrate as the terminal electron acceptor, producing nitrite. Therefore, we asked the simplistic question, "What proteins are absent from Sden that are present in the other 9 species in GS1?" To answer this question, we used Starlight to identify the collection of ortholog graphs for which exactly one species was absent, for example, those fully connected graphs with nine nodes. The left of Figure 9.4 shows some of these graphs. We then applied a simple filter to hide any graph in this collection that included a protein from Sden. The ortholog graphs remaining after this filtering step were the collection of proteins that were completely conserved in all nine of the other species in GS1, but absent from Sden. Figure 9.4 illustrates this filtered collection on the right (nodes are color-coded by the functional category of their proteins).

Once this set of ortholog graphs was identified, browsing their functional categorization was done based on information from Pfam. Figure 9.5 shows the nodes reorganized into clusters, where the groups are labeled with Pfam functional information, and the protein nodes are color-coded by species. Empty

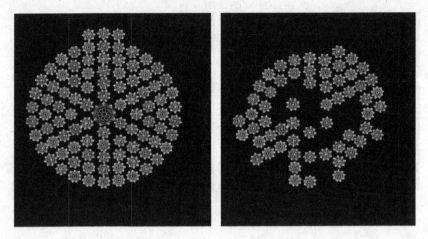

Figure 9.4. Ortholog graphs from GS1 having nine nodes.

circles represent a functional group that included Sden proteins, and thus all those orthologous proteins have been hidden from view (or filtered out). In this way, we built a list of orthologs and their functions that were common to many *Shewanella* species, but absent from Sden.

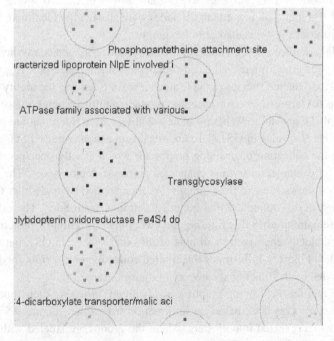

Figure 9.5. Functional categorization of proteins in the nine-node graphs.

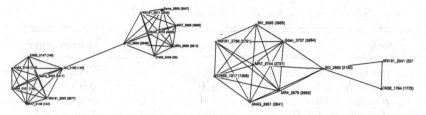

Figure 9.6. Detail of complex ortholog graphs.

A second line of exploration using the ortholog graphs highlighted the value of visual interface to this data set. The essential features of many of the ortholog graphs cannot be described by any simple topological description and therefore cannot be found easily (or at all) without a visual representation. Figure 9.6 illustrates some examples of these more complex orthologs. These groups were not maximal cliques, and were not fully connected, but were easily detected in Starlight by visual inspection. For example, the left panel of Figure 9.6 shows a group consisting of two reasonably well-defined and nearly fully connected subgroups (the right and left poles of the "barbell"). However, there was a link between these poles, suggesting the presence of paralogs in some of the species. In this case, six species were represented in each of the subgroups, with an MR1 protein in one and a PV4 protein in the other forming a link between the subgroups. Phylogenetic analysis of these proteins might reveal an evolutionary relationship involving gene duplication, gain, or loss to explain this complex set of links.

Another complex ortholog graph involved the cytochromes, which are proteins involved in electron transfer during respiration. The right panel of Figure 9.6 illustrates an ortholog graph of cytochrome. This graph has two proteins from CN32 and two proteins from W3181, suggesting a gene duplication event. Manual curation of these proteins indicated that CN32 and W3181 proteins in the larger subgroup were likely orthologs to the MR4, MR7, ANA3, Sfri, and SONE proteins, whereas the CN32 and W3181 proteins in the small subgroup on the right were paralogs. Starlight captured these features by displaying the two duplicated proteins as nodes joined to the group as a "tail."

9.3.2 Interactive and Iterative Hypothesis Discovery

This section focuses on the value of connecting data-intensive analyses to a high-performance compute infrastructure via MeDICi to drive iterative, real-time hypothesis discovery. We used MeDICi to create a single analysis pipeline for a two-stage iterative analysis of ten *Shewanella* genomes. This analysis

Table 9.3. Shewanella *species in genome set 2 (GS2)*

Species	Num Proteins	Abbreviation
S. putrefaciens CN-32	4000	CN32
Shewanella sp. ANA-3	4420	ANA3
S. oneidensis MR-1	4401	SONE
S. denitrificans OS217	3780	Sden
S. loihica PV-4	3885	PV4
S. amazonensis SB2B	3668	Sama
S. baltica OS185	4458	OS185
S. sediminis HAW-EB3	4499	Ssed
S. woodyi ATCC 51908	4930	Swoo
S. pealeana ANG-SQ1	4295	Spea

pipeline combined 1) the remote homology detection capabilities of SHOT to give a cursory view into the possible functions and relative abundance of functions within each species, and 2) mapping of orthologs between the *Shewanella* species to explore the differences and similarities between the species relative to the functions identified in the first step. Figure 9.7 illustrates this pipeline.

For this case study, an updated set of ten *Shewanella* species' genomes (GS2) were used. Because these genomes were obtained at a later date than GS1, there were slight differences in the number of proteins identified in some of the species. Table 9.3 lists the formal species names, protein counts, and abbreviated names for the GS2 data set.

For the first analysis phase, the SHOT classifier had already been trained on a basis set of 4,352 proteins of known structure and function from the SCOP [26] database. The roughly 42,000 proteins from the GS2 data set were analyzed

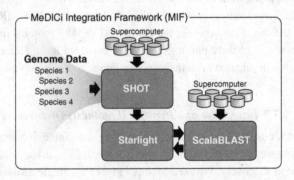

Figure 9.7. MeDICi Integration Framework.

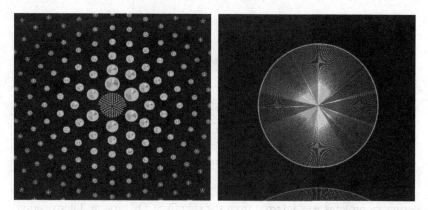

Figure 9.8. Exploring remote homolog graphs.

against this classifier using SHOT to determine the relationship between each of these proteins and the 4,352 "basis" proteins from the SCOP database.

This was done by first calculating BLAST scores for all of the 42,000 proteins of interest versus the 4,352 SCOP proteins. This was done using ScalaBLAST on a multiprocessor platform. These scores were used to populate a vector representation of each of the GS2 proteins. SHOT calculated the inner products between these vector representations and the support vectors from the trained classifier to determine remote homology scores. This provided an efficient categorization of the *Shewanella* proteins based on remote homology to SCOP proteins of known structure and function.

To benchmark the performance of SHOT on parallel systems, SHOT calculations were performed using a dual-dual core AMD Opteron cluster housed in the Wiliam R. Wiley Environmental Molecular sciences Laboratory (EMSL) using a varying number of cores. Using 128 cores this task completed in 22 minutes and using 700 cores the classification task finished in 4.5 minutes. The accompanying ScalaBLAST calculations required to populate the SHOT vectors were included in these run times. Because these applications scale efficiently in parallel, it should take proportionally less time on thousands of processors, if connected to a larger dedicated machine for larger analysis tasks. This calculation would have taken days on a single workstation, making it a prohibitive step in the overall workflow. Using multiprocessor architectures eliminated this bottleneck and allowed us to incorporate SHOT into a real-time workflow.

Our analysis produced thousands of graphs similar to the one illustrated in Figure 9.2. The left of Figure 9.8 shows an example of such a collection. From this view, the user can zoom in or out, or filter based on textual attributes of the edges or nodes. In these graphs, the possible functional role of the

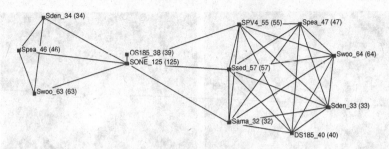

Figure 9.9. Refining a hypothesis with ortholog graphs.

periphery proteins was inferred from the central SCOP protein. Interrogation of our SHOT output in this way identified more than 500 proteins in GS2 with remote homology to the ferric enterobactin receptor (FepA), a protein known to be involved in iron sensing and iron transport in microbes [27]. The right panel of Figure 9.8 shows the radial graph with FepA in the center.

The second phase of our analysis addressed determining the relationship between these ~500 proteins among the ten species. These proteins were passed to ScalaBLAST and InParanoidC++ to generate ortholog graphs. Exploring these ortholog graphs revealed a complex graph (Figure 9.9) that contained proteins involved in the biogenesis of pili. Pili are appendages required for the formation of biofilms – structures composed of many cells held together and protected by an extracellular polymer. Because *Shewanella* species have the ability to transfer electrons to an electrode, *Shewanella* biofilm formation on iron oxide surfaces formed a simple fuel cell [28]. By combining our observations of remote homology to iron sensing, and orthologous proteins related to pili formation, we started to develop a hypothesis focused on proteins involved in pili formation that may sense iron in the environment and trigger biofilm formation. In this way, we developed a testable hypothesis arising directly from the data itself, not from a predetermined line of inquiry. Furthermore, the protein orthologs shown in the graph in Figure 9.9 reveal that this protein was present in only eight of the species and that there has been an apparent gene duplication event resulting in two similar copies (paralogous proteins) in four of the species. These observations suggested additional testable hypotheses that 1) those species with two copies of this protein may have an enhanced ability to form biofilms in response to iron, and 2) the two species that did not appear in the ortholog graph may have lost this ability.

Note that many other cursory hypotheses were attempted from the SHOT output visualization before we arrived at the ones previously described. Because the second phase was interactive and very fast, we were able to test and refine many sample hypotheses in a short time. This allowed us in the space of a few hours to converge on a testable set of hypotheses from exploratory interactions with the data. In effect, because we did not start with a hypothesis, the patterns in the data itself suggested interesting relationships that warranted further investigation. This was a truly data-driven hypothesis discovery exercise.

9.4 Discussion

Data analysis in bioinformatics, and to a large extent biology in general, continues to be driven by the increasing availability of sequence data and will for a long time to come. Efficiently processing these large data sets will remain a growing priority for the foreseeable future. To address these needs, we implemented and assembled an efficient set of computational tools that took advantage of multi-processor platforms. Optimized ortholog detection software was implemented based on the well-tested open source algorithm InParanoid. High-throughput BLAST was realized using ScalaBLAST. Remote homology detection was driven by a combination of ScalaBLAST and SHOT, both running on HPC architectures. This boost in computational efficiency effectively reduced the analytical time for multiple whole-genome analysis to the point where it was integrated into a real-time iterative analytical process.

During our work developing high-performance algorithms for biology, it became clear that the HPC applications themselves were not enough – solving the throughput challenge alone only pushed the computing bottleneck downstream. For example, parsing hundreds of thousands (or millions) of BLAST output records from a multiple whole-genome analysis into a typical spreadsheet application to search for patterns was impractical and inefficient. Thus, one goal of this research was also to demonstrate how visual representations of the complex relationships found in such large-scale analyses could play a significant role in alleviating this bottleneck. Visual approaches to organizing these large genomic data sets have the potential to greatly enhance the researcher's ability to find patterns that lead to testable hypotheses. Therefore, this work presented an analytical process in which high-performance computing and visual analytics came together to provide the user with a highly interactive environment for evaluating patterns in large, complex genomic data sets and HPC analysis results.

Specifically, visual representation of the orthologous relationships between proteins encoded by several *Shewanella* species made it possible to identify patterns that were readily recognized visually, but nearly impossible to describe in topological terms. In some cases, these relationships were straightforward to interpret biologically (as likely gene duplications/deletions), leading to insight that could not have been easily gained from automated processes. For instance, automated methods would have failed to identify the complex orthologous and paralogous relationships in the cytochrome proteins described in the first case study. *Shewanella* species in particular encode many cytochrome proteins with subtly (but importantly) different function, specialized for respiration under various environmental conditions. The variability in respiratory capability of the species under study was manifest in complex evolutionary inheritance of cytochromes. Although automated methods might miss much of the rich detail displayed in the ortholog graphs, a human analyst can quickly recognize the presence of linked subgroups of cytochrome proteins. With Starlight, it was also possible to integrate additional data into the visual representation of our HPC analysis output. The incorporation of protein functional information meant that we could combine graphical and text-based filtering to explore the presence/absence of functions relative to the species' metabolic capabilities. Specifically, we could use the ortholog graphs to identify completely conserved or unique proteins among the genomes, and examine their functional role (for instance, to explore why Sden appears to have lost the ability to reduce nitrate). Furthermore, integrating additional data sources, such as gene expression profiles and global proteomics data, was straightforward, and could provide the means to investigate differences between species based on a fusion of protein homology data, functional annotation, gene expression, and protein expression from a spectrum of experimental conditions.

One limitation of this approach was that scalable HPC algorithms can overwhelm serial visual applications with the volume of output. Our analyses of *Shewanella* genomes required operation of Starlight near the memory limits of the machine on which it was running. Thus, graph layout and other processes required to transform the HPC output to. a visual form could become a bottleneck or limiting factor for larger-scale biological analyses, so continued development in this area is needed. One potential area for development to alleviate this problem would be a parallel engine to drive graph layout, data ingestion, indexing, and filtering.

Starlight was only one of the possible applications that could drive the visualization in such an analytical pipeline. The modular nature of MIF would allow users to drive other visual platforms using a similar approach.

We used the MeDICi Integration Framework to build an iterative, automated pipeline that combined different high-performance analytical tools that were common steps in many different types of biological analysis. This pipeline demonstrated that high performance computing resources can be used to reduce the run time of expensive computations on multiple whole genomes, but the real power of this approach was that it can be changed to suit a broad variety of other lines of investigation. Our case studies demonstrated particular workflows of interest, but it could be changed to add or remove steps in the analysis process as new analysis is needed.

One of the goals of these methods was to present a real-time analysis of large-scale biology data. ScalaBLAST + inparanoid C++ presumed, however, the availability of dedicated compute resources. If parallel visualization applications were used instead of serial ones, this need would be even greater. For some small compute clusters, this was a reasonable requirement, but as the scaling demand increased, finding a cluster that allows on-demand access (as opposed to batch-mode access) became problematic. The need for on-demand computing is a key difference between exploratory, data-driven sciences and computational sciences that focus on first-principles and equation-driven calculations. For HPC architectures to have the greatest impact for biology and other exploratory domains in this age of data-driven exploration, new paradigms need to be developed for giving on-demand compute access from large-scale machines.

9.5 Conclusion

This chapter demonstrated how data-intensive computation can be integrated into analytical workflows for biological sciences. One strength of this approach was that high-performance architectures significantly reduced the time for computational tasks making it possible to embed them in real-time analysis. Combining this with visualization allowed users to operate on very large data sets using sophisticated analysis to *discover* a hypothesis from data, rather than looking for supporting evidence of a hypothesis. Freeing the user to look at much larger data sets meant they are much more likely to find the unexpected. This concept can be translated to many other data-driven science and intelligence domains. In effect, this technique of combining high-performance computing, scalable applications, and visualization using MIF lead to a new way of *discovering* hypotheses in real-time at the multiple genome scale using data-intensive computing.

Acknowledgments

MeDICi, the MeDICi Integration Framework, ScalaBLAST, and SHOT were partially funded through the Laboratory Directed Research and Development (LDRD) at Pacific Northwest National Laboratory (PNNL). ScalaBLAST and SHOT were also partially supported by the U.S. Department of Energy (DOE) Office of Advanced Scientific Computing Research. SHOT received additional support from the National Science Foundation under contract 53836A. Significant portions of the work were performed in conjunction with the Computational Science Grand Challenge Program at the Wiliam R. Wiley Environmental Molecular Science Laboratory, a U.S. DOE national scientific user facility at PNNL in Richland, Washington. PNNL is perated for the DOE by Battelle under contract DE-AC06–76RLO-1830.

References

1. Markowitz, V., Chen, I. M., Palaniappan, K., Chu, K., Szeto, E., Grechkin, Y., Rattner, A., Anderson, I., Lykidis, A., Mavromatis, K., Ivanova, N., and Kyrpides, N. "The Integrated Microbial Genome System: An Expanding Comparative Analysis Resource." *Nucl. Acid. Res.* 38 (2010): D382–D390.
2. Koonin, E. "Orthologs, Paralogs, and Evolutionary Genomics." *Annu. Rev. Genet.* 39, (2005). 309–338.
3. Brent, M. "Steady Progress and Recent Breakthroughs in the Accuracy of Automated Genome Annotation," *Nat. Rev. Genet.* 9 (2008): 62–73.
4. Pagel, P., Mewes, H., and Frishman, D. "Conservation of Protein-Protein Interactions- Lessons from Ascomycota." *Trends Genet.* 20 (2004): 72–76.
5. van Noort, V., Snel, B., and Huynen, M. "Predicting Gene Function by Conserved Co-Expression." *Trends Genet.* 19 (2003): 238–42.
6. Thornton, J., and DeSalle, R. "Gene Family Evolution and Homology: Genomics Meets Phylogenetics." *Annu. Rev. Genomics Hum. Genet.* 1 (2000): 41–73.
7. Ekins, S., Mestres, J., and Testa, B. "*In silico* Pharmacology for Drug Discovery: Methods for Virtual Ligand Screening and Profiling." *Br. J. Pharmacol.* 159 (2007): 9–20.
8. Altschul, S., Gish, W., Miller, W., Meyers, E., and Lipman, D. "Basic Local Alignment Search Tool." *J. Mol. Biol.* 215 (1990): 403–10.
9. Oehmen, C. S., and Nieplocha, J. "ScalaBLAST: A scalable Implementation of BLAST for High-Performance Data-Intensive Bioinformatics Analysis." *IEEE Trans. Parallel Dist. Sys.* 17 (2006): 740–49.
10. Webb-Robertson, B. J., Oehmen, C. S., and Shah, A. "A Feature Integration Approach for a Generalized Support Vector Machine Pairwise Homology Algorithm." *Comput. Biol. Chem.* 32 (2008): 458–61.
11. Alexeyenko, A., Tamas, I., Liu, G., and Sonnhammer, E. "Automatic Clustering of Orthologs and In-Paralogs Shared by Multiple Proteomes." *Bioinformatics* 22 (2006): e9–e15.
12. Li, L., Stoeckert, C., and Roos, D. "OrthoMCL: Identification of Ortholog Groups for Eukaryotic Genomes." *Genome Res.* 13 (2003): 2178–89.
13. Remm, M., Storm, C., and Sonnhammer, E. "Automatic Clustering of Orthologs and In-Paralogs from Pairwise Species Comparisons." *J. Mol. Biol.* 314 (2001): 1041–52.
14. Storm, C., and Sonnhammer, E. "Automated Ortholog Inference from Phylogenetic Trees and Calculation of Orthology Reliability." *Bioinformatics* 18 (2002): 92–99.

15. Tatusov, R., Koonin, E. , and Lipman, D. "A Genomic Perspective on Protein Families." *Science* 278 (1997): 631–37.
16. Wall, D., Fraser, H., and Hirsh, A. "Detecting Putative Orthologs." *Bioinformatics* 19 (2003): 1710–11.
17. Zhou, Y. and Landweber, L. "BLASTO: A Tool for Searching Orthologous Groups." *Nucl. Acid. Res.* 35, (2007): W678–W682.
18. Zmasek, C. and Eddy, S. "RIO: Analyzing Proteomics by Automated Phylogenomics Using Resampled Inference of Orthologs." *BMC Bioinformatics* 3 (2002): 14.
19. Chen, F., Mackey, A., Vermunt, J., and Roos, D. "Assessing Performance of Orthology Detection Strategies Applied to Eukaryotic Genomes." *PLoS ONE* 2, (2007): e383.
20. Hulsen, T., Huynen, M., dee Vlieg, J., and Groenen, P. "Benchmarking Ortholog Identification Methods Using Functional Genomics Data." *Genome Biol.* 7 (2006): R31.
21. Risch, J., Rex, D., Dowson, S., Walters, S., May, R., and Moon, B. "The STARLIGHT Information Visualization System." In *IEEE International Information Visualization Conference (IV' 97)*, London, UK, 1997, p. 42.
22. Finn, R., Tate, J., Mistry, J., Coggill, P., Sammut, J., Hotz, H., Ceric, G., Forslund, K., Eddy, S., Sonnhammer, E., and Bateman, A. "The Pfam Protein Families Database." *Nucl. Acid. Res.* 36, (2008): D281–D288.
23. Gorton, I. Wynne, A., Liu, Y., and Yin, J. "Components in the Pipeline." *Software IEEE* 28, no. 3 (May–June 2011): 34–40.
24. Fredrickson, J. Romine, M. Beliaev, A. Auchtung, J. Driscoll, M. Gardner, T. Nealson, K. Osterman, A. Pinchuk, G. Reed, J. Rodionov, D. Rodrigues, J. Saffarini, D. Serres, A. M. Spormann, I., and J. Tiedje. "Towards Environmental Systems Biology of *Shewanella*." *Nat. Rev. Microbiol.* 6 (2008): 592–603.
25. Hau, H. and Gralnick, J. "Ecology and Biotechnology of the Genus *Shewanella*." *Microbiol.* 61 (2007): 237–58.
26. Andreeva, A., Howorth, D., Chandonia, J., Brenner, S., Hubbard, T., Chothia, C., and Murzin, A. "Data Growth and Its Impact on the Scop Database: New Developments." *Nucl. Acid. Res.* 36 (2008): D419–D425.
27. Ma, L. Kaserer, W. Annamalai, R. Scott, D. Jin, B. Jiang, X. Xiao, Q. Maymani, H. Massis, L. Ferreira, L. and Newton, S. "Evidence of ball-and-Chain Transport of Ferric Enterobactin through Fepa." *J. Biol. Chem.* 282 (2007): 397–406.
28. Biffinger, J., Pietron, J., Ray, R., Little, B., and Ringeisen, B. "A Biofilm Enhanced Miniature Microbial Fuel Cell Using *Shewanella* Oneidensis DSP 10 and Oxygen Reducing Cathodes." *Biosens. Bioelectron.* 22 (2007): 1672–79.

10

Data-Intensive Visual Analysis
for Cyber-Security

William A. Pike, Daniel M. Best, Douglas V. Love,
and Shawn J. Bohn

10.1 Introduction

Protecting communications networks against attacks where the aim is to steal information, disrupt order, or harm critical infrastructure can require the collection and analysis of staggering amounts of data. The ability to detect and respond to threats quickly is a paramount concern across sectors, and especially for critical government, utility, and financial networks. Yet detecting emerging or incipient threats in immense volumes of network traffic requires new computational and analytic approaches. Network security increasingly requires cooperation between human analysts able to spot suspicious events through means such as data visualization and automated systems that process streaming network data in near real-time to triage events so that human analysts are best able to focus their work.

This chapter presents a pair of network traffic analysis tools coupled to a computational architecture that enables the high-throughput, real-time visual analysis of network activity. The streaming data pipeline to which these tools are connected is designed to be easily extensible, allowing new tools to subscribe to data and add their own in-stream analytics. The visual analysis tools themselves – Correlation Layers for Information Query and Exploration (CLIQUE) and Traffic Circle – provide complementary views of network activity designed to support the timely discovery of potential threats in volumes of network data that exceed what is traditionally visualized. CLIQUE uses a behavioral modeling approach that learns the expected activity of actors (such as IP addresses or users) and collections of actors on a network, and compares current activity to this learned model to detect behavior-based anomalies. Traffic Circle is a raw network flow visualization tool that is architected to provide detailed views of very large volumes of traffic (in the hundreds of millions of records per view) in such a way that analysts can identify features that could otherwise be obfuscated through analysis of aggregates alone.

The tools we describe are designed to analyze network flows, a construct that aggregates individual packets into sessions that summarize the communication between two IP addresses over a particular combination of source and destination port. We use network flows because they are ubiquitous; most enterprises have deployed network flow collection sensors as a way to gather a useful, albeit imperfect, summary of network activity. In our case, the end user organizations for our analysis applications commonly use flows generated by sensors at an enterprise's internet gateway as as an entry point into analysis to find interesting patterns, features, or trends. Flows contain connection-level information (essentially, header data summarizing a connection) and each flow might summarize a large number of underlying packets. Although packet-level analysis can provide insight into the contents of a communication (which flows typically do not), as summaries over all the packets communicated during a session between two network hosts flows provide a first-order data reduction. In addition, as network traffic is increasingly encrypted, access to communication content is no longer guaranteed. Therefore, methods that rely solely on connection-level variables are increasingly necessary. Network flows remain a useful element of a cyber security analysis environment simply because a compromised machine is only useful to an attacker if he can reliably communicate with it. Thus, malicious code should leave some trace on a communication network.

10.2 Motivation

Ensuring the security of a computing network requires the timely discovery, and ideally prevention or deterrence, of malicious activities that can represent threats to information or infrastructure. Although rule-based techniques (such as signature-based intrusion detection systems) can assist in detecting instances of known malicious activity, detecting new threats (instances of which have never been seen, and for which a signature does not exist) poses significant computational challenges. Detecting statistical anomalies in traffic volumes is generally insufficient, because large numbers of false positives or false negatives can result. In the former case, flagging anomalies in diverse and evolving hosts can burden an analyst charged with resolving them because anomalous activity alone is not necessarily malicious. In the second case, sophisticated threats can be buried in seemingly normal-looking traffic. In fact, it is the goal of the sophisticated attacker to evade detection by making the traffic his malware generates appear normal.

Our approach to data-intensive analytics acknowledges that human analysts are by necessity part of the discovery, resolution, and response process. Visual interfaces are therefore necessary to provide analysts with the means to assess patterns, identify data features that may be hard to detect except through human perception, and apply judgment to determine whether an anomaly is malicious or benign. However, three primary challenges complicate visual analysis of computer network traffic: data volume, time sensitivity, and the need to focus analytic effort.

10.2.1 Data Volume

It is common for an enterprise network to generate thousands of flow records each second, producing billions of flows (amounting to hundreds of gigabytes of data or more) each day. Although some threats may emerge quickly, requiring the analysis of just a few days of data at most, of frequent concern is the "low and slow" exploit that may take weeks, months, or years to develop. A patient attacker, in a deliberate attempt to avoid detection by taking advantage of the data-intensive analysis problem, may scan a network for vulnerabilities through just a few packets per day, week, or year – hiding the events his code generates in massive volumes of legitimate traffic. Given the potential for long durations over which data must be analyzed to detect such attacks, the data store from which an analysis may draw can contain terabytes to petabytes of data. Moreover, the number of unique actors observed on a network challenges contemporary approaches. For some of the end user organizations using the tools we developed for them and discuss in this chapter, tens of millions of unique IP addresses are seen each month. (The problem of vast numbers of discrete actors becomes even more challenging in IPv6 addressing.) Data volume is a leading reason that traditional cyber analytic tools operate in an offline, post mortem mode: the volume of data simply overtakes the analytic process. Not only must new data be examined (both automatically and manually) for potential threats, but historical data must be available for efficient retrieval when the analyst wants to review it for earlier indicators or compare it to current events.

Processing, visualizing, and interacting with data sets containing billions of records per day introduces specific analysis challenges. Visualization of discrete records is rarely an effective entry point into large data sets. Most systems for depicting raw event logs are only effective for data sets with tens of thousands to hundreds of thousands of records. Beyond these sizes, rendering times and occlusion cause challenges for visual analysis. Moreover, reducing large data sets down to subsets suitable for such tools means that very small portions of the source data are actually explored by an analyst; filters must be applied to either reduce the time period under study to one that is brief enough to contain just the amount of data a tool is capable of displaying, or to select flow records on the basis of a limited set of attribute-value pairs (such as particular port numbers). In either case, visualizing such subsets can remove the needed temporal and logical context of the flows under study. Performing discovery on small subsets is inefficient and, by preventing indicators only observable over broad data sets from being detected, quite difficult. The analytic process itself is hindered when analysts must continually "dip in" to their data repository to retrieve new subsets but are unable to keep all of the data of interest in view at once.

10.2.2 Time Sensitivity

Network security is inherently a time-sensitive endeavor. Analysts are faced with the challenge of identifying potential threats or vulnerabilities as early as possible, so that significant compromise of data or resources is prevented or mitigated. Frequently, data collection and analysis infrastructures are designed to support only forensic analyses of data that may be hours or days old by the time it is reviewed by analysts. Visualization tools often reinforce this analysis approach by operating solely in a batch mode, allowing analysts to issue queries against a repository to retrieve historical information. Tools like intrusion detection systems (IDSs) assist in real-time analysis by providing alerts based on predefined conditions (useful for detecting events like SYN flooding or null HTTP headers). The signatures on which these alerts are based are frequently static and, although they can be useful indicators for malicious activity, do not effectively summarize the state of a network for an analyst. The post-mortem analysis that batch-mode visualization enables often occurs too late for the analyst to take proactive measures; damage may have already been done and the network is in triage mode.

The goal of most of the analysis groups with which we work is to analyze data as soon after its collection as possible. This does not mean that every network flow needs to be reviewed by an analyst. Rather, our analysts seek broad awareness of the state of their enterprise sufficient to give them confidence that current activities are within bounds of acceptability and help them identify where potential problems might be incipient. Creating such awareness requires that summaries of network activity be calculated in real time and that visual displays capable of communicating changes in real time be created. When analysts perceive patterns or trends of concern, they need to be able to drill into the summaries to recover additional details and explore the raw data from which these summaries are derived. Linking visualizations capable of summarizing aggregate events in vast amounts of network traffic succinctly with those that enable detailed exploration of raw data can give analysts the power not just to detect events quickly, but also to resolve them efficiently.

10.2.3 Focusing Analytic Effort

A third analytic challenge, and one that derives from the data volume problem, lies in giving analysts cues about potentially fruitful paths of investigation. Given the billions of transactions available per day for analysis, where should the analyst who is looking for new threats begin? Given a particular indicator detected by an IDS, where else might activities related to that potential threat lie? Anomaly detection at the level of a gateway or router can help point analysts toward activities of interest, but identifying statistically significant anomalies at the gateway can require large shifts in traffic that a savvy attacker will seek to avoid. Low and slow attacks that attempt to hide in normal-looking traffic become extremely difficult to detect.

Our analysts frequently ask for "jump-off" points for their work. Given a tip or a clue, analysts can drill into the data and judge the potential impact of a threat. Generating these tips in a manner that minimizes false positives and maximizes return on analytic investment is critical for the successful adoption of visualization tools. One comment we heard many times when talking with analysts was the desire to know what is normal for their network. If they can efficiently compare current activities to known normal (or at least acceptable) profiles for users, hosts, or groups on their network, analysis of the deviations from expected behavior can give a strong starting point for investigation. More than just useful for anomaly identification, behavioral models also have a predictive capability. Using models to help predict future states can help organizations move beyond the "catch and patch" security posture common today. The result is a new ability to proactively respond to nascent threats based on the combination of model predictions and observed activities.

10.3 Medici

10.3.1 Architecture Overview

At the Pacific Northwest National Laboratory, the applications we build are increasingly dependent on processing and visualizing data from multiple heterogeneous sensors and simulations. We find that applications over multiple scientific and analytic domains have similar needs to ingest large volumes of data, perform complex and often computationally expensive analysis to reduce the data to some human-readable form, and deliver the results to multiple visualization displays. To ease the development and deployment of complex, high-performance analytic and scientific applications over multiple domains, we have created a single middleware platform, called Middleware for Data Intensive Computing (MeDICi).

MeDICi consists of three architectural elements:

1. The MeDICi Integration Framework (MIF), which provides a Java-based API, runtime, and associated tools for visually building and deploying complex processing pipelines.
2. MeDICi Workflow, which enables a workflow designer to allow a scientist or analyst to visually create an application from a set of components predefined in MIF.
3. A facility for the capture and management of application metadata called MeDICi Provenance.

These components are loosely coupled and may be used in a number of combinations for any given application.

A typical usage scenario involving all three architectural elements is as follows: Software developers create processing logic by programming a set of cooperating modules and encapsulating them as components. These components are stored in a library so that they can be retrieved later. Each component, where appropriate for the application, takes advantage of API methods to capture and store provenance information in the repository. An analyst then draws upon this library of components using the Workflow Designer tool that allows her to query the store and drag components onto a canvas, visually creating a new application.

A central design principle of MeDICi is to incorporate existing open source and commercial off-the-shelf (COTS) software products in order to provide high-performance and enterprise-ready infrastructure. We then build simplification layers and value-add features that are specific to the domains we support. Thus, MIF is built on top of a widely used Enterprise Service Bus (ESB), Mule [1], which provides a multi-threaded service-oriented platform in which services (called modules in MIF) can communicate over virtually any communication protocol or messaging scheme. These modules can be easily "wired together" using a simplified Java API to create robust and modular event-driven processing pipelines. MeDICi Workflow improves usage of the OASIS standard Business Process Execution Language (BPEL) [2] by providing a simplified graphical language that is then transformed to standard BPEL and deployed to a BPEL engine. MeDICi Provenance uses an open source RDF repository to store metadata about workflows, allowing scientists and analysts to review the exact conditions in which a processing result was obtained.

For the network visualization applications being discussed here, the MIF API was used to build the analytic pipeline, without the use of the other two architectural elements; thus, the remainder of the discussion will focus on the usage and implementation of MIF for this network visualization application. A more complete description of MeDICi, including details of each architectural element, can be found in [3].

10.3.2 Application Characteristics

We maintain that multiple visualization techniques with different strengths must be combined to create a full picture of network situational awareness. This approach requires an underlying distributed software architecture that is robust, scalable, and deployable in a production environment. Specifically, MIF supports these features required by cyber visualization applications:

- A wide array of visualization tools are supported, which can be easily added and removed from the system.
- Analytic routines that filter and aggregate data before it is visualized can be readily created and added to a processing pipeline.
- Multiple programming languages are supported so that existing or legacy programs can be incorporated into pipelines with new processing modules.
- Multiple communication protocols are supported so that modules and programs running external to MIF can send messages over the most convenient channels.
- The underlying runtime environment is able to process data at a high rate and have the ability to scale horizontally to accommodate additional sensor streams and processing routines.

Also, MIF's flexible service bus supports the addition of arbitrary heterogeneous sensor streams. Therefore, this application can be extended to include additional sensors and processing routines. In fact, a predecessor to MIF was used to build a Distributed Intrusion Detection System (DIDS), which was deployed as a test application in a production environment at a large networked conference [4]. This system had many of the same features of enterprise performance and modularity. However, several improvements have since been made to MIF that make it even easier to construct a pipeline. For example, we have created a simplified Java API to aid the construction of a distributed application. We also have created a graphical component builder that allows the

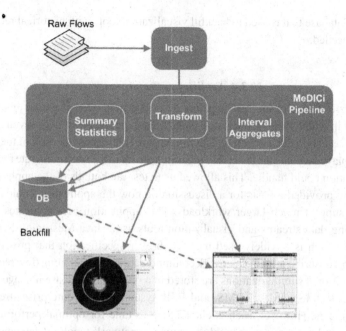

Figure 10.1. MeDICi pipeline.

programmer to generate most of the infrastructure code needed to construct a pipeline while focusing on module implementation.

10.3.3 Application Construction

MIF provides a flexible framework for creating analytic workflows optimized for high-volume data streams such as network flows. In a MIF pipeline, in-stream analysis components consume data from upstream producers and provide derived results to downstream consumers. In a cyber analytics workflow (Figure 10.1), a MIF ingester pushes data from flow sensors through a processing pipeline that first transforms various flow record formats into the particular internal schema used by each analysis tool (allowing multiple third-party tools to be plumbed into the same data pipeline). Downstream consumers create summary statistics and aggregate traffic into adjustable time bins, both of which are used in the CLIQUE models described in the following sections. The pipeline also distributes data to the real-time visualization tools described in the sections that follow; these tools implement a MeDICi listener that receives and processes flow records. Finally, the pipeline stores the data that passes through it in a database that is used to backfill visualization tools with historical records when needed.

10.3.4 Application Performance

The performance of the MIF pipeline described here was measured against a dataset in which flow records were captured at a public event over seven days. For these tests, a day's worth of data from a particularly busy portion of the data was replayed against the described pipeline sped up to the maximum rate that the application could handle. This allowed us to test the bounds of the application and also provided a basis for a discussion on how the application could scale out to support much larger workloads. This application communicates with incoming data streams and visualization tools using Java Messaging Service (JMS), which is a widely used message broker specification that provides a publish-subscribe model of network communication. All incoming flow records and additional summarizations are stored in a relational database management system (RDMS). JMS, RDMS, and ESB systems are all enterprise-strength technologies. However, each is challenging to tune for optimal performance on its own because each is highly sensitive to network topology, latency, and the intricacies of vendor-specific configuration options. This task is made even more difficult when an application is built on all three and communicating with an arbitrary number of visualization displays whose behavior may affect the overall system. Because of these difficulties, software vendors often generate high-performance numbers by testing their products using trivial applications with short bursts of data. By contrast, the intention of these tests is not to produce the highest possible throughput numbers for an idealized MIF application, but to represent the performance of a reasonably well-tuned, real-world distributed network analysis system.

These tests were performed with three separate server-based software packages: MIF, the ActiveMQ JMS server, and a Postgres database running on a Dell 7500. This is an upper-end desktop machine, but also has a similar hardware configuration as compute cluster nodes in common use within our organization's current generation of state-of-the art commodity clusters. Therefore, it is a good choice for a testing platform as it is also a likely deployment platform. Specifically, the computer has a dual quad core 2.80 GHz Intel Xeon® processor with 16 GB of memory. Although MIF does not require a large amount of memory, it does benefit from a large number of processor cores. This is because each module in a MIF pipeline (and the corresponding service running in Mule) is actually deployed as its own server with a dedicated thread pool. This allows each module to dynamically adapt to higher volumes of data by increasing the number of available threads. During the tests, CPU and memory usage was monitored to help determine where any bottlenecks occurred. In addition to the pipeline previously described, two additional short programs were created: an ingester, which simply reads flow records from files on disk and sends them at an increased rate over a JMS topic to the pipeline and a "performance monitor," which is a standalone application that receives messages from the pipeline and reports both an overall flow record processing rate (measured in records per second) and a rate for the most recent 30-second interval. The ingester and performance monitor were run on a separate machine from the MIF pipeline in order to ensure that their CPU usage did not interfere with that of the other components. Because each individual flow record is small (each record in this dataset averages 236 bytes), the ingester uses nonstandard JMS configurations to improve performance: (1) transacted mode, in which groups of JMS messages are batched and sent as a single network message and (2) asynchronous mode in which the sender does not wait for acknowledgement of a message from the receiver before sending subsequent messages.

The network flow data used to test MeDICi throughput in this application is real-world data from a large enterprise. The traffic volume varies greatly over the course of a day. Over the busiest four-hour period, the total average rate of flow records was 83 records/second, while during the busiest hour, the rate increased to 145 records/second. This system was first tested at this "actual maximum" rate, at which the system performs well and an observation of CPU usage shows that MIF, JMS, and RDMS are not taxed at all. Next, the maximum throughput was tested by doing runs in which the ingester is set to send data at increasing rates over several runs of the dataset. For the best run, the system reported a maximum average throughput of 2,781 records per second, which translates to processing more than 240 million transactions per day on a single node. The highest throughput 30-second interval was 3,350 records per second. During this time, neither of the computers involved reached a CPU usage above 50 percent, leading us to conclude that the network may be the bottleneck in this case. Reasonable, although nonexhaustive, efforts were made to tune JMS performance and, to a lesser extent, Postgres performance as well. MIF performance was tuned by modifying the size of a module's thread pool and by changing the size of the JDBC connection pool that was used to insert records in the database.

Because our tests showed that a single node could process approximately one-tenth of the network flow data we typically see in a large multi-site enterprise, MeDICi provides acceptable performance: a ten-node cluster is a sufficient, and

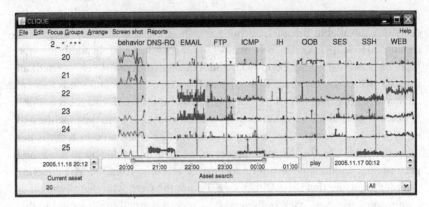

Figure 10.2. CLIQUE interface.

reasonable, network flow processing infrastructure. Alternatively, because such a cluster would represent the minimum computational resources necessary to keep up with network traffic, additional compute resources would enable more complex automated data analysis to be moved from visualization displays to the service bus to improve client response time and make the analysis algorithms available to a wider array of client tools.

10.4 Clique

Achieving real-time situational awareness of network activity requires techniques for summarizing large amounts of network traffic and for presenting those summaries in an easily understood interface. Although visualization of raw flows in large volumes can help analysts understand the current state of their networks and detect anomalous events, visual techniques that aggregate flows to higher-level abstractions can help analysts better cope with data scale. We have developed a behavioral summarization tool called CLIQUE, which bases its interface on LiveRac [5], that generates statistical models of expected network flow patterns for individual IP addresses or collections of IP addresses (each of which we term an "actor"), against which current activity is compared (Figure 10.2). CLIQUE uses MeDICi's ability to perform in-stream analyses to present real-time views of network behaviors.

The majority of changes made to LiveRac were done to the model and controller for the interface. Major changes include:

- Columns and rows were updated to feed off of data from the database (columns) and lists of user configurable groups (rows).

- Addition of the ability to listen to MeDICi's feed of data and update the interface without further database calls.
- Calculation and display of behavioral plots.

The objective of CLIQUE is to help humans discover and detect potentially malicious events in vast amounts of streaming data. Previous research in this area has focused on two standard approaches for event identification in transactional data: signature-based methods and statistical anomaly detection [6]. Signature-based approaches are successful at identifying instances of known patterns, whereas anomaly-based approaches use general heuristics and statistical variances to identify patterns of interest. In practice, however, neither method alone is sufficient.

Recognizing that a gap exists between signature- and anomaly-based approaches, we implement a modeling approach that can be used in either a supervised or an unsupervised mode. Rather than producing visual displays that depict all of the raw data, we use a multi-level classifier and temporal model builder to reduce and condense the data visualized to an amount more suited to human interaction. The goal is to classify the data into patterns that represent categories of behavior inherent in computer network traffic. These patterns are then further classified, based on temporal sequence, to create higher-level abstractions of the activity in a network. This multi-level classification approach, coupled to a visual front end, allows the end user to view high-volume data in a much more condensed, information-rich fashion than is possible with raw flow visualization; this approach also attempts to capture the structure of an actor's traffic such that the behavioral representations serve as complete and useful summaries of the activities in which an actor is engaged.

Behavioral models such as those produced in CLIQUE are useful for anomaly detection, because they can be used to compare expected behavior against actual behavior. Rather than simply comparing expected traffic levels to observed signatures or applying a single policy-based model to each actor, CLIQUE behavioral models take a functional approach to anomaly identification. Such models learn the typical behavior of each actor over multiple kinds of activity (including port ranges and traffic types) and use these baseline representations as a predictor (over minutes, hours, days, or more) for that actor's traffic. These models are also helpful because they can also help identify what is *not* happening in an actor's traffic, which can be as useful an indicator as what *is* happening that shouldn't be. Times when the model predicts a certain kind of activity that doesn't occur can point to behavioral changes indicative of a potential threat (of course, adding contextual information to these models that indicates, for instance, that an actor is on vacation can help resolve such anomalies).

10.4.1 Behavior Modeling

CLIQUE builds behavioral models for each actor on a network. Models are built in real time in response to user interactions, rather than being predefined. This approach allows models to be created for arbitrary collections of IP addresses on a network. The analyst configures CLIQUE initially by specifying groupings to use when CLIQUE launches. For instance, the analyst might configure CLIQUE to show behavioral summaries for aggregations of IP addresses such as buildings in an enterprise, or subnets, or organizational units. Later, we describe how drilling down through the CLIQUE interface allows the analyst to decompose these actor groups in subgroups and (eventually) retrieve models for individual IP addresses.

Figure 10.3 outlines the process for creating behavioral models and calculating behavioral deviations. The behavior modeling process begins with identifying natural clusters of flow records. A streaming classifier within the MeDICi pipeline creates categories of flow records based on shared attributes (step 1 in Figure 10.3). We classify each flow into one of sixty-five categories developed by cyber-security analysts using a set of rules based on port, protocol, and TCP flags. When each flow enters the pipeline it is assigned a class. For a specific IP or group of IPs, we sum the number of occurrences for each category at a user-defined temporal resolution. For the purposes of the current work, we use an interval of 1 minute. This interval was chosen based on analyst assessment of the smallest useful time window over which network activity might need to be assessed. To allow for other interval selections, the pipeline configuration could be updated or aggregation of intervals could be done.

10.4.1.1 Symbolic Aggregate ApproXimation

Although we classified each flow into one of the characteristic categories of activity on a network, we have not yet reduced the number of flows to be analyzed. To accomplish this reduction, we use a technique called SAX – Symbolic Aggregate approXimation that allows streaming dimensionality reduction and generation of a representation (word) based on time series discords [9, 10].

The use of SAX begins in step 3 of Figure 10.3 where data is sent to the SAX module from the CLIQUE data model. For each channel (the temporal activity for a given category), the interval aggregations and the average historic interval aggregations are sent to the module. This provides the current and historic state for the channel at the visible time window. The output of the SAX module is a given actor's behavior. The actor's overall behavior can be considered

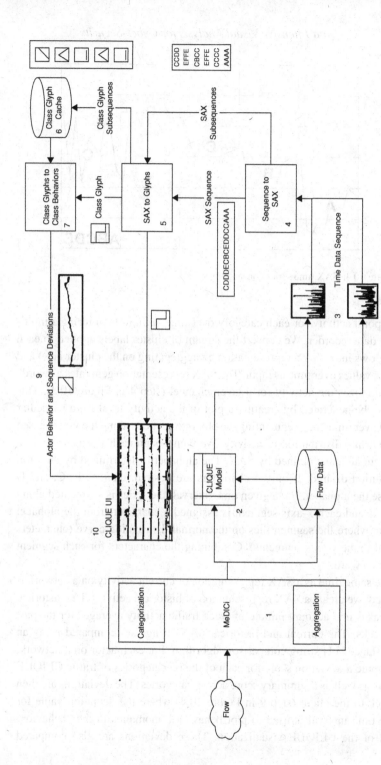

Figure 10.3. Behavior modeling process flow.

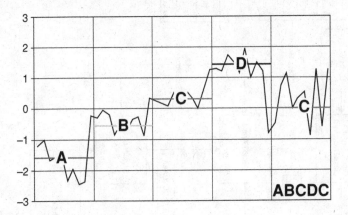

Figure 10.4. SAX time series conversion.

the temporal activity for each category over time, akin to monitoring a multi-channel data recorder. We convert the stream of cluster labels applied to each actor's flows into a SAX representation by aggregating on the cluster label and using the values over time as input. The SAX representation generates a "word" that symbolizes the activity for a given channel (step 4 in Figure 10.3). This word can be generated by creating a plot of the activity level for a particular channel over time, then segmenting the plot into sections along the y-axis based on the normal distribution of activity. We then assign each y-axis segment a letter from alphabet defined by SAX. The alphabet is determined by the level of resolution desired. If only 4 characters are desired, then A, B, C, and D comprise the alphabet. For a given time interval, the series is segmented along the x-axis and each x-axis segment is assigned a character from the alphabet based on where the segment lies on the normal distribution curve (characters assigned to the y-axis segments). Combining the characters for each segment produces a word.

At the same time as a SAX representation of current activity on a network is generated, we create a SAX representation of historical activity. The historical model takes into account minute-of-week traffic activity averages for the past three weeks. The current and historical SAX strings are compared using an Edit Distance [11] string comparison algorithm. For each actor on a network, we compute a deviation score for each of the 65 categories of traffic CLIQUE monitors as well as a summary score across categories. The deviations are then sent back to the client (step 9 in Figure 10.4) where the deviation value for a given time interval is used to plot behavioral anomalies in the "behavior" column of the CLIQUE visualization. These deviations are also compared against alert thresholds that an analyst has previously established and control the color scheme used in the background of each cell.

10.5 Interaction

CLIQUE uses the LiveRac rubber-sheet interaction technique. To aid scalability; analysts can view highly generalized summaries of traffic in a heatmap style display. They then can zoom into a single heatmap cell to see greater detail in a variety of statistical charts; as analysts zoom in, they first see "sparklines" and then full data tables – the level of detail adapts to the level of zoom as seen in Figure 10.5. CLIQUE shows flow activity levels for each actor across a range of predefined categories (such as web, ftp, and email) as well as a summary "behavioral" signal that reflects the deviation of that actor calculated from the SAX module. This behavior model, which can evolve over time, gives the analyst a sense of what is normal or expected for each actor.

Users can set thresholds in CLIQUE that alert them when an actor's traffic departs from expectations. For each category, a number of levels can be defined. Each level in turn can be assigned a value and color to encode that value. The threshold verification algorithm can be based on several factors in the data (min, max, mean, and so on). When the selected factor is within a threshold range, the background of the given cell is colored with the chosen encoding. This color-coding allows quick understanding of the current state for each category for each actor. For example in Figure 10.5, several cells are shaded darkly, depicting issues, whereas others are shaded lightly, signifying a valid state. Behavior can also have a threshold encoding defined to alert users when deviations have gone past the threshold.

10.5.1 Results

A key attribute of the tool is the ability to determine the normal state of a given network. Any departure from normal triggers an alert that can be further investigated. If an actor is showing as normal yet channels are showing past thresholds it may be an indication that thresholds need to be reevaluated. One can observe the normal state of the network at a high level and drill into groups to view finer detail when needed.

10.6 Traffic Circle

Analysis of aggregates, as is performed in CLIQUE and other tools such as Isis, [12] is one way to create visual representations that scale effectively.

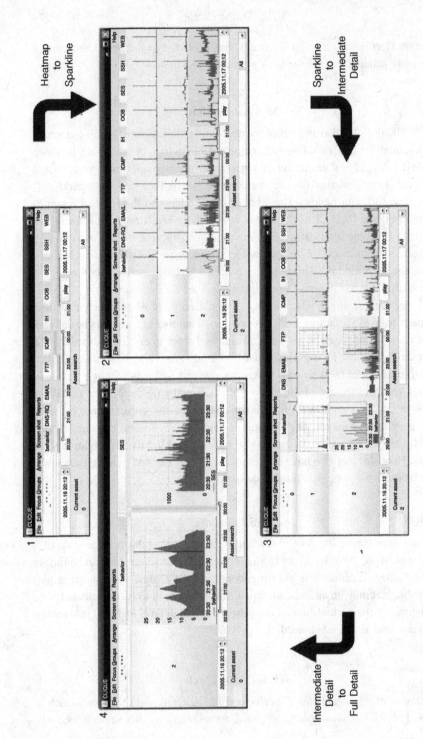

Figure 10.5. CLIQUE interface showing semantic zooming.

Depictions of summary statistics such as counts scale indefinitely as long as the underlying mechanism used to generate those statistics similarly scales. However, aggregates alone can occasionally obfuscate events in large data volumes. Sometimes, understanding the characteristics of individual transactions or their temporal pattern is necessary to resolve a behavioral anomaly discovered in CLIQUE.

To address this limitation, we have constructed a visual interface called Traffic Circle that complements CLIQUE by presenting detailed plots of individual flows. Our aim in developing Traffic Circle was to display as much flow data as possible in an interactive, exploratory interface. In their effort to understand "normal" traffic, our analysts want to learn as much as possible about the state of their networks, and raw plots of flow activity can help them learn what normal looks like and spot off-normal conditions. Typically, occlusion and rendering issues mean that plots of raw data may not scale beyond tens of thousands to hundreds of thousands of flows. This scaling challenge means that, in some enterprises, analysts can see at most a few seconds of traffic at once before the limits of the visualization tool are exceeded.

Our motivation in developing Traffic Circle is that, although summarization techniques like CLIQUE are effective at providing overviews of very large traffic volumes, there are always features in data that the human perceptual system is able to detect more readily than an automated system would – particularly those unexpected features that we would not even have known to train an automated system to look for. By displaying large amounts of network traffic in an interactive plot – up to hundreds of millions of individual flows – we are able to support the deeper exploration of features initially discovered in CLIQUE and allow analysts to step back and see large segments of their network traffic transit their screen in real time. Such massively scalable plots introduce their own visualization challenges. Displaying large flow volumes on standard resolution displays can create occlusion problems, resulting in an undifferentiated mass of visual features that prevents the analyst from perceiving clear patterns. In addition, rendering and interacting with displays depicting millions or more flow volumes can be sluggish.

We have developed Traffic Circle to mitigate each of these challenges. To display large flow volumes on standard resolution, Traffic Circle includes a mechanism for assigning flows to "layers" based on common attributes; these layers can be toggled on and off to help reduce occlusion issues. Traffic Circle has also been successfully demonstrated on very large-resolution displays (up to 15.5 million pixels), helping to reduce occlusion even when many layers are visible at once. To render and interact with millions of flow records, we leverage hyper-threading to render large data sets efficiently. Flows are partitioned across

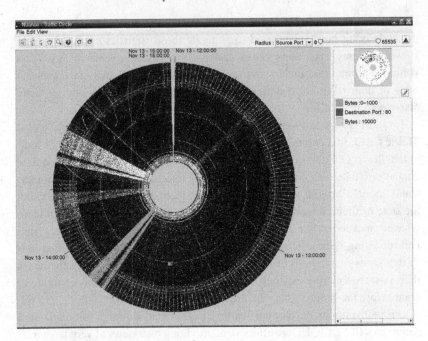

Figure 10.6. Traffic Circle interface

all available threads, with each thread responsible for drawing just those flows in its partition.

10.6.1 Interface

To the analysts with whom we worked in developing Traffic Circle, time is the primary attribute used to understand flow data. They wanted an easy way to perceive temporal patterns in their data, with the ability to drill down into very short time periods or scale up to very long time periods. Traffic Circle uses a circular "time wheel" metaphor to display flow records as arcs (Figure 10.6). Traffic Circle's time wheel metaphor is consistent with an analog clock. The earliest time in the data set under examination is located at the top of the circle, to the right of the small gap. Time flows clockwise around the circle and ends at the top to the left of the gap.

Flows are ordered around the wheel by their start time, and their arc length corresponds to duration. The radial position of a flow is determined by a user-selectable attribute such as source or destination port or packet count. The attribute to which the radius maps is selected via a drop-down list at the top right of the user interface. Next to the drop-down list is a double-headed slider that enables the analyst to use a fisheye zoom capability to reveal additional detail where it is occluded (such as at the center of the circle). (A rectilinear plot option is also available and is discussed in the following section.)

In addition to loading static data sets from the backfill database shown in Figure 10.1, Traffic Circle can also operate in real time by receiving flow records from the MeDICi pipeline. When in streaming mode, the circle slowly rotates clockwise, adding new data to the beginning and removing data from the end. In this mode, it serves as a live situational awareness display that gives the user a near-real-time display of current activities. We find it particularly effective as an ambient display in the analyst's workspace; by observing the plot's activity over a period of days, the analyst can learn what typical activity looks like and can therefore spot off-normal events readily. When occupying a secondary or tertiary display in the workspace, the analyst can use peripheral vision to assess whether the plot currently "looks like it should" for the flow sensors that are feeding it. When features appear that look off-normal, the analyst can monitor their evolution while performing other work.

10.6.2 Interaction

A key motivation for using a circular interface is the affordance it provides for direct manipulation to zoom in and out in time. Analysts can "spin the wheel" to adjust the time period shown (from seconds through years), without the need to readjust mouse position. Additionally, Traffic Circle draws upon the ability to spot periodic elements that spiral plots have been shown to provide (albeit a lesser degree due to being a single circle) [13]. This ability helps in identifying features such as beaconing or port scanning that could occur for more than very short or very long periods. Traffic Circle provides a natural method of time zooming; the user simply grabs a time label on the edge of the circle and drags it around the circle. Time can be added or removed from both ends of the visible data. The user grabs a time label on the right side of the circle to interact with the start time and drags clockwise to add time and counter-clockwise to remove time. The user grabs a label on the left side of the circle and drags counter-clockwise to add and clockwise to remove time from the end time.

Traffic Circle uses traditional pan/zoom functionality as well as a radius and time zoom. By default, the value of the radius at the center of the circle is zero and the value at the outside edge is the maximum data value for the selected parameter. For example, if the user has selected to order the radius by "source port" and the largest source port in the loaded data is 5,000, then the outside edge of the radius corresponds to 5,000 and the center to 0. The user can independently adjust the inner and outer radius values to be viewed within the current range causing the data to spread out across the radius and producing less overplotting. Data that are located near the center of the circle view are compressed as the circumference in the center of the circle is shorter than on the outside of the circle. To minimize this effect, users can turn on a fisheye mode that stretches the data to fill the circle as the radius sliders at the top right of the interface are adjusted. Traffic Circle can also reverse the order of the radius.

Analysts use filters based on flow parameters to color or hide certain kinds of traffic, reducing noise and revealing features that are otherwise occluded. The filter panel, on the right side of the interface, lists the filters that are currently active. The filters are ordered so that the top filter in the list takes priority over any filters below it. The data are rendered in order starting with the bottom filter, ensuring that the topmost filters are not occluded by data that matches a filter that is lower on the list. Each filter behaves like a layer, allowing the analyst to toggle the filter between three states: on, off, and hidden. In the "on" mode, the color corresponding to the filter is used to paint the flow arcs that match that filter. In the "off" mode, the arcs corresponding to the filter are drawn in their default white (uncolored). In the hidden mode, the arcs corresponding to the filter are hidden from view. By selectively hiding layers, analysts can wade through large amounts of traffic efficiently and can overcome occlusion problems resulting from overplotting.

A radial selection device allows the analyst to retrieve additional information on a flow collection depicted in Traffic Circle. Summary tables that aggregate flow characteristics for a given selection can be retrieved, and through those tables the analyst can drill down to raw flows.

Although the main display mode of Traffic Circle is circular, there is also a rectilinear mode in which Traffic Circle displays data as a traditional scatterplot, with time on the x-axis and an analyst-selectable attribute of the flows on the y-axis. The usefulness and simplicity of rectilinear plots has made them a standard plot for network flow data. For some users the rectilinear plot option provides a more familiar interface, although it removes the "spinning" inter-action affordance for time zooming found in the radial plot. The user must instead repeatedly pick up and reposition the mouse to adjust the time period. Both views of the data incorporate the layering and time selection needed for exploratory analysis.

The circular plot, by providing an alternative to a Cartesian plot, provides a pattern identification aid. Simply changing the way that data are portrayed for an analyst from a Cartesian to a radial plot can present features that encourage exploration. Certain features appear more readily in either the circular or the rectilinear mode.

10.6.3 Performance and Scalability

Traffic Circle has been operationally demonstrated at data volumes upward of 125 million flows per analysis session, and uses a multi-threaded architecture to provide interactive exploration of large data sets. We have used a high-performance database from Netezza to enable query responses in interactive time as the user manipulates the interface. The scalability of Traffic Circle means that analysis is not bound by small data extracts that may prevent the full picture of a threat from being understood.

Issues with plotting flow data in a circular view include render time and the length of the arcs at different radius positions. The amount of time to render arcs is greater than the amount of time to render lines. Comparably, this means that the circular view renders more slowly than the rectilinear view. To address this issue, Traffic Circle uses a multi-threaded drawing engine to minimize the render time and maintain interactivity at large data volumes.

Screen resolution and display size become relevant when visualizing one glyph per flow. As display size and resolution decrease, overplotting increases. Visualizing data sets containing more than 1 million records on a standard desktop display results in overplotting, sufficient to entirely obscure any discrete features. To address this challenge, we have begun experimenting with running Traffic Circle and CLIQUE on large, high-resolution displays. In the powerwall view shown in Figure 10.7 capable of rendering 15.5 million pixels, we are interacting with upwards of 5 million flows at once. The ability to detect visually individual features at this data volume becomes possible.

10.7 Case Study

The following scenario depicts a possible interaction with the tools described to explore a cyber event. This scenario is informed by our interactions with analysts in cyber security organizations and captures how Traffic Circle and CLIQUE fit into analyst workflows. The ability of Traffic Circle and CLIQUE to support both real-time and forensic analyses enables analysts to detect current events and use historical data to understand them in context. In this scenario, both Traffic Circle and CLIQUE are installed on an analyst's workstation. The MeDICi framework is configured to output data to the tools and a backend database.

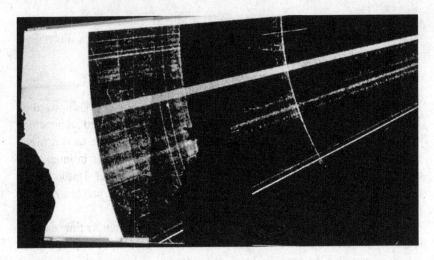

Figure 10.7. Traffic Circle rendered on a high-resolution Powerwall.

The analysis begins with CLIQUE and Traffic Circle both operating in streaming mode. The analyst is going through her normal daily routine: investigating items, answering emails, and performing other tasks. On one of the displays, Traffic Circle and CLIQUE update with the current network traffic on a time interval defined by the analyst, in this case 1 minute. As the analyst works, she notices that the color encoding for the behavior cells in one of the IP address aggregations she monitors – for Building A on her organization's campus – has changed from green to yellow. (Analysts can use any aggregation of IP addresses they wish.) This change signals to the analyst that behavior has started to deviate from the normal calculated by the SAX algorithm. The analyst makes a note to watch the group, but does nothing yet. As time progresses, the encoding shifts to red, signaling that the behavior for that group is highly deviant from its norm.

She leaves this instance of CLIQUE open on her desktop to monitor real-time traffic and opens a second CLIQUE window to explore the new anomaly more closely. The analyst adjusts the CLIQUE timeline to incorporate a larger amount of time to show the progression of Building A's behavior. She drills down into the Building A group by double-clicking its row. CLIQUE expands the heatmap to show one row for each room in the building. The analyst can now see that the behavior cell for Room 10 is colored red, whereas the other rooms are mostly gray and blue – this indicates that Room 10 is causing the majority of the behavioral deviation for the group, starting at 7:00 AM. Looking at the individual traffic type charts for Room 10, the analyst notes that typical behavior comprises web traffic. However, today there seems to be a large amount of SESsion (SES) traffic on port 445. SES traffic represents valid session traffic that could not within another category.

The analyst recalls a report that recently went out from Gartner about port 445 traffic and a vulnerability in Microsoft's Message Block Protocol (SMB) [14]. Because of what the tools are reporting and the recent news, she decides to investigate further.

CLIQUE has provided the entry point to the problem: a given machine is acting outside of its normal behavior on port 445. To explore the data comprising this event in more detail, the analyst turns to Traffic Circle. Traffic Circle is running in real-time mode on her desktop, and she observes the patterns to determine whether this view of all traffic looks similar to its typical view. She applies a filter to highlight port 445 traffic for all machines on her network and observes that the density of flows on port 445 appears to be increasing over the past few hours. To investigate the early stages of this event, the analyst adjusts the time wheel to show the same time range as CLIQUE is displaying. She pauses, the streaming updates to Traffic Circle so that she can examine data from earlier today.

She filters the current Traffic Circle view, which had been showing all network flows from across her organization, to show just traffic whose source or destination is an IP address in the address space assigned to Building A. She loads a summary statistics table for the flows she has highlighted – those on port 445. Traffic Circle aggregates these statistics by remote IP address, so she sorts the table by the number of flows to each remote IP. She sees that the majority of port 445 traffic is going to a small handful of remote IPs.

The analyst decides to double check her assessment by examining the rest of the port range to determine if there is an increase in activity across the range or just with port 445. She toggles off the port 445 filter and sees that the remaining traffic seems as she expects it. The traffic appears to be distributed evenly across the port range with the majority of sessions being short in duration. She creates a new filter to contain this other traffic on its own layer, and toggles the new layer off to show just port 445 traffic. The analyst selects a particularly busy section of the circle and highlights the traffic.

Using the attribute space drop-down list, the analyst switches the radial axis to show local IP addresses as the radius of the circle. The previously highlighted flow records remain highlighted but are shown in the new attribute space. It is immediately apparent to the analyst that the majority of the traffic is along a single line in that attribute space, signifying that the port 445 traffic is all coming from the same source.

The analyst creates and applies a new filter for the remote IP range in question, filtering out all other flow data. The analyst can now explore what other traffic is going to that IP range. She also saves the collection of filters she has made, as a record of her work and as a discovery aid she can share with her team. She can pass this filter set on to a colleague who will explore the traffic between the local and remote IPs she identified in more detail.

10.8 Related Work

As the number and sophistication of cyber attacks increase, the challenge for businesses to protect their networks has become more difficult. As a result, there have been several contributions to the domain of flow analysis and visualization to assist with the problem. Some, like Traffic Circle and CLIQUE, make use of flow data to create various charts depicting attributes of network traffic [15–17]. Others look at the problem a different way and show the connectivity of different systems, vulnerabilities, and the attack paths that can be derived from that data [18–20]. A variety of complementary approaches should be used in any operational activity.

Neither Traffic Circle nor CLIQUE display network connectivity graphs showing possible connections from one IP to another. The Bundle Diagram available in FloVis [20] is one such tool that visualizes flows between IP addresses by bundling these edges together on a circular plot. By bundling the edges, FloVis simplifies the visualization and minimizes overplotting. The input to FloVis is processed SiLK flows that have been placed into a relational database, rather than real-time data as in our approach.

Another connectivity graph, used to visualize attacks, is VisFlowConnect [20], which does not bundle edges such as FloVis. However, this system does have the ability to accept streaming NetFlow records from a socket. Because of the streaming nature of VisFlowConnect, it could easily be incorporated into the MeDICi architecture, adding another capability to the suite of tools all operating on the same data. Although the edge bundling in FloVis can be easier to navigate and find patterns in than a nonbundled plot, it may be harder to incorporate such plots into our MeDICi architecture because of the preprocessing required.

Like Traffic Circle, many existing flow visualizations are 2-D rectilinear graphs that show some attribute along the y axis, and time along the x axis. An example of this is the Activity Plot in FloVis, which shows IP addresses and their activity over time [20]. The plot uses color to encode attributes to allow the user to see issues at a glance. Another use of this type of visualization is seen in Abdullah et al., which uses such plots to detect intrusion [15].

CLIQUE uses 2D rectilinear plots exclusively. Similar to Abdullah et al., the plots are mostly flow counts over time, with the addition of a behavior column. Intrusion is a subset of activity that can cause deviations from normal for a given actor. The FloVis Activity Plot uses a similar visualization as the heat map created by CLIQUE, which uses thresholds to determine color encoding. Changing the encoding to depict an activity metric in CLIQUE could be possible with minor changes.

A third type of visualization can be termed "nonstandard" plots. Tools in this category would consist of visualizations such as Flodar [17], the follow on work on Flodar by Blake [21], NetBytes in FloVis [20], and Traffic Circle. Flodar and Blake use a platter visualization to show network traffic and the activity of a given IP address on that network. Blake contributes the ability to accommodate dynamic networks. The platter uses time as a radius and plots intervals toward the center of the platter. IP addresses are color encoded based on their role in the network. By remaining active the column (for an IP) remains on the outermost edge of the plot. The platter also visualizes data in three dimensions, having the height of a given column represent the amount of activity for a given IP.

NetBytes uses 3-D space to visualize historical perspective instead of animation [20]. The purpose of using a static plot is to minimize change blindness that can be introduced with the use of animation.

10.9 Future Work

The behavioral modeling approach implemented in CLIQUE lends itself to other domains, and we intend to explore applications of the modeling technique in analyzing the transactional activity of Supervisory Control and Data Acquisition (SCADA) systems and the power grid. To improve our models' sensitivity and their ability to summarize accurately the activities of an individual actor, we plan to incorporate other types of log files into our models. Records such as syslogs and other host application events can provide additional nuance to the models. The application of sequence detection techniques from bioinformatics can also be used to identify commonly recurring subsequences in our vocabulary (which might be benign), subsequences that are known to be indicative of malicious activity, and very rare subsequences (which might be suspicious new threats).

A further challenge with behavioral modeling is ensuring that behaviors that analysts do not want included in the model are removed from the source traffic. The risk of not doing so is that malicious activities are unwittingly learned as normal traffic. We are exploring techniques that allow analysts to flag certain suspicious traffic as traffic that should not to be incorporated into the model and to use the CLIQUE classifier in a semi-supervised mode that allows analysts to remove entire clusters of traffic that do not have a ready benign explanation.

Although CLIQUE and Traffic Circle operate over the same live data streams and backfill database, we anticipate coupling them more tightly. It should be possible to instantiate Traffic Circle directly from within a CLIQUE cell, launching a detailed flow chart from a CLIQUE aggregate.

10.10 Conclusion

Combining Traffic Circle and CLIQUE in a near real-time environment, provided by MeDICi, enables network support staff to visualize traffic as it occurs. By providing this capability, potential issues can be investigated as soon as behavior deviates from normal. We have discussed how CLIQUE can provide a jump-off point for investigation in other tools that do not abstract the level of information such as Traffic Circle. Traffic Circle enables an investigator to quickly view potential threats contained within raw flow records and apply many different attribute spaces and color encoded filters. The three tools together present an environment for defense-in-depth network visualization.

References

1. "Mule Enterprise Service Bus: What is Mule ESB?" Accessed July 23, 2010, http://www.mulesoft.org/what-mule-esb.
2. "OASIS Web Services Business Process Execution Language: Specification version 2.0." Accessed July 23, 2010, http://docs.oasis-open.org/wsbpel/2.0/wsbpel-v2.0.html.
3. Gorton, I., Wynne, A., Almquist, J., and Chatterton, J. 2008. "The MeDICi Integration Framework: A Platform for High Performance Data Streaming Applications." In *Proceedings of the Seventh Working IEEE/IFIP Conference on Software Architecture (February 18–21, 2008). WICSA'08.* Washington, D.C: IEEE Computer Society, 95–104.
4. Wynne, A., Gorton, I., Almquist, J., Chatterton, J., and Thurman, D. 2008. "A Flexible, High Performance Service-Oriented Architecture for Detecting Cyber Attacks." In *Proceedings of the 41st Annual Hawaii international Conference on System Sciences* (January 07–10, 2008). HICSS. Washington, D.C: IEEE Computer Society, 263.
5. McLachlan, P., Munzner, T., Koutsofios, E., and North, S. 2008. "LiveRAC: Interactive Visual Exploration of System Management Time-Series Data." In *Proceeding of the Twenty-Sixth Annual SIGCHI Conference on Human Factors in Computing Systems (Florence, Italy, April 05–10, 2008). CHI '08.* New York, NY: ACM, 1483–92.
6. Cahill, M. H., Lambert, D., Pinheiro, J. C., and Sun, D. X. "Detecting Fraud in the Real World." In *Handbook of Massive Data Sets*, edited by J. Abello, P. M.

Pardalos, and M. G. Resende, 911–29. Norwell, MA: Kluwer Academic Publishers, 2002.

7. Dutta, M., Mahanta, A. K., and Pujari, A. K. "QROCK: A Quick Version of the ROCK Algorithm for Clustering of Categorical Data." *Pattern Recogn. Lett.* **26**, 15 (Nov. 2005): 2364–73.

8. Domingos, P., and Hulten, G. 2000. "Mining High-Speed Data Streams." In *Proceedings of the Sixth ACM SIGKDD international Conference on Knowledge Discovery and Data Mining* (Boston, Massachusetts, United States, August 20–23, 2000). KDD '00. New York: ACM, 71–80.

9. Keogh, E., Lin, J., and Fu, A. D. "HOT SAX: Efficiently Finding the Most Unusual Time Series Subsequence." In *Proceedings of the Fifth IEEE International Conference on Data Mining* (November 27–30, 2005). ICDM'05. Washington, D.C.: IEEE Computer Society, 226–33.

10. Lin, J., Keogh, E., Lonardi, S., and Chiu, B. 2003. "A Symbolic Representation of Time Series, with Implications for Streaming Algorithms." In *Proceedings of the 8th ACM SIGMOD Workshop on Research Issues in Data Mining and Knowledge Discovery* (San Diego, California, June 13–13, 2003). DMKD '03., New York, NY: ACM, 2–11.

11. Levenshtein, V. I. 1966. Binary Codes Capable of Correcting Deletions, Insertions and Reversals. *Soviet Physics Doklady.* **10** (1966): 707–10.

12. Phan, D., Gerth, J., Lee, M., Paepcke, A., and Winograd, T. "Visual Analysis of Network Flow data with Timelines and Event Plots." In *Proceedings of Visualization for Computer Security* (Sacramento, CA, October 29, 2007). VIZSEC'07. Berlin, Springer-Verlag: 85–99.

13. Weber, M., Alexa, M., and Müller, W. 2001. "Visualizing Time-Series on Spirals." In *Proceedings of the IEEE Symposium on information Visualization 2001* (October 22–23, 2001). INFOVIS'01. Washington, D.C.: IEEE Computer Society, 7.

14. Pescatore, J. *More Port 445 Activity Could Mean Security Trouble.* Technical Report. Stamford, CT: Gartner, 1997.

15. Abdullah, K., Lee, A., Conti, G., and Copeland, J. A. "Visualizing Network data for Intrusion Detection." In *Proceedings of the 2005 IEEE Workshop on Information Assurance and Security* (US Military Academy, West Point, 2005). New York: IEEE, 2–3.

16. Plonka, D. 2000. "FlowScan: A Network Traffic Flow Reporting and Visualization Tool." In *Proceedings of the 14th USENIX Conference on System Administration* (New Orleans, Louisiana, December 03–08, 2000). System Administration Conference. Berkeley, CA: USENIX Association, 305–318.

17. Swing, E. "Flodar: Flow Visualization of Network Traffic." *IEEE Comput. Graph.* **18**, no. 5 (Sep. 1998): 6–8.

18. Nanda, S. and Deo, N. "A Highly Scalable Model for Network Attack Identification and Path Prediction." In *Proceedings of the IEEE SoutheastCon* (Richmond, VA, March 22–27, 2007). New York, NY: IEEE, 663–68.

19. Noel, S., Jacobs, M., Kalapa, P., and Jajodia, S. 2005. "Multiple Coordinated Views for Network Attack Graphs." In *Proceedings of the IEEE Workshops on Visualization For Computer Security* (October 26–26, 2005). VIZSEC., Washington, D.C: IEEE Computer Society, 12.

20. Taylor, T., Paterson, D., Glanfield, J., Gates, C., Brooks, and S., McHugh, J. "FloVis: Flow Visualization System." In *Proceedings of Cybersecurity Applications and Technologies Conference for Homeland Security* (Washington, DC, March 03–04, 2009). CATCH'09. Los Alamitos, CA: IEEE Computer Society, 186–98.

21. Blake, E. H. 2004. "An Extended Platter Metaphor for Effective Reconfigurable Network Visualization." In *Proceedings of the information Visualisation, Eighth international Conference* (July 14–16, 2004). IV. Washington, D.C.: IEEE Computer Society, 752–57.

Index

Index

Printed in the United States
By Bookmasters